Voices of Resistance

Voices of Resistance

Interdisciplinary Approaches to Chican@ Children's Literature

Edited by Laura Alamillo, Larissa M. Mercado-López, and Cristina Herrera

ROWMAN & LITTLEFIELD
Lanham • Boulder • New York • London

Published by Rowman & Littlefield
A wholly owned subsidiary of The Rowman & Littlefield Publishing Group, Inc.
4501 Forbes Boulevard, Suite 200, Lanham, Maryland 20706
www.rowman.com

Unit A, Whitacre Mews, 26–34 Stannary Street, London SE11 4AB

Copyright © 2018 by Laura Alamillo, Larissa M. Mercado-López, and Cristina Herrera

All rights reserved. No part of this book may be reproduced in any form or by any electronic or mechanical means, including information storage and retrieval systems, without written permission from the publisher, except by a reviewer who may quote passages in a review.

British Library Cataloguing in Publication Information Available

Library of Congress Cataloging-in-Publication Data

ISBN 978-1-4758-3403-1 (hardcover)
ISBN 978-1-4758-3404-8 (paperback)
ISBN 978-1-4758-3405-5 (electronic)

∞™ The paper used in this publication meets the minimum requirements of American National Standard for Information Sciences—Permanence of Paper for Printed Library Materials, ANSI/NISO Z39.48–1992.

Printed in the United States of America

Contents

Foreword—U.S. Poet Laureate Juan Felipe Herrera   vii

Introduction   ix

SECTION I: TRACING CHICAN@ IDENTITY AND CONSCIOUSNESS   1

1. Entre Tejana y Chicana: Tracing Proto-Chicana Identity and Consciousness in Tejana Young Adult Fiction and Poetry   3
   Larissa M. Mercado-López

2. Imagineering a New Mexican American Girl: Josefina Montoya (1824)   17
   Patricia Marina Trujillo

3. A Bone to Pick: Día de los Muertos in Children's Literature   33
   Roxana Loza and Tanya González

4. Águila: Personal Reflections on Reading Chicanx Picture Books from the Inside Out   47
   Lettycia Terrones

SECTION II: NEGOTIATING GENDER AND SEXUALITY   59

5. A Portrait of the Artist as a Muchachito: Juan Felipe Herrera's *Downtown Boy* as a Poetic Springboard into Critical Masculinity Studies   61
   Phillip Serrato

6	Not-So-Sweet *Quince*: Teenage Angst and Mother-Daughter Strife in Belinda Acosta's Young Adult Novel, *Damas, Dramas, and Ana Ruiz* Cristina Herrera	77
7	"You Wanna Be a Chump/or a Champ?": Constructions of Masculinity, Absent Fathers, and Conocimiento in Juan Felipe Herrera's *Downtown Boy* Sonia Alejandra Rodríguez, PhD	91
8	Representations of Sexual and Queer Identities in Chicana/o-Latina/o Children's Literature Cecilia J. Aragón	105

SECTION III: TRANSFORMATIVE PEDAGOGIES: REFLECTIONS FROM INSIDE AND OUTSIDE THE CLASSROOM — 121

9	Chillante Pedagogy, "She Worlds," and Testimonio as Text/Image: Toward a Chicana Feminist Pedagogy in the Works of Maya Christina Gonzalez Elena Avilés	123
10	Was It All a Dream? Chicana/o Children and Mestiza Consciousness in *Super Cilantro Girl* (2003) and "Tata's Gift" (2014) Katherine Elizabeth Bundy	137
11	Translanguaging *con mi abuela*: Chican@ Children's Literature as a Means to Elevate Language Practices in Our Homes Laura Alamillo	151
12	Identity Texts in Linguistically and Culturally Sustaining Classrooms: Chican@ Children's Literature, Student Voice, and Identity Lilian Cibils, Enrique Avalos, Virginia Gallegos, and Fabián Martínez	163

Index	179
About the Editors	189
About the Contributors	191

Foreword

ENTHRALLING: NOTES

"Chinela!" I read out loud, as mamá Lucha pointed to the image of a slipper, next to the CH letter in Spanish in the slim hardcover book she held up inside our makeshift trailer on the outskirts of Escondido, California, in the fifties. "Chi. . . ."

"Chinela!" I repeated until finishing with the musical piano-like "Zilófono" at the end of the alphabet. Moralistic stories followed—the one about two trees, the nurtured one that reached the sky, and the abandoned one? It splayed out its cracked and broken, jagged limbs and bent back its crest toward a cliff. All this from a cracked and worn, sixty-year-old Spanish language primer that mamá purchased downtown at la segunda, a second-hand store. Used—and from another century, my first book. Beyond that, for a migrante, a campesino boy on the road, there was the familiar horizon of cornfields, newborn colts, spiders, and ants—and in the oblong, distant, and strange city, sizzling on Saturday night, there were the spangled neon words balanced on the movie house signs that I could not fully read—or understand.

How to understand? How do we notice closely, hold up in our imagination, talk about, gather, and read the endless pages of the endless line (it seems) of Chican@ children's books and Young Adult (YA) novels at the beginning of a new century? (My tilted, hand made trailita and the scarce materials for a Chican@ and child recede into the past.) How do we notice and make "sense" of this new wave of text, imagineering, language- play, and the relationships between culture and power, gender blender remix, the jitter of traditions that are not static, rigid, and monumental as we once thought, like the Quinceañera. What is going on in the pages of this new kind of book about Chican@ lives and how do we put things together (like my trailer) from page to community, from casa to escuela, home to school and back?

Back to you, it is in your hands, these kinds of reflections and many more, these essays, these pláticas, soulful conversations—with this volume edited by Alamillo, Mercado-López, and Herrera (not related). These new literary critics and culture visionaries alert us to the recent rise of books written for Chican@ youth and to a new way of seeing too. How do we see and read ourselves in this radically new room of conversations and stories? How do we write ourselves into the key centers of society, into the schools, libraries, classrooms, and little houses like mine many years ago? How does the text, the actual words, the images blurring into phrase, and the gestures of the major characters inhabiting the books—how do they say things, mean things in and of themselves, and how are they (in some odd way) loosely threaded to all of us, pulling in, for, out, and against the larger grid of power? And—how do we speak of the writing about ourselves? Let me answer this with the metaphor of the "tree" from mamá Lucha's bitten and frayed Spanish primer—*we have nurtured the tree of knowledge in the last half century, that is, our place as literary critics, writers, speakers, as artists—here is a gifted, incisive, and luminous testament to such a blossoming accomplishment.*

"Chinela," I said. Then, after reading and speaking out loud the words to mamá Lucha, at the end, I said, "Zilófono." Then I pointed to the images again, touching the pages, smiled, smiled because somewhere inside of me there were chinelas now and there was a zylophone with many keys that I could play—and to this day, I compose with their music, and the music and words all around me, enthralling.

—Juan Felipe Herrera, Poet Laureate of the
United States, 2015–2017

Introduction

In 2010, the Tucson Unified School District in Tucson, Arizona, issued a ban on the highly successful Mexican American Studies program, citing the textbooks' perceived anti-American ideology that opponents argued called for the overthrow of the U.S. government (Planas, "Arizona Law," 2015). What subsequently followed were additional policies that censored course reading lists, effectively leading to the banning of prominent Chican@-authored books, including foundational texts such as Rudy Acuña's *Occupied America: A History of Chicanos* and Elizabeth Martínez's *500 Años Del Pueblo Chicano/500 Years of Chicano History in Pictures*.

Shortly after, courses focused on Mexican American history were eliminated, students' papers were subjected to monitoring for anti-American sentiment, and students were met with hostile resistance from administrators and conservative border vigilante groups. Border states including Arizona, California, New Mexico, and Texas have long histories of policing Mexicans and Chican@s on the U.S.–Mexico border, so it is unsurprising that the ban on Mexican American Studies coincided with the passing of Arizona's SB 1070, a bill that essentially legalized racial profiling to target immigrants of Mexican and Latin American descent for deportation under the guise of maintaining "safe neighborhoods" (Morse, "Arizona's Immigration," 2011).

The simultaneous implementation of these policies and bans revealed not only a fear of a growing demographic in those states, but made more visible the systematic ways in which institutions attempt to render invisible the bodies, lives, and stories of Chican@s. The Mexican American Studies curriculum in Arizona not only provided counterstories that forged spaces of curricular inclusion for students who were a minoritized majority in their state, but exposed them to histories of Chican@ activism that ignited their political and activist consciousness upon the implementation of the ban, resulting in collective student efforts to oppose a measure that had permitted state authorities to confiscate books while students sat in class.

Additionally, educators across the country seized the opportunity to reinvigorate conversations in their schools about the politics and practice of teaching race, ethnicity, and culture in the classroom; in response, underground libraries of banned literature sprung up in schools and community spaces, which also served as sites for banned literature readings.

In addition to historical and sociological texts, importantly, Chican@ youth literature and books with young Chican@s in central roles, such as Matt de la Peña's *Mexican White Boy* and Rudolfo Anaya's *Bless Me, Ultima*, were included on some of these lists ("Tucson's Banned Book List," 2012), thus disconnecting students from literature that was relevant to not only their cultural lives, but to their adolescent lives.

Educators also connected the ban to other methods of exclusion, including former and ongoing restrictive language policies in P–12 education that exclude the languages and knowledge systems of many Chican@ youth. These informal and formal educational practices take place in curricula that invisibilize the primary language(s) of children and Chican@ youth literature and obscure the heterogeneity of the Chican@ community and the fluid language practices in the lives of Chican@ children.

While most work on youth literature has emphasized "multicultural" literature as a means of being inclusive, we recognize that our present moment—one that is rife with continued anti-Mexican sentiment but that has given rise to our first Chicano National Poet Laureate—demands a more focused study of children's and young adult literature by and about Chican@s. This book reexamines how we view multicultural and diversity literature and how we recognize literature that impels social transformation.

It reaffirms the need to acknowledge Chicano@ children's literature as a means to achieve equity and social change. It is a hopeful time within the field of Chican@ children's literature. In addition to the recognition of a Chicano Poet Laureate, Juan Felipe Herrera, and the most recent Newbery award recipient, Matt de la Peña (first Latino awardee), as Guadalupe Garcia McCall, recipient of the Pura Belpre Award, and Ashley Hope Pérez, recipient of a Printz Honor award, indicate publishers are providing intentional spaces for publishing literature with Chican@ themes.

Cinco Puntos Press, Piñata Books, Lee & Low books, and independent Chican@ publishers such as Maya Christina Gonzalez's Reflections Press aim to produce quality literature considering insider perspectives as a way of reclaiming marginalized histories and centering Chican@ lives in all their complexities. Scholarship on Chican@ children's literature has grown within academia, but until now, the scholarship has been scattered across journals and submerged within larger studies of "multicultural literature" or even "Latino children's literature."

Voices of Resistance considers the potential of Chican@ literature to effect socially and politically transformative change through stories that reflect the diverse intricacies that can be found in Chican@ children's social, cultural, and linguistic lives.

CHICAN@ CHILDREN'S LITERATURE: CONTEXT AND CANON

Chican@ children's literature encompasses a wide range of experiences grounded in sociocultural/historical context. The purpose of this collection is to highlight and recognize the heterogeneity within this body of literature and give special attention and credit to the range of experiences within the Chican@ community.

In this work, scholars from various fields come together to describe how Chican@ children's literature raises questions on themes related to identity, social inequality, marginalization, raciolinguistic ideologies, and leveraging the *conscientizacao* or consciousness (Freire, 1993) in the Chican@ community. By focusing on the wide range of perspectives within Chican@ children's literature, the contributors present alternative voices *beyond* dominant voices in the field of children's literature.

From investigating the representation of masculinity in books written by our Chicano poet laureate, Juan Felipe Herrera, to identifying and theorizing the artivism of Chicana illustrators like Maya Christina Gonzalez, the contributors expose the rich tradition of Chican@ children's literature, focusing on the various iterations of the Chican@ experience written by Chican@ writers.

Within the field, Chican@ children's book authors tell stories stemming from their own personal experiences, from what they observe in their community, schools, or homes and leveraging these experiences in the literature. Producing books that young children and young adults relate to resists the context of restrictive language policies, social and educational marginalization of Chican@ youth, inaccurate textbooks on Mexican–American history, and anti-Mexican rhetoric by prominent political figures.

Presenting positive images and uplifting stories for young Chican@ children has the potential to normalize positive and nondeficit views of Chican@ families. Trailblazers like Children's Book Press, Piñata Books, Cincos Puntos Press, and others recognize the linguistic variation within Chican@ children's literature and strive to publish authentic and accurate language experiences in the Chican@ community.

More recent publishers like Lee & Low Books are paying more careful attention to the imposition of Castilian Spanish in translated books by selecting authentic bilingual speakers who understand the heteroglossic, linguistic variation within the Chican@ community. They aim to produce literature that truly speaks to the heterogeneity within the community and are thoughtful to this often-ignored feature of the Chican@ experience.

The thoughtful and mindful attention to cultural and linguistic variation allows for fresh voices to enter the field of this literature. More critical attention to variation in sexual/gender identification and family structure raises more awareness of the diversity of Chican@ experience, and goes beyond perpetuating notions of diversity as solely pertaining to language and culture.

As these scholars investigate queerness and LGBTQ issues in Chican@ children's literature, the contributors elevate the discussions on *diversity* in our schools and communities. Scholars go beyond heroes and holidays in their analysis, and in some cases, discuss the implications for schooling. Some say this positive change has come slowly. Barrera and Garza de Cortes (1997) describe this aim toward accuracy and authenticity as "one Chicano at a time."

Although the depiction of Mexican Americans in literature has improved, reoccurring themes in Latino literature may reinforce the stereotypical notions of Chican@s as exotic, foreign, or different. Terms such as Latino children's literature can also potentially lump the experiences of all Latinos into one category. More recent research in the field (Clark, Bustos Flores, Smith, & Gonzalez, 2016) reflects on the various terms used to describe it. There is consensus that there is a need "to understand that labels in their context from a knowledge base and choose the one that best defines them" (xxi).

We are aware of the labels placed on Chican@ children in schools. Labels like English Learners, Standard English Learners, and Limited English Proficient further perpetuate deficit notions of the linguistic practices of Chican@ children in schools and perpetuate a monoglossic view of bilingualism. Labels deny the existing knowledge and expertise Chican@ children bring into the classroom from their homes and communities.

Because of imposed labels, there is a need to use terms grounded in social justice, and to push, question other labels used in the field. This collection challenges this grouping of voices and instead offers an alternative way to look at Chican@ children's literature. Most importantly, it insists on claiming and giving intellectual consideration to a rich Chican@ children's literary tradition, long overlooked by scholars in multiple fields.

We anticipate this collection as the first in bringing together various voices and perspectives analyzing Chican@ children's literature from Women's Studies, Chican@ Studies, Education, Theater, and others. This array of voices is needed in order to be inclusive of more experiences in the field, offering unique perspectives on how the literature can be consumed, examined, and introduced to young adults and children.

VOICES OF RESISTANCE: A THEMATIC OVERVIEW

The chapters in this collection are written by scholars that span the fields of literature, education, gender, and Chican@ Studies. Section I, "Tracing Chican@ Identity and Consciousness," offers chapters that explore and challenge the boundaries of Chican@ identity and that expand historical narratives about the origins of Chican@ consciousness. In chapter 1, "Entre Tejana y Chicana: Tracing Proto-Chicana Identity and Consciousness in Tejana Young Adult Fiction and Poetry," Larissa M. Mercado-López discusses Ashley Hope Perez's recent YA novel, *Out of Darkness*, a text that gives voice to groups that have been marginalized within dominant narratives of colonial and imperial histories.

Continuing, Patricia Trujillo investigates what she refers to as "literary gentrification" to discuss the only Nuevo Mexicana character in the well-known American Girl book series in chapter 2, "Imagineering a Mexican American Girl: Josefina Montoya (1824)." Chapter 3 by Roxana Loza and Tanya González, "A Bone to Pick: Día de los Muertos in Children's Literature," analyzes the well-known children's picture book, *Rosita y Conchita*, as an example of a decolonizing narrative of the Mexican Day of the Dead. Chapter 4 by Lettycia Terrones, "Águila: Personal reflections on reading Chicanx picturebooks from the inside out," engages in personal and critical responses to Chicanx picturebooks to account for the diversity of Chicanx lived experiences.

In Section II, "Negotiating Gender and Sexuality," contributors insist on examining Chican@ children's literature with a keen focus on intersections of sexuality and gender with ethnic/racial identity. Chapter 5, "A Portrait of the Artist as a Muchachito: Juan Felipe Herrera's *Downtown Boy* as a Poetic Springboard into Critical Masculinity Studies," by Phillip Serrato, explores multivaried expectations of masculinity and boyhood that the young protagonist must maneuver.

Chapter 6 by Cristina Herrera, "Not-So-Sweet Quince: Teenage Angst and Mother-Daughter Strife in Belinda Acosta's Young Adult Novel, *Damas, Dramas, and Ana Ruiz*," argues that the young adult writer, Belinda Acosta, demystifies the quinceanera "tradition" to account for a more nuanced understanding of gender, coming-of-age, and identity. Following this is chapter 7 by Sonia Alejandra Rodriguez, "You wanna be a chump/or a champ?: Constructions of Masculinity, Absent Fathers, and Conocimiento in Juan Felipe

Herrera's *Downtown Boy*," which further investigates warring images of masculinity that are complicated by the absence of paternal figures.

Finally, in chapter 8, "Representation of Sexual and Queer Identities in Chicana/o-Latina/o Children's Literature," Cecilia Aragon urges a critique of queerness and sexuality in Chican@ children's literature, a topic that has historically been overlooked in the field.

Section III, "Transformative Pedagogies: Reflections from Inside and Outside the Classroom," presents chapters that call for a nuanced exploration of identity and selfhood. Chapter 9 by Elena Avilés, "Chillante Pedagogy, 'She Worlds,' and Testimonio as Text/Image: Toward a Chicana Feminist Pedagogy in the works of Maya Christina Gonzalez," explores the significance of Maya Christina Gonzalez's artwork and writings that create alternative sites of Chicana selfhood. In chapter 10, "Was It All a Dream? Chicana/o Children and Mestiza Consciousness in Super Cilantro Girl (2003) and 'Tata's Gift' (2014)," Katherine Elizabeth Bundy explores identity formation and dream states in texts by Juan Felipe Herrera.

In chapter 11, "Translanguaging con mi abuela: Chican@ Children's Literature as a Means to Elevate Language Practices in Our Homes," Laura Alamillo unpacks the role of the Abuela figure in children's literature as agent of speech and resistance. Lilian Cibils, Virginia Gallegos, Enrique Avalos, and Fabián Martínez conclude the book with chapter 12, "Identity Texts in Linguistically and Culturally Sustaining Classrooms: Chican@ Children's Literature, Student Voice, and Belonging," which insists on the need to include linguistically and culturally affirming children's texts in the classroom.

Crossing disciplinary and thematic boundaries, the chapters in this volume not only urge the inclusion of Chican@ children's literature in the fields of education, literature, and ethnic and gender studies, but they speak to the need to acknowledge Chican@ children's literature as a highly politicized, revolutionary, and dynamic body of work that has evolved as an established canon.

As our title indicates, Chican@ children's literature voices a resistance to the many interlocking trappings of oppression faced by our community, and in this resistance offers new ways of being Chican@ in the twenty-first century.

IMPLICATIONS FOR THE CLASSROOM

At the forefront of the collection is the education of Chican@ children and how the use of Chican@ children's literature transforms classroom pedagogy. As readers explore the themes presented in the collection, it is also important to consider how the literature can be used to transform educational outcomes for Chican@ children who are also emergent bilingual children. Keeping in mind how the authors introduce the specific literature with the highlighted themes educators can also explore how these themes can be discussed with young children.

REFERENCES

A Copy of Tucson's Banned Book List. (2012). In NewsTaco. Retrieved from http://www.newstaco.com/2012/01/31/a-copy-of-tucsons-banned-book-list

Barrera, R. B., & Garza de Cortes, O. (1997). Mexican American children's literature in the 1990's: Toward authenticity. *Using multiethnic literature in the K-8 classroom*, 129–54.

Barrera, R. B., Quiroa, R. E., & West-Williams, C. (1999). Poco a poco: The continuing development of Mexican American children's literature in the 1990s. *New Advocate, 12*, 315–30.

Bishop, R. S. (2003). Reframing the debate about cultural authenticity. in Fox, Dana L. and Kathy G. Short (Eds), *Stories matter: The complexity of cultural authenticity in children's literature*, 25–37. Urbana, Illinois: National Council of Teachers of English.

Clark, E. R., Flores, B. B., Smith, H. L., & González, D. A. (2015). *Multicultural literature for Latino bilingual children: Their words, their worlds*. Rowman & Littlefield.

Freire, P. (1993). *Pedagogy of the oppressed. 1970.* New York: Continuum, 125.

Morse, A. (2011). Arizona's immigration enforcement laws. *National Conference of State Legislatures*. Retrieved from www.ncsl.org

Planas, R. (2015). Arizona law that banned Mexican-American studies may be discriminatory, court rules. *Huffington Post*. Retrieved from www.huffingtonpost.com/

Section I

TRACING CHICAN@ IDENTITY AND CONSCIOUSNESS

The most recent census data reveal that one in four children enrolled in school in the United States is Latino, and of the 55 million Latinos counted in the 2014 census, just over 60 percent are of Mexican descent. This suggests that students of Mexican descent, or Chican@s, maintain a significant presence in K-12 classrooms in the United States. Pan-ethnic terms such as "Hispanic" and "Latino," however, obscure the differences that exist among Latinos, as well as render invisible the real anti-Mexican sentiment that continues to fuel efforts to eliminate Ethnic Studies courses, implement racial profiling laws, and ban books. Thus, the terms Chicano, Chicana, and Chicanx continue to be relevant as children of Mexican descent trace their histories and construct their own ways of identifying as Chican@s. The chapters in this section trace some of the contours of Chican@ identity, exploring its legal, linguistic, and visual constructions in Chican@ young adult and children's literature.

The chapters in this section speak to the complexities of defining and representing Chican@ identities, communities, and traditions. Larissa M. Mercado-López's chapter, for example, challenges the historical origins of Chicana consciousness by putting Ashley Hope Perez's *Out of Darkness* in conversation with pre-Chicano movement poetry. Similarly, while the book series' character is technically Mexican, Patricia Trujillo's chapter expands the historical tracing of Chican@ history by situating the American Girl Josefina Montoya series "on a trajectory of becoming an American Girl"; she declares the Josefina Montoya series to be an important contribution to the representation of New Mexican girls in Chican@ literature. In their analysis of *Rosita y Conchita*, Roxana Loza and Tanya González read the book and the Day of the Dead holiday through a decolonial lens to highlight the permeability of borders within the text and surrounding Chican@ identity. Finally, Lettycia Terrones' chapter surveys both text and images in Chicanx picture books to assess authentic representations of Chicanx identities, discussing how this literature can engage educators in transformational educational praxis for effecting social change.

This section challenges, widens, and illuminates concepts and varying representations of Chican@ identity and consciousness, making the case for close studies of specifically *Chican@* texts that center Chicano@ experience in the analysis, as opposed to conflating it with a pan-ethnic "Latino" experience. As these chapters uncover, Chican@ children's literature reveals the fluidity of what it means to be Chican@ and the challenges of representing authentic lived experiences.

Chapter 1

Entre Tejana y Chicana: Tracing Proto-Chicana Identity and Consciousness in Tejana Young Adult Fiction and Poetry

Larissa M. Mercado-López

Eh, Tejana!
Hateful words hurled in scorn
Branding a Texas born
Mexicana.

Oh, that Texan
Spanish and Indian,
Brown-skinned American—
A Mexican;

O, Tejana!
Robbed of the land you love,
Betrayed by the hand of
Santa Ana,

Mexicana,
Proud of race and breeding
But proudest of being
Hailed Tejana!
—Lupe Salazar, Age 18, 1936

In 1936, eighteen-year-old Lupe Salazar was one of the winners of the San Antonio Public Library's Young Pegasus contest, a poetry competition that continues today. The poem in the book featuring the winners' pieces is preceded by an epigraph that reads:

TEJANA means Texas born, but like GREASER and GRINGO, it is used as a term of insult or contempt. Nortenos (sic), or Mexican people of Northern Mexico, particularly remind Texas born Mexicans that though their parents are Mexicans,

they aren't. Neither are Mexican-Texan Americans in the same way as citizens of the United States, they simply are TEJANOS, aliens in Mexico and in the U.S.A.
But I am proud of being a Texan. (n.p.)

Here, Lupe Salazar, whose full first name is most likely Guadalupe, exhibits the complicated experience of a U.S.–Mexico borderlands identity, particularly in a state that was an important site of colonization and that just 100 years before the publication of this poem used to be Mexico.

In her poem, Tejana, Texan, Mexican, and "Brown-skinned American" are used to exemplify the ways in which her racialized and gendered identity is negotiated in response to situational and cultural contexts. From "Eh, Tejana" at the beginning of the poem to "proudest of being/Hailed Tejana" at the end, the Tejana identity evolves from one of scorn that is "branded" upon Salazar to one of self-reclamation and empowerment, firmly grounded in her connection to Mexico and shaped by critical recognition of the history of the colonial Southwest.

This poem, as well as Salazar's "Gringo!" that will be discussed later, signals a nuanced understanding and consciousness of racial and ethnic identities as they are informed by concepts of belonging and authenticity conceptualized by subjects on both sides of the border. Her use of descriptors such as "Mexicana," a "brown-skinned American," and "Spanish and Indian" exemplifies Chicana theorist Gloria Anzaldúa's (2012a) concept of mestiza consciousness, a "consciousness of the borderlands" that embraces duality and hybridity, and demands nonbinary ways of thinking about the self; most Chicanas, women of Mexican descent living in the United States, are mestizas.

Mestiza consciousness is not only a recognition of the mestiza's identity as both colonizer and colonized, it is also a way of reconciling the two into an empowered third identity. For Salazar, claiming a Tejana identity is her way of reconciling her seemingly oppositional identities of Texan and Mexican; in fact, her use of "Lupe," as opposed to what is most likely her birth name "Guadalupe," is one signal of this reconciliation.

I bring forward this previously unstudied poem from the archives and put it into conversation with Chicana theory to raise questions about what it means to be Chicana and to have a Chicana consciousness prior to the Chicano movement of the 1960s and 1970s. Literary works written by Tejanas such as Jovita González's *Caballero: A Historical Romance* (1996), coauthored with Eve Raleigh and originally written in the 1930s and 1940s, and Leonor Villegas de Magnón's *The Rebel* (1994), originally written in the 1920s, have been hailed as "proto-Chicana" works (Rodriguez, 2008) that demonstrate early evidence of a Chicana consciousness.

The chapter also focuses on Tejanas, or women of Mexican descent who identify as Texan, but I am limiting my reading to adolescents within the genre of Young Adult (YA) literature. Texas has been the setting for several recent Chicana YA novels, including Guadalupe Garcia McCall's *Under the*

Mesquite, *Summer of the Mariposas*, and *Shame the Stars*, and Ashley Hope Pérez's YA historical fiction novel, *Out of Darkness*. In *Shame the Stars* and *Out of Darkness*, early twentieth-century race relations and politics figure prominently, providing a snapshot of a history whose struggles continue to be experienced today.

Considering that Texas is currently embroiled in a battle over allegedly inaccurate and racist textbooks that are expected to be adopted for use in Mexican American Studies classrooms, it is especially critical that young readers have access to books written by and for Chicanas—books that tell Texas history from the perspective of those in an ongoing resistance to colonialism.

Though *Out of Darkness* was written in the twenty-first century about an event that occurred in 1937, the use of historical documents to portray the era and its careful depiction of Naomi Martinez, a teen girl born in Mexico and who grew up in San Antonio and spends most of the book living in East Texas, gives the story a strong sense of credibility and presents opportunities for further study of Texas history from nondominant, and female, perspectives.

I am complicating and expanding the study of Tejana identity and consciousness further, however, by focusing on the genre of YA literature, compelling its inclusion within the Chican@ literary landscape as another source for tracing trajectories of collective identity formation and giving voice to voices marginalized within dominant narratives of colonial and imperial histories.

This chapter situates Ashley Hope Pérez's YA historical fiction novel *Out of Darkness* in conversation with early Tejana youth poetry. Through a Chicana feminist reading of contemporary fictional narratives of pre-Chicana movement histories, this chapter exemplifies how youth literature incorporates voices that are not traditionally considered to be "authoritative" and whose positions in the interstices of consciousness give us a fuller understanding of the experiences of Chicanas.

Chicana feminist youth literature can have serious implications for its young Chicana readers already living in the in-between spaces of childhood and adulthood and Chican@ and U.S. mainstream cultures. Importantly, using Gloria Anzaldúa's concept of mestiza consciousness, I argue for the inclusion of *young* Tejana feminist consciousness in our conceptualization of Chicana feminist consciousness.

CHICANA YA LITERATURE AS AN INTERVENTION STRATEGY

I precede my discussion of Pérez's work with a brief discussion of Chican@/Latin@ YA lit as an intervention strategy, as conceptualized by teachers for their classroom, authors for their audience, and scholars of youth literature.

Literary scholars of youth literature discuss the need for "Hispanic" representation in YA to compel students to read, to feel recognized by seeing characters like themselves in stories, and even to mitigate high school dropout rates (Barry, 1998). Much of the rationale for teaching multiethnic YA rests on perceived academic deficiencies. However, teachers of students of color are in positions in which they can seize upon opportunities for using YA literature to not only compel students to read but also to understand structural and historical oppressions at this especially formative time in their lives.

Pointing to critical works by Latinas in YA literature, Cristina Herrera (2016) notes that "women writers of color have turned to children's and young adult writing to invoke critical consciousness at a young age" (p. 100). In her analysis of Guadalupe Garcia McCall's *Summer of the Mariposas*, Herrera argues that the novel is a "Chicana feminist text" that "rejects the patriarchal myth" of La Llorona that historically "depicts women and girls as untrustworthy and 'bad' if they fail to abide by prescribed gender codes" (p. 98).

The feminist intent of the book is supported by García McCall, herself, who identifies her young female students' frustration with not finding girls represented in "adventure books" as the impetus for writing *Mariposas* (p. 100). Texts such as Sandra Cisneros' *House on Mango Street* are often considered to be feminist, consciousness-raising texts; however, in the case of *Mango*, it was not Cisneros' intent to write specifically for children or YAs. Nonetheless, *Mango* is one of the most widely read books in K-12 classrooms across the country, and it should be included in the articulation of the landscape of Chican@ children's literature.

Chican@ youth literature scholar Phillip Serrato also recognizes the utility and significance of youth literature in the consciousness formation of children and YAs. In his discussion of Chicana feminist children's book writers Pat Mora and Ana Castillo, Serrato (2010) identifies the political implications of Chican@ children's book writing, explaining that "writing books for younger readers creates a valuable opportunity to expand the reach of their critical projects to include an audience still in the midst of its intellectual and social formation" (p. 133).

Serrato further points to the potential for scholars and educators "to turn to their [Mora and Castillo] books for children for a demonstration of the capacity of children's literature to serve as a venue for the articulation and implementation of progressive gender politics" (p. 133).

Chican@ youth literature, because of its visible grappling with issues of identity and injustice, offers educators and readers even more opportunity to engage in critical literacy practices. According to Morgan (1998), "Critical literacy teaching begins by problematising the culture and knowledges in the text—putting them up for grabs, critical debate, for weighing, judging, critiquing" (p. 157). Through such practices, students can also put their discussions of the text into critical engagement with their social text/world, expanding the reach of the book and its applicability.

Out of Darkness is a riveting fictional account of the events leading up to and surrounding the 1937 New London School House Explosion, which killed hundreds of children and school staff. At the center of this novel is Naomi Martinez, her half brother and half sister Beto and Cari, who are twins, Naomi's white stepfather Henry, and Wash, a young black boy who befriends Naomi, Beto, and Cari, and with whom Naomi falls in love.

New London, Texas, is depicted as a booming oil town that draws workers from across the state, providing them with home-owning opportunities and a sense of community. But the town is highly segregated, virtually devoid of black residents. In fact, black Texans in that region lived in the fictional neighboring town of Egypt Town, whose name is perhaps a nod to the enslavement of the Israelites in Egypt and the town's residents' histories of enslavement. Naomi, one of the few brown children in New London, quickly finds herself unable to fit neatly into racial categories, directly challenging the racial binary that draws the lines between who does and does not belong— who is and is not safe.

Returning to my thesis and further clarifying its scope, this chapter focuses specifically on Naomi's experiences within Texas' segregated education system and as a victim of sexual violation to argue that by naming Naomi a Chicana, we can more firmly place her within the trajectory of Chicana identity, consciousness, history, and violence. Thus, in conversation with Lupe Salazar's poetry, her story can be used to enrich our understanding of anti-Chican@ sentiment prior to the Chican@ movement from an epistemically rich perspective—that of an adolescent, one that is not usually included in authoritative historical narratives of Texas.

MESTIZA IDENTITY AND THE IMPERIAL EDUCATION SYSTEM

In *Out of Darkness*, Naomi is described from Henry's perspective as dark— "shades darker" than her mother—with "a mouth full of Spanish" (p. 28). In Gloria Anzaldúa's *Borderlands* (2012a), Anzaldúa describes the mestiza as an embodiment of both the Spaniard and the Indian, the colonizer and the colonized.

Her repeated references to darkness as a marker of indigeneity further emphasize the significance of color in the experience of mestizaje, the primary characteristic of Chicana identity. The association of Chicana identity with a particular mestizaje of cultures and races, then, begs the question of whether or not contemporary usages reflect this broader conceptualization.

In a recent twitter conversation, Chicano YA literature author Joe Jimenez tweeted: "Chatting with @ashleyhopeperez. Is a Mexican-American character in a novel about 1937 East Texas Chicana? #outofdarkness. #sabookfest" (Jimenez, 2015). Jimenez's tweet, suggesting that the question was unresolved by the author, raises interesting questions about the limits of current usage of the term Chicana.

Marta Ester Sánchez (1986) defines "Chicana" as "a woman of Mexican heritage who lives in the United States" (p. 338), a definition that emphasizes heritage and location, and that reflects most of the definitions that can be found across various sources. However, others suggest that the term has been stigmatized due to its associations with a "radical" movement, yet while they strive for a definition with wider applicability, they also want it to reflect a more politicized articulation.

Xicana writer Ana Castillo (1995) explains:

> many women of Mexican descent in the nineties do not apply the term Chicana to themselves seeing it as an outdated expression weighed down by the particular radicalism of the seventies. The search for a term which would appeal to the majority of women of Mexican descent who are also concerned with the social and political ramifications of living in a hierarchical society has been frustrating. (p. 10)

Here, Castillo speaks to the desire to retain the political imperative of Chicana identity, by connecting the "outdated" and "radical" expression of the 1970s to the struggles and identity politics that shape Chicana activism today. Castillo takes the term a step further by using the word "Xicana" to signify "Chicana feminist," an attempt to recoup a lost indigenous heritage (p. 11), the indigeneity that Anzaldúa closely associates with the marker of brownness.

The twentieth- and twenty-first-century debates around defining Chicana identity circle back around to questions of who has the power to define, and what is revealed when those identities are used as lenses for understanding experience. I argue that it is critical to name Naomi a Chicana, not only because under more general definitions it is accurate, but also because it makes her more visible within the dominant black/white racial paradigm. Though Naomi does not reflect upon nor claim a politicized experience or identity, others impose their politics on her, compromising her safety, peace, and agency over her body.

The contention over Naomi's racial identity is conveyed by the collective voice of the students, named "The Gang" in the novel. The Gang mulls over Naomi's identity, stating that "a few of us decided that she wasn't a Mexican at all since the little kids [Beto and Cari] weren't brown. The explanation was that her mama was white but there's been a nigger in the wood stack" (p. 59).

They continue, explaining that the town could not decide where she belonged: some argued that she "ought to be out learning with the coloreds," but others argued that "she was a Mexican and that it was hardly fair to make a Mexican go to a darkie school" (p. 59). The debate over Naomi's identity and her place within the school system exposes the ways in which Mexican children were invisible within school segregation rhetoric and policy.[1]

Likewise, Salazar's (1935) poem "Gringo" reveals racial tensions in an altercation presumably between two schoolchildren. The poem reads:

> "Greaser!" shouted the towhead lad,
> "Gringo!" screamed the dark-skinned child;
> Which hated most was hard to tell—
> What turned them both so wild?
>
> If one of them was better,
> Who was it, please tell me who?
> For is it not the inferior,
> Who makes the most ado? (n.p.)

In the poem, Salazar uses phenotypic markers to racialize the white "towhead lad" and the Mexican "dark-skinned child." Unlike what she does in her later poem "Tejana," Salazar does not condemn either one; instead, she questions the character of both children, though her title's emphasis on the "gringo" seems to suggest one to be the antagonizer. In her introduction to the Young Pegasus 1935 booklet, children's librarian Leah Johnson observes that the young poets in the collection "are thinking about their future. But perhaps a little, too, they are thinking about the past as it contrasts with their future" (n.p.). However, for Salazar, a teen living in the segregated Southwest, "Gringo" reflects a present experience.

Describing Salazar's poem as "pos[ing] . . . a question as old as time itself but always with a fresh application," Johnson focuses on the philosophical question of inferiority rather than on the first question in the poem that seeks an understanding of race relations. Salazar's desire to know "What turned them both so wild?" speaks to the failures of the education system to miseducate children about the history of colonization.

As Pérez explains in the Author's Note, "The educational experiences of Naomi, Wash, and the twins allowed me to incorporate glimpses of the tripartite segregation system present in Texas before the Civil Rights Movement, a system that separated children into 'white,' 'colored,' and 'Mexican' schools" (p. 399). Naomi demonstrates acute awareness of her experiences of racism in a "Mexican" school when she recounts her schooling in San Antonio, insisting that the white teachers "hated" the Mexican kids, giving elementary school books to the Mexican students in high school and teaching them skills that were not "useful" (p. 89). This is juxtaposed with her experience in New London, where she attends a "white" school.

It takes Mexican Naomi to disrupt and push the boundaries of the black/white racial paradigm that firmly guided the law and shaped social relations in East Texas. The experiences of adolescents attending school under racist laws give us insight into lived experiences of discrimination and segregation that come to be part of the consciousness of those who shape future policy. Further, they enable us to see the early pivotal moments of critical social and political awareness.

In her essay "The New Mestiza Nation: A Multicultural Movement," Anzaldúa (2012b) examines the propagation of white supremacy through the suppression of people of color knowledges, histories, and perspectives in K-12 and higher education. She asserts, "The new conservatives want to keep higher education a Euro-Anglo institution. They want to keep a Euro-Anglo country, expanding a Euro-Anglo world, imperializing into the Third World" (p. 206).

Claiming "multicultural education as a centerpiece of the Mestiza nation" (p. 204), she struggles against "literary assimilation," instead seeking personal and political validation, "transformative pedagogical and institutional practices," and "scholarship that challenges existing power hierarchies" (p. 204). In short, a decolonial education. Naomi's educational experiences, as depicted in the novel, serve to demonstrate how the continued colonization of Mexicans and other children of color can inform attitudes toward Chicanas today.

The link between the experiences of the past and present is clear in one of the novel's scenes, in which Naomi is in a bathroom and witnesses an exchange between presumably two teachers. In their conversation, the women refer to Naomi as "Dark" and "Maybe a little retarded" (p. 103). They continue describing her as "fast in other areas of life" and "want[ing] the boys to look" (p. 103).

Placing the hypersexualization of Naomi within the context of 1937 is revealing, as the year 1937 falls on the heels of Mexican Repatriation, from 1929 to 1936, which forced the return of people of Mexican descent to Mexico. The suspicion of Naomi as a sexual lure, as the rest of their conversation reveals, speaks to the fear of Mexican women's sexual domination of white men.

The hypersexualization of Mexican women has been well-documented by scholars (Carlos Velez-Ibanez, 1980; Espino, 2000; Gutiérrez, 2008) whose works expose how the fear of Mexican women's reproduction and the growing population of people of Mexican descent in the United State led to practices of forced sterilization by U.S. doctors. In her research, Ochoa (2015) looks at the intersection of Latina teen mothers, teachers' perceptions of the mothers as hypersexual and indifferent toward their education, and curriculum policy. Her work reveals how the prevailing notions of Latina sexuality can figure significantly in Latinas' schooling experiences.

The exchange between the women in the novel, then, speaks to the ways in which Mexican women/Chicanas have and continue to combat others' presumptions of their sexuality and educational aspirations. After witnessing the exchange, Naomi "fight[s] to get free of their words" (p. 108), and soon after deflects Wash's question about having "sweethearts" (p. 107), indicating a struggle to "free" herself of the sexualized image imposed on her and to honor the love she has for Wash.

Taking Naomi's mestiza identity a step further by renaming it as Chicana allows for us to more firmly place her within the longer and broader struggles of Chicanas. The intersections of gender, sexuality, and race that shape Naomi's experiences heighten her consciousness of what it means to be a girl of Mexican descent in a white town. The poetry of Lupe Salazar provides a more critical perspective and enunciation of Chicana consciousness. Together, Naomi's story and Salazar's poetry reveal the intense conflict that defined this time in Texas history.

As Naomi's experiences with Henry reveal, it is within the character of Naomi that colonialism, sexuality, and violence converge; her lack of agency due to her age and secondary citizen-status as an "alien" as a young girl of Mexican descent in a segregated town further subject her to an experience of violation that can be figured into the trajectory of the sexual conquest of Chicanas.

CHICANA ALIENATION AND SEXUALITY IN THE ONGOING COLONIAL PROJECT

The connection between Naomi's sense of alienation and her violation at the hands of Henry is not unlike the sexual conquest of indigenous women at the hands of the Spaniards in the name of "progress."[2] The concept of feeling or being "alien," particularly in one's own homeland, is a salient feature of Chicana identity. Anzaldúa (2012) refers to the experience of being a mestiza in the borderlands as feeling "Alienated from her mother culture, 'alien' in the dominant culture" (p. 42). Likewise, in "Tejana" Salazar describes Tejanos as being "aliens in Mexico and in the U.S.A." (n.p.).

Indeed, San Antonio Public Library Children's Librarian Leah Johnston speaks to Salazar and Naomi's feelings of alienation. In her foreword at the beginning of the 1935 Young Pegasus, Johnson speaks of Salazar's poem, "Tejana," insisting that "'Tejana' is herself [San Antonio] speaking. She, too, has always been a little alien in the land of her adoption" (n.p.).

The comparison is useful, as both Naomi and San Antonio are unwillingly displaced and rehomed, both having been part of Mexico and Texas, and still struggling to achieve a sense of belonging. Describing a similar existence, Anzaldúa (2012) explains, "As a Mestiza I have no country, my homeland cast me out" (p. 102); the parallel experiences of feeling or being without a country, or a home, further connects Naomi to Chicana history and the Chicana psyche.

In the novel, Naomi is continuously subjected to the advances of her stepfather, Henry, who begins the molestation while Naomi's mother, Estella, is still alive and they are living in San Antonio. When Naomi and the family are moved to East Texas, the combination of Henry's alcoholism, grief over the death of his wife, Naomi's mother, and the urging of a local pastor creates a sense of patriarchal entitlement that emboldens Henry to prey upon young Naomi. Throughout the story, Naomi devises plans to stay out of Henry's path and to mitigate his efforts to be alone with her. Her own home is an uneasy space where her siblings have security but where she fears for her own safety.

In one scene, Naomi suspects that Henry is drunk and considers going to bed without brushing her teeth to avoid interacting with him; instead, she decides to finish washing the dishes to keep him from becoming angry. Still wearing her mother's dress she had tried on earlier, Naomi stands at the kitchen sink, where Henry approaches her and rubs his body against hers, repeating Estella's name. Naomi fights him off, to which he responds, "Oh, honey, go on and be mad, that makes you look even more like your ma. She liked to pretend to fight, too" (p. 196).

The novel continues, "He grinned at her as if none of her resistance had registered" (p. 196). Henry's reading of Naomi's resistance as "pretending" reflects the teachers' descriptions of Naomi as inherently hypersexual and "wanting" sexual attention, further tightening the shackles of racist and sexist discourse that shapes her existence in East Texas. Unlike her siblings, and even after adopting Henry's Anglo last name, Naomi is unable to transcend the markings of sexuality and the historical imprint of conquest on her brown body.

In fact, it is only in the hollow of a tree that Naomi finds peace; it is a space not associated with race, where she and Wash can express their love for one another. As Naomi crosses the lines of sexuality with herself, discovering her own sexual pleasure, and with Wash, she vows that "she would not allow even the shadow of a thought of Henry into their tree" (p. 209). As an "alien" in East Texas, this is the only space where she feels belongingness.

At one point in the novel, Henry finds out that Naomi has been shopping for their groceries in Egypt Town because the local shop owner does not allow her to patron his store. He angrily reminds her, "This is East Texas, and there's lines. Lines you cross, lines you don't cross" (p. 133). The lines, ambiguous and ever-shifting, create the "alien element" of the borderlands (Anzaldúa, 2012, n.p.) that Naomi finds difficult to navigate. The tree, hollowed after years of decaying, is the one place of unarguable certainty.

However, it is a tree that figures prominently in Naomi's demise at the end of the novel. After the New London school has exploded the town goes on a witch-hunt for Wash to hold him accountable for the deaths and destruction, including the death of Cari. Naomi and Beto attempt to escape with Wash but are confronted by Henry, who leads them deep into the forest and forces Beto to tie Wash to a tree. At this tree, Wash is forced to watch Henry brutally rape Naomi as punishment for her rejection of Henry and her love for Wash. Exclaiming, "What do you do with a field you own? You plow it" (p. 380), Henry proceeds to rape and beat Naomi, ordering Beto to watch. At last, Henry pulls the trigger, killing both Wash and Naomi.

Naomi's death, in many ways, symbolizes the impossibility of her liberation. As a Chicana in the segregated Southwest, she has no home, limited agency, and little legal protection. As an adolescent, Naomi experiences an additional layer of ownership by Henry—as his "field" that he is entitled to "plow." The use of slave imagery and the rhetoric of ownership and possession amplify Naomi's utter powerlessness as an adolescent, a person of color, and racially ambiguous under the law.

CHICANA YA LITERATURE FOR A LIBERATORY FUTURE

Today, Naomi lives on in the cases of young Chicanas who have been victimized by rape. In fact, less than 200 miles away from New London is Cleveland, Texas, another East Texas town that was the site of a vicious gang rape of an eleven-year-old Chicana, the daughter of Mexican immigrant parents, involving eighteen boys and men.

Newspapers shared the comments made by local residents: "They said she dressed older than her age, wearing makeup and fashions more appropriate to a woman in her 20s. She would hang out with teenage boys at a playground, some said" (McKinley, 2011). Resident Angie Woods also asserted, "Them boys didn't rape her. She wanted this to happen" (Siemaszko, 2011). This case, and many others, begs the inclusion of Naomi's story within the literary trajectory of the Chicana history.

Claiming Chicana identity, as outlined by Anzaldúa, can be the beginning of a transformation of consciousness into an "'alien' consciousness" that can heal the split of dualistic paradigms that she identifies as the "root" of racial and sexual struggles. She explains, "A massive uprooting of dualistic thinking in the individual and collective consciousness is the beginning of a long struggle, but one that could, in our best hopes, bring us to the end of rape, of violence, of war" (p. 102).

Though Naomi does not survive at the end of the novel, reading Naomi as a Chicana can enable readers to begin to see the social and legal paradigms that made the recognition of her personhood impossible. And it is then that Naomi is no longer a victim of rape and patriarchal conquest, but a true borderlands subject whose life is one of the many being reclaimed by the anticolonial Chicana feminist movement—a movement in pursuit of the end of rape, of violence, of war.

Educators looking for fictional and nonfictional accounts of young Chicana in early Texas should consider *Out of Darkness* and the poetry of Lupe Salazar. These works directly grapple with the effects of colonialism, racism, and violence, in the lives of young people, while also speaking to their adolescent desires for love, safety, and peace.

Though *Out of Darkness* presents some challenges in terms of the graphic depiction of sexual violence, the scenes can be opportunities to facilitate students' confrontations of the horrors of the past to better understand the struggles of the present. This is especially critical during a time when Texas is embroiled in a war over inaccurate and racist textbooks that are being considered for inclusion in Mexican American Studies classes in Texas' public high schools ("Proposed Mexican American Studies," n.d.).

We can only hope that Tejana-Chicanas today can use their dual consciousness to critique anti-Mexican rhetoric and to reconcile their identities as young poet Lupe Salazar has done in her poem "Tejana." As Naomi's story and Lupe's poetry have demonstrated, the voices of young Chicanas are not only worthy of being heard, they also generate critical knowledges that enhance our understandings of Chicana identity and experience today.

NOTES

1. Mexicans were formally recognized as white in 1930, but in 1954, *Hernandez v. Texas* determined that Mexican Americans, though racially white, constituted a separate class from whites and African-Americans that subjected them to discrimination, and were entitled to equal protection under the law (*Hernandez v. State of Texas*, n.d.).

2. See Andrea Smith's *Conquest: Sexual Violence and American Indian Genocide* (2005) for more on the role of rape in the colonization of the Americas.

REFERENCES

Anzaldúa, G. (2012a). *Borderlands/La Frontera: The new mestiza* (4th ed.). San Francisco, CA: Spinsters/Aunt Lute Books.

Anzaldúa, G. (2012b). The new mestiza nation: A multicultural movement. In AnaLouise Keating (Ed.), *The Gloria Anzaldúa Reader* (pp. 203–16). Durham, North Carolina. Duke University Press.

Barry, A. (1998). Hispanic representation in literature for children and young adults. *Journal of Adolescent & Adult Literacy, 41*(8), 630–37.

Castillo, A. (1995). *Massacre of the Dreamers: Essays on Xicanisma*. New York: Plume.

Espino, V. (2000). "Woman sterilized as gives birth": Forced sterilization and the Chicana resistance in the 1970s. In V.L. Ruiz & C. Noriega (Eds.), *Las Obras: Chicana politics of work and family* (pp. 65–82). Los Angeles: UCLA Chicano Studies Research Center Publications.

Gutierrez, Elena R. (2008). *Fertile Matters: The Politics of Mexican-Origin Women's Production.* Austin: University of Texas Press.

Herrera, C. (2016). Cinco hermanitas: Myth and sisterhood in Guadalupe García McCall's *Summer of the Mariposas*. *Children's Literature, 44*(1), 96–114.

Jimenez, J. [JoeJimenezSATX]. (2015, April 2). Chatting with @ashleyhopeperez. Is a Mexican-American character in a novel about 1937 East Texas Chicana? #outofdarkness. #sabookfest. Retrieved from https://twitter.com/JoeJimenezSATX/status/716327882063106048

McKinley, J. (2011, March 8). Vicious assault shakes Texas town. *The New York Times*. Retrieved from http://www.nytimes.com/2011/03/09/us/09assault.html?_r=0

Michels, P. (2016, May 11). *Proposed Mexican American studies textbook: Chicanos want to 'destroy this society'*. Retrieved from https://www.texasobserver.org

Morgan, W. (1998). Critical literacy. In W. Sawyer, K. Watson, & E. Gold (Eds.), *Re-viewing English* (pp. 154–63). Sydney: St Clair Press.

Ochoa, G. (2015). Gendered Expectations and Sexualized Policing: Latinas' Experiences in a Southern California High School. G. Conchas and M. Gottfried (Eds.) *Inequality, Power and School Success*. New York, NY: Routledge.

Pérez, A. (2015). *Out of darkness*. Minneapolis, MN: Carolrhoda Lab TM.

Salazar, Lupe. (1935). "Gringo!" *Young Pegasus prize poems*. San Antonio, TX: San Antonio Public Library.

Salazar, Lupe. (1936). "Tejana." *Young Pegasus prize poems*. San Antonio, TX: San Antonio Public Library.

Sánchez, M. E. (1986). *Contemporary Chicana poetry: A critical approach to an emerging literature*. Berkeley: University of California Press.

Serrato, P. (2010). Promise and peril: The gendered implications of Pat Mora's *Pablo's Tree* and Ana Castillo's *My Daughter, My Son, the Eagle, the Dove*. *Children's Literature, 38*, 133–52.

Siemaszko, C. (2011). Rape of girl, 11, tears apart Texas town as many insist on blaming the victim. *The New York Daily News*. Retrieved from http://www.nydailynews.com/news/national/rape-girl-11-tears-texas-town-insist-blaming-victim-article-1.112143

Smith, A. (2005). *Conquest: Sexual violence and American Indian genocide*. Durham, NC: Duke University Press.

Velez-Ibanez, C. (1980). Se me acabó la cancion: An ethnography of non-consenting sterilizations of Mexican women in Los Angeles. In A. DelCastillo & M. Mora (Eds.), *Mexican women in the United States: Struggles past and present* (pp. 71–91). Los Angeles, CA: Chicano Studies Research Center Publications (UCLA).

Chapter 2

Imagineering a New Mexican American Girl: Josefina Montoya (1824)

Patricia Marina Trujillo

I visited American Girl Place at Water Tower Place in Chicago, IL, during the summer of 2016. I happened to be in Chicago on a short-term fellowship at The Newberry Library. My research at the Newberry was in effort of recovering Nuevo Mexicana voices and stories in two archival collections dating from the late territorial/early statehood period (1870–1912) of New Mexico. I spent hours surveying documents for any sign of women in letters, cuadernos (ledgers/notebooks), and other ephemera. I was elated anytime I found a woman's name, or even a mention of a woman in the collections. Blurry eyed, and at times emotionally exhausted, I kept up my search for any sign of women of color, let alone girls of color, in the files of prominent men of New Mexico.

Though I did find some documents, most were business correspondence or letters between family members. These findings are significant, but I think Chicana feminist literary scholars can commiserate with the feeling of want, of desire, to find a journal or collection of stories that represent our foremothers' practices and stories. Imagine my surprise when one day on the way home from the library I walked into the opulent spectacle that is American Girl Place to find exactly what I had been looking for in the archives, except at American Girl Place, it came by way of a Josefina's Nighttime Accessories kit.

The accessory kit includes a "Faux-leather notebook" which are part of "the 'things' [Josefina] likes to have close by at night: A candle in a silver candle-stick, a quill pen and inkwell to practice her penmanship, a faux-leather ledger the Montoya's use to keep track of business, and her beloved doll, Niña, made by Mamá" (Americangirl.com; see website for images of the products). The toy accessory that really caught my eye was the cuaderno filled with poems, proverbs, songs, and sayings written by women in 1824

New Mexico! The book is approximately 1½ inches by 2 inches and filled with the shared generational knowledge of fictitious women in the Josefina Montoya American Girl book series. I couldn't help but simultaneously delight in this tiny book's existence and shake my fist at the conspicuous commodification of my desire for New Mexico women's history.

Josefina Montoya, the first "Hispana" represented in the high-end, heirloom American Girl doll collection, is a nine-year-old girl growing up in 1824 New Mexico who has access to things like those packaged as part of Josefina's Nighttime Accessories, sold for $48. Even if we real New Mexican girls do not have this access, the imaginary world of Josefina provides a simulated material experience of interacting with history. The development of the doll was a joint venture of the original doll makers, the Pleasant Company, the multinational corporation Mattel, various authors, illustrators, and a board of advisors assembled to "ensure that the stories were accurate and culturally authentic" (Jones and LaPierre, 1999, p. 4).

American Girl dolls in the historical dolls line (currently marketed as the BeForever dolls) retail at $115, with accessories averaging $18–48, and clothing averaging between $28 and $36 an outfit. Each doll line has specific furniture, which in the case of the Josefina doll can cost up to $159 for a carved wooden petaquilla (chest). American Girls' brand of conspicuous consumption in children's literature is important to examine for many reasons: this chapter will explore how the Josefina doll and her accompanying books embody a simultaneous sense of fulfilling cultural desire for representation and opportunity for the positive intervention of play, all the while providing a narrative of New Mexico as an always-already colonized space.

The larger venture of the Josefina doll, her accouterments, her growing library, and her accessories spatialize authenticity that "marks a bond between tourism and colonialism as alternate forms of the appropriation and redistribution of space according to relations of power" (Spurr, 1997, p. 21). In this schema, girls who have access to the doll are unwittingly participating in a relational power structure that the interaction of playing with Josefina and reading her stories give girls (and their parents) a controlled narrative about Chicano history: even though Josefina is technically a Mexican girl in 1824, in Josefina's world she will always already be on a trajectory to becoming an American Girl through colonization.

But for the girls who cannot afford a Josefina doll, it is particularly significant to understand how the Josefina books, sold at $9.99 each, are the most affordable and central aspect to distributing the recast myths about New Mexico space that codify symbolic landscapes in the product line. Even with all of these complications, the book series that accompanies the doll constitutes a critical intervention in Chicana/o young adult literature. American Girl has produced a six-book serialed collection, along with three separate mystery novels, that narrate Josefina's life through ages nine and ten.

Though not written by a Chicana author, the Josefina Montoya book collection is significant in that it represents the first (and so far, the only) book series with a Nuevo Mexicana protagonist for young adult readers. First published in 1997, the Josefina books fill a historic literary gap in Chicana young adult literature as one of the most well-funded historical research projects documenting the lives of everyday people in the Mexican period of New Mexico. Josefina's books create dynamic tensions in the study of Chicana young adult fiction that force us to consider the complications of positive and technically historic representations of characters, considerations for work researched by Chicana/o scholars but written by a white author, set on a landscape absent of conflict.

By rendering New Mexico conflict free, Valerie Tripp, author of the Josefina series, enacts a form of literary gentrification. Gentrification is the "transformation of space underwritten by an explicit marketing text, a strategy of 'place advertisement' accentuated by compelling products" (Mills, 1993, p. 152). This spatial order is a project of "Imagineering" invested in authenticating an organization of space to "naturalize a mythical version of the way the world works" (Mills, 1993, p. 168). Imagineering (imagination + engineering) is a term first coined by Walt Disney in the 1950s and remains a central business practice for the corporation.

The Disney Corporation is simultaneously praised and condemned by cultural critics for the model of entertainment firms they have established worldwide by merging diverse populations and spatial configurations to emphasize "simulated pleasures that rely on artificially produced entertainment landscapes that prioritize virtual realities over seemingly authentic experiences" (Grazian, 2008, p. 33). Imagineering overtly functions by providing outlets for desire through affective forces, and creating spaces—real and imaginary—like the American Girl Place and the narrative world of the dolls they market.

Dr. Rosalinda Barrera, one of the members of the Josefina advisory board, recalled that during research and development (R&D) of Josefina much of the narrative organization surrounded the concept of what could and could not be "SKU-ed," that is, made into a Stock Keeping Unit (SKU), the industry term for a product that can be bar-coded (R. Barrera, personal interview, July 16, 2008). According to Felipe R. Mirabal (2004), another of the members of the Josefina advisory board,

> Each [Josefina] book was carefully designed to contain details so that the doll figure of Josefina would be outfitted with clothes and accessories to accompany

each book. Each of the accessories had to be historically accurate, contain "play time," and be manufactured cheaply. [. . .] The challenge was to make history marketable and profitable. It was, in fact, the commodification of culture. (p. 1)

Though Mirabal was not accustomed to this type of business venture, this process is part of a larger corporate children's consumer culture studied as a paradigm in childhood studies and childhood education. Shirley R. Steinberg and Joe L. Kincheloe (2004) coined the term "Kinderculture" to describe the children's consumer culture that "commodifies cultural objects and turns them into things to purchase rather than objects to contemplate. Kinderculture thus is subversive but in a way that challenges authority in an effort to maintain rather than transform the status quo" (p. 11).

The exact amount of funding for the R&D of the Josefina doll is unknown, but Mirabal identifies how this funding also addresses a critical gap in the literature: "What is unique to the construction of the fictional character of Josefina is the fact that this project is probably the most well documented story of the everyday person of the Mexican period" in New Mexico (4–5). But Steinberg and Kincheloe (2004) would assert:

> Corporate cultural pedagogy has "done its homework"—it has produced education forms that are wildly successful when judged on the basis of their capitalist intent. Replacing traditional classroom lectures and seat work with dolls with a history, magic kingdoms, animated fantasies, interactive videos, virtual realities, kickboxing TV heroes, and an entire array of entertainment forms produced ostensibly for adults but eagerly consumed by children, corporate America has helped revolutionize childhood. (p. 16)

Josefina becomes a prime example of an Imagineered "corporate curriculum" aimed to teach girls a sanitized version of how New Mexico was incorporated into the United States (p. 18).

IMAGINEERING JOSEFINA'S HISTORICAL SPACE

Set in 1824 two years after Mexican independence from Spain, twenty-four years prior to the United States occupation of Mexico, and just three years after the opening of the Santa Fe Trail from St. Louis, MI, into Chihuahua, MX, Josefina's narrative mythologizes a utopic New Mexican time period Imagineered to have very little political unrest. As Pleasant Rowland writes in a letter to Dr. Rosalinda Barrera, former Dean of the College of Education at Texas State University and one of the members of the Josefina advisory board, "We have chosen this period, when Anglo influence was just beginning, in order to highlight the depth and richness of Spanish and

Indian heritage in this part of the country" (P. Rowland, Personal letter, July 12, 1995).

The narrative emerges prior to the War against Mexico in 1846, where suspicion of the newcomers (*americanos*) can be figured in terms of building trust as mere business transactions rather than as colonial relations. Josefina, thus, is described in a product line with "books and merchandise that 'tell the truth' in the broadest sense, by presenting a realistic portrayal of New Mexican history and a positive image of its people" (P. Rowland, Personal letter, July 12, 1995). The R&D of Josefina can be understood, in part, as an endeavor to find a historical loophole that would not require the American Girl authors to engage U.S. colonialism explicitly, where New Mexico history renders people rather than the Nuevo Mexicanos rendering history.

As Veronica E. Medina (2007) contends, "Setting Josefina in New Mexico in 1824, rather than after the US-American invasion of Mexico in the mid 1840s, is convenient for American Girl. It allows them to ignore the legacies of internal colonization that have plagued Mexicans and Mexican Americans" since 1848 (pp. 25–6). Medina also asserts that this placement in time avoids the book series having to address the institutionalization of Manifest Destiny in 1845 when it became official federal policy (p. 13). Medina seeks to place Josefina in the historical narratives that most often define Chicana/o ethnic and racial identity in the United States.

The Treaty of Guadalupe-Hidalgo, after all, is the treaty that marks the moment that Mexican Americans become U.S. ethnic minorities. Despite AG's attempt at decontextualization from historical conflict, the coloniality of New Mexican space emerges in the six-book series as they reflect "all those nostalgic responses to globalisation which mourn the loss of the old spatial coherences. It is a nostalgia for something that did not exist" (Massey, 2005, p. 65).

As mentioned earlier, Josefina's library includes ten significant works of fiction: the six book series, three mystery novels, and the short story collection. I will concentrate here on the book series that includes the titles: *Meet Josefina: An American Girl, Josefina Learns a Lesson: A School Story, Josefina's Surprise: A Christmas Story, Happy Birthday, Josefina!, Josefina Saves the Day: A Summer Story*, and *Changes for Josefina: A Winter Story*. They were written by Maryland author Valerie Tripp and illustrated by British artist Jean-Paul Tibbles. Both author and illustrator spent extended periods of time in Santa Fe, NM, to get "a feeling for Josefina's world" (*Josefina's Short Story*, p. 219).

The books can be read separately or as a longer work and are numbered Book 1 to Book 6. In the Josefina series, each text begins with an explication of the death of Josefina's Mamá. The cause of her death is never explained but we are told, "Josefina and her sisters thought of Mamá every day, with longing and love" (*Learns a Lesson*, p. 3). Collectively, the books tell the story of Josefina through two years on her rancho. The following summary of the Josefina books is provided in *The Teacher's Guide* (1999):

> Josefina Montoya is a nine-year-old Hispanic girl growing up on her family's *rancho* in northern New Mexico. Her six books take place between 1824–1826, just after Mexico wins independence from Spain and the Santa Fe Trail opens up trade with the United States.
>
> Two related themes dominate the six books: tradition and change. When the first book opens, Josefina's mother has recently died, and Josefina and her three older sisters [Ana (married with two boys), Francisca (15), and Clara (12)] are struggling to keep things as they were when Mamá was alive. They and their father rely on family, faith, and traditions for strength and comfort as they face this profound change in their personal lives.
>
> As the same time, the world around Josefina is changing, too. In 1824, New Mexico is part of the country of Mexico. Families like Josefina's speak Spanish, practice the Catholic faith, and follow Spanish and Mexican ways of life. But the opening of the Santa Fe Trail has brought Americans into New Mexico with new ideas and goods, and different ways of doing things. Josefina and her family must find a way to accept these changes while holding on to what is precious from the past. (p. 2)

Even in this brief overview of the books, the changes brought about by the death of Mamá are paralleled to the pending changes of space we know (even though Josefina and her family do not) are coming for New Mexico as it becomes territorialized and then incorporated into the United States. One central character that is not mentioned in this overview is Tía Dolores, Mamá's sister. In the first book, *Meet Josefina*, Dolores comes back to live in New Mexico after tending to her elderly aunt for ten years in Mexico City.

For Tripp, Tibbles, and the Josefina advisory board (see Trujillo, 2008, for a full list of Advisory Board), the texts work to balance multiple, often opposing messages about New Mexican space. Though rendered in a time period imagineered as utopic, the tensions of space, "The coming together of two [or more] self-consistent but habitually incompatible frames of reference causes *un choque*, a cultural collision" (Anzaldúa, 1999, p. 100). The tensions in the Josefina texts collide on a theoretical terrain that balances New Mexican cultural epistemologies, contemporary multicultural pedagogies, contemporary feminist pedagogies, and a narrative structure of hegemonic literary modernity.

In the book series, the contemporary concern for producing multicultural literature that is respectful and celebratory of the subject culture is at odds with the zealous modern concern for the New Mexican authenticity. "The spatial construction of authenticity is a cultural phenomenon . . . in modern literature.... The importance of spatial arrangement itself is a 'mediating cultural code'" (Spurr, 1997, p. 21). In making "these stories of the past come alive for American girls," the authors of the Josefina series render colonial tensions implicitly and explicitly.

The Pleasant Company "Summary of Proposal" for "The New Mexico Series," dated July 26, 1995, provides a feasibility report on producing a New Mexico themed doll by identifying three "turning points in the history of Hispanic New Mexico: the early colonial period, the 1820s, and the 1840s" (Pleasant Company, 1995, p. 2). The summary states that the early colonial period is interesting because of Spanish colonization in 1598, the 1680 Pueblo Indian Revolt, and the subsequent recolonization by the Spanish in 1692. But it was not ideal for AG because documentation was sparse and developing a collection would be "overwhelming" (Pleasant Company, 1995, p. 2).

The 1840s was considered because it signals the time when the AG character would become a "true American Girl" but was decided against for three main reasons: (1) the material culture was becoming Americanized and was "not as distinctly Spanish" as in earlier time periods, (2) New Mexico became a territory "through a military invasion during the Mexican War" and war was already a theme in the Felicity/Revolutionary War, Addy/The Civil War, and Molly/World War II series, and (3) "1844 clusters uncomfortably with Kirsten's 1854 and Addy's 1864" (2). Ultimately, the company chooses the 1820s because:

> For more than a century after recolonization, life in New Mexico changed little. The next major turning point occurred in 1821, when Mexico won independence from Spain and immediately threw open its borders to foreign trade. The Santa Fe Trail opened in 1821–1822, bringing U.S. traders in ever-increasing numbers from Missouri to New Mexico. It was the beginning of the tricultural mix—Hispano, American Indian, and Anglo—that so distinguishes New Mexico today, and amicable relations between New Mexicans and the early American traders helped ease New Mexicans' fears after the U.S. takeover in 1846. The *1820s is an appealing setting* for an AGC series about a Hispana girl because the material culture is still relatively free of American influences, yet Americans are present and change is in the wind. Moreover, historical documentation for this era is more plentiful and reliable than for earlier periods, and clothing styles are quite distinct from those of other AGC characters. (my italics, Pleasant Company, 1995, p. 2)

The company's proposal hinges on an ideology that choosing the best "time" will allow them to more authentically represent the best "space" of New Mexico. New Mexico is *apart* from the United States, "still relatively free of American influences" but *a part* of the United States because of the increasing number of Anglos coming in from the Santa Fe Trail. Master narratives of the region's history are engaged: New Mexico as unchanging and the tricultural myth of Hispano, American Indian, and Anglo harmony. American colonial myths are insinuated: New Mexicans wanted to become Americans, and the concept of a peaceful colonization after the Mexican American War.

All of these mythologies of New Mexico support the creation of the 1820s as the setting, and in this configuration, Edward Soja's (1989) ontology of space can be invoked. He writes "Spatiality is reduced to a mental construct alone, a way of thinking, an ideational process in which the 'image' of reality takes epistemological precedence over the tangible substance and appearance of the real world" (p. 125). American Girl's decision to choose the 1820s over the 1840s exemplifies Soja's assertion.

Not choosing the 1840s because war was already represented in three other AG doll series—the Revolutionary War, the Civil War, and World War II—makes the choice seem "harmless" because it is allowing a different kind of narrative outside of war. The omission of the Mexican American War and Manifest Destiny is rendered as a narrative choice rather than a configuration of space that excludes an unpopular war where issues of U.S. imperialism would have to be addressed. Unlike the three wars that are narrativized, the United States' attack on Mexico cannot be easily rendered in mere terms of patriotism, unquestioned victories, and moral righteousness.

The "uncomfortable clusters" of a potential Josefina of 1844 with Kirsten's 1854 and Addy's 1864 point to similar issues of narrative choices that steer us away from Soja's tangible substance of reality. They break up Kirsten Larson's narratives of American exclusion as a non-English-speaking Swedish immigrant in Minnesota, and Addy Walker's narratives of escaping slavery, being separated from her family, and living in exile during the Civil War. American Girl avoids an "overly negative" rendering of American space by not adding another girl into the Kirsten/Addy sequence that already challenges notions of hegemonic American girlhood.

Though Kirsten is assimilated as an English speaker by the end of her series, she asserts differential notions of white ethnicity in the Midwest. And even though Addy is freed at the end of the series, she begins it as an escaped slave who embodies defiance to white Anglo dominance. Choosing a different time for Josefina renders U.S. history as merely punctuated with conflicts rather than allowing a simultaneous conceptualization of multiple girls living in multiple spaces with multiple conflicts at the same time.

The concern is to "keep our [AG's] history honest and our product line appealing" (Pleasant Company, 1995, p. 1). This benevolent narrative choice folds social space into mental space, into transparent "concepts of spatiality which all too often take us away from materialized social realities" (Soja, 1989, p. 125). In the AG series, the mental spaces are achieved through the strategic temporal positioning of space which, in regard to the geopolitical arena, tells the story of "the United States moving from a subaltern position in the world order, at the beginning of the nineteenth century, to an imperial force during the twentieth century" (Mignolo, 2000, p. 128).

Josefina's 1824, meant to be a "positive" representation of space, is complex in its renderings of Mexican social space influenced by American Indian cultures and Spanish colonial legacies. Acosta-Alzuru's assertion that Josefina is "apart" from the American Girls series because of her lack of "American-ness" neglects how New Mexico in 1824 was already being spatialized within the United States' colonial vision.

First, it is unclear historically if inhabitants of the region would use "Nuevomexicana/o" as a regional identifier but Gabriel Meléndez (2000) notes in "Nuevo México by Any Other Name," that Benjamín M. Read, Nuevo Mexicano historian, argued in 1911 that "the descriptor Nuevo México was in common usage among Franciscan missionaries [by the mid to late 1500s]" (p. 145). Josefina was born a Spanish subject prior to Mexican independence.

At the time of her stories, Josefina would identify nationally as a Mexican citizen (Mexicana). It seems, however, that she may have also understood herself in terms of her *New* Mexican-ness, or as part of "*un otro, o nuevo México*," a phrase in use ascribed to Spanish explorers as early as 1539 (Meléndez, 2000, p. 145). Erlinda Gonzalez-Berry and David Maciel (2000) write of the early 1800s in New Mexico as a period of emerging social and economic autonomy: "Confronting their isolation and neglect during this period, Nuevomexicanos began expanding their horizons and seeking out trading and mercantile possibilities beyond Mexico's borders" (Gonzales-Berry and Maciel, 2000, p. 13).

Trade routes—the Camino Real and the Santa Fe Trail—are central to the configurations of Josefina's New Mexico, just as they were to actual New Mexico. The trails engaged Nuevo Mexicanos in processes of space that were dialectical. However, we can read space along these trails as paths to a taming of narrative space in the Josefina series where "co-existing spatial heterogeneity [is rendered] as a single temporal series" (Massey, 2005, p. 71). This imposition of a single universal of time traps Josefina as a character always configured on a path to colonization.

On December 2, 1823, President James Monroe articulated U.S. policy on the new political order developing in the rest of the Americas and the role of Europe in the Western Hemisphere in an address to Congress. The Monroe Doctrine eventually became the document that allowed for U.S. "intervention," that is, the territorialization and subsequent colonization of vast areas in Latin America including Cuba, Nicaragua, Haiti, Panama, Puerto Rico, and the Dominican Republic.

Though the doctrine never comes up explicitly in the Josefina narratives, the policy is indicated in terms of American economic expansion into New

Mexico and by the conflation of Mamá's absence with the space of pre-U.S. contact New Mexico. From Mamá's absence, Tía Dolores stands for a space more ideal to the U.S. national desires of expanding capitalism.

Mamá's death precedes the narratives and is represented as a sorrow always in the family's hearts (*Meet Josefina*, p. 7). Josefina longs "for life to be the way it was when Mamá was alive" (*Meet Josefina*, p. 13). Tía Dolores, who has lived in Mexico City for ten years prior to moving in with Josefina's family, offers the family new hope in their desire to feel happy. She represents the "modern" and metropolitan counterspace to Mamá.

Whereas Mamá's ways are symbolic of the past, synonymous with nature and rurality, Tía Dolores embodies change and progress tied to spatial sophistication in terms of culture and urbanity. She is a *new* New Mexican subject who introduces Josefina and her sisters to multiple forms of literacy that Mamá did not: reading, writing, music, and business. She is traveled and well read. In Book 5, while the girls are fascinated by various goods available at the plaza, "Tía Dolores was distracted by some books" (*Saves the Day*, p. 21).

On the other hand, "Mamá didn't read or write. Mamá didn't ask anyone to teach us to read or write," Francisca explains to Josefina, "It'll be just one more way she'll fill our heads and our hearts so that we'll have no room left for Mamá" (*Learns a Lesson*, pp. 51–2). In creating this distinction between Mamá and Tía Dolores, rural/urban, nature/civilized, oral/written, and tradition/innovation, Valerie Tripp asserts a geopolitical narrative process "of making and unmaking the Americas" (Mignolo, 2000, p. 127). This process "is part of the larger one, the formation and transformation of the modern/colonial world system of imperial allocation of cultures (e.g., territorializing people in relation to their language and their location in the planet)" and interjects an unyielding cultural desire for no longer existing space (ibid).

In offering Dolores as the space of culture, Tripp conflates Mamá's space of nature onto Josefina. The central conflict of her character is summed up in the descriptions of her narratives on the AG website: "Josefina's love of nature follows Mamá's traditions. But can she also embrace new traditions?" (www.americangirl.com). This conflict arises for Josefina in each text in different ways, particularly because she is tentative around strangers. Mamá's New Mexico is represented as a static time to be transcended, rather than a dynamic space in process.

Mamá comes to represent the defeated Spanish colony and Dolores, the newly established, free-trading country of Mexico. "She's used to live in Mexico City, where there are lots of grand people and grand houses" (*Meet Josefina*, p. 65). The latter signals the more desired configuration of space for the economic advantage of the anticipatory capitalists to the North. Mamá is "shy and obedient" like Spanish New Mexico that kept its borders closed to trading with the United States, making it "illegal for [the americanos] to come to New Mexico" (*Short Stories*, p. 20; *Meet Josefina*, p. 10).

Dolores is "adventurous," and her class position and literacy provided her access to information about the cultural and political climate that she lived through in witnessing the Independence of Mexico (*Short Stories*, p. 20). Dolores' New Mexico is a space configured with the policies of the Monroe Doctrine in mind, and like Mamá she is configured on an established timeline, "In these conceptions of singular progress (of whatever hue), temporality itself is not really open. The future is already foretold; inscribed into the story" (Massey, 2005, p. 68). Dolores' New Mexico, thus, is rendered within the U.S. colonial imaginary as "a part" of the modern/colonial inscription of the story that insures unfettered dominance by the United States indefinitely.

In Book 2, *Josefina Learns a Lesson*, Tía Dolores introduces the concept of trading with Americans. Dolores suggests to Papá that the family could "use the old sheep to get new sheep," she continues with her plan for acquiring more sheep for the family's flock. She shares her plan, "We'll keep as few as possible for our own use, and trade most of the blankets to the villagers for new sheep. We can trade with the Indians at the *pueblo*, too."

When Papá points out the flaw that their neighbors at the pueblo weave their own blankets and asks why they would want more, Dolores asserts, "To trade with the americanos. . . . My father told me that they are glad to trade their goods for blankets. They value the blankets for their warmth and strength and beauty" (*Learns a Lesson*, pp. 22–3). Abuelito is a trader on the Camino Real and provides the context for Dolores' knowledge.

Thus, the americanos are figured early in the book series as the resolution to the economic hardship brought about by a storm that drowned the family flock. This subplot continues throughout the book series: in Book 4, *Happy Birthday, Josefina*, Papá visits with his friend Esteban at the nearby pueblo. Josefina is allowed to go with her father to visit with her best friend, Mariana, but she knows that her father has come to trade with Esteban and to strategize with his friend about trading with the Americans. "'I hope trading with the americanos will be a good thing,' Papá said. Esteban nodded to show that he shared Papá's hope" (*Happy* Birthday, p. 43). The brief exchange sets the stage for Book 5, *Josefina Saves the Day*, where the whole Montoya family travels to Santa Fe to meet the American wagon train arriving on the Santa Fe Trail.

Unlike Mamá and Tía Dolores, Josefina emerges as a third space, "a divergent and supplementary category for social identity" and for spatial identity (Sandoval, 2000, p. 46). She negotiates her identity from what she remembers of her mother and what she learns from her aunt. In Book 5, Josefina accidentally encounters the first americano introduced in the book series, Patrick O'Toole, a trail scout from St. Louis, MO.

When Josefina hears him whistling she calls out to him thinking he is her sister, "The whistler was a young man Josefina had never seen before. . . . The young man was a stranger. And not just any stranger, either" (*Saves the Day*, p. 3). He was an americano looking for her Abuelito to conduct business. Josefina's sisters are curious as to how "shy" Josefina came to know the americano before anyone else; after he and their grandfather leave the room, they ask. "'So!' said Francisca to Josefina. 'Where did you find the americano?' 'Well, I guess he found me,' said Josefina" (*Saves the Day*, p. 14).

This description of the meeting supports the American Girl trajectory of history as peaceful interactions between groups that meet by chance rather than design. But it is actually Josefina who calls out to Patrick, making the initial connection, and leads him to her grandfather's home; in addition, she continues to help Patrick out with cultural differences in his communication style.

When Patrick tries to engage Abuelito in business without first having a friendly conversation, as was custom, Josefina intervenes. "No one saw Josefina tug on his sleeve. When Patrick glanced at her, she frowned and shook her head just the smallest bit to tell him no" (*Saves the Day*, p. 9). Throughout Book 5, Josefina continues to work as an intermediary between the americano, Patrick, and her family.

Josefina comes to represent a differential consciousness that mediates between her traditional New Mexican space (Mamá) and her burgeoning space as a capitalist (Tía Dolores). She even enters into trade with Patrick directly to purchase his fiddle for Papá. Right as the "americanos driving the wagons whooped and hooted and whistled and threw theirs hats into the air," Josefina and her sisters are given purchasing power (*Saves the Day*, p. 18). Dolores shares "'Your papa and I think that you girls deserve something for all the hard work you've done weaving,' she said. 'We've decided that you may each choose one of the blankets you wove, and you may sell it or trade it for anything you wish'" (*Saves the Day*, p. 20).

At first, the sisters all want different items that reflect their personalities: Clara, "practical and sensible" wants new knitting needles, Francisca, "headstrong, independent" and concerned with her looks wants a mirror, and Josefina, hopeful and heartful, wants a toy farm. And not just any farm, a farm that reminds Patrick "of how the farms look back home in Missouri" (*Saves the Day*, p. 24). Patrick and Josefina have an interesting exchange after Josefina remarks that she would like to shrink small enough to fit into the toy house:

> "I'd like to go inside the house. I've never seen such a steep roof and so many big windows!"
>
> "It's different, isn't it" said Patrick. "Here in New Mexico your houses are low. They look like they grew right up out of the ground because they're made

out of earth, and they don't have any sharp corners. Where I come from the buildings seem to want to stick up and call attention to themselves. Sort of like the people, I guess." (*Saves the Day,* p. 24)

In this feat of Imagineering, Tripp introduces a toy for Josefina to play with to teach her about another place, St. Louis, normalizing the impending encroachment by the americanos, and also using *historical fiction* to normalize the ventures of the Pleasant Company. The book, *Imagineering: A Behind the Dreams Look at Making the Magic Real* (1996), indicates that architectural Imagineering is invested in creating a "'forced perspective,' the art of making something appear taller than it actually is" (Imagineers, 1996, p. 84).

Patrick's description of the buildings and people interjects a forced perspective on the spatial position of the americanos as sticking up and calling attention to themselves, this is reinforced by the hooting and hollering from the men on the wagon trains. On the other hand, the description of adobe homes renders them low and close to the ground and once again invokes the connection between women/nature and men/culture.

Even though Clara, Josefina's practical sister, warns her that the purchase would be a waste of her blanket, "Josefina couldn't help wanting the farm" (*Saves the Day*, p. 24). As she and her family move on without the farm, Josefina's father whispers to her "If that's what you want, then that's what you should get," Papá said. "Don't let anyone talk you out of your heart's desire" (*Saves the Day*, p. 25).

In creating dimensionality, which is what the American Girl Collection seeks to do with its dolls and accessories and what Walt Disney sought to do in his theme parks, Imagineering takes a girl from observer of space to participant in a themed space. "The imagery is not confined to the parameters of" the pages of the book. The reader is "bombarded" with products that make the experience come to life. "The key to making this work is for each element to mesh with the story" (Imagineers, 1996, p. 90).

Imagineering is simultaneously invested in grand scale building and detailed minutia needed to create themed space. "In Imagineering architecture, the obvious function of a building is secondary to its primary purpose: to tell a story" (Imagineers, 1996, p. 84). With American Girl, the narratives and the associated products tell the stories (plural) of girls emerging from one singular story of America.

As Pleasant Rowland explains in a letter to an advisory board member, "I hope these materials also give you a sense of our commitment to helping today's young girls claim their history and heritage." Rowland frames the process of multiple girls narratives imposed on the singular trajectory of history in one of the first documents developing Josefina. For all the work to authenticate Josefina's New Mexico, the Pleasant Company fails to truly address the possibilities of space.

Doreen Massey (2005) would argue "this way of imagining space can lead us to conceive of other places, peoples, cultures simply as phenomena 'on' this surface. It is not an innocent maneuver, for by this means they are deprived of histories" (Massey, p. 4). In the company's desire to create a singular historic space for actual American girls, they neglect how the space that they create simultaneously denies their histories (plural).

After spending a couple of hours at the American Girl Place in Chicago, engagement in histories of the complex subjectivities of Mexican American girls paled in relationship to the conspicuous consumption. As I left the story, um, I mean store, I finally got to "meet" the American Girl Doll of the Year 2013—Saige Copeland. I had heard about her, another New Mexican American girl, but this time she is white and uncomplicated. She gets to live in the present tense as a contemporary "Doll of the Year" in the company's American Girl Today doll series.

Her narratives empower her to fight injustices, create art, and influence educational policy. It makes me wonder how Josefina can be imagined in the contemporary moment. Maybe she would hang out in archives? Maybe she would write children's books? Or walk out of high-end heirloom doll stores thinking of all the ways she could encourage other girls to play without having to erase or ignore their histories.

REFERENCES

Acosta-Alzuru, C., & Roushanzamir, E. P. L. (2003). 'Everything we do is a celebration of you!:' Pleasant Company constructs American girlhood. *The Communication Review, 6*, 45–69.

Acosta-Alzuru, M. C. (1999). *The American girl dolls: Constructing American girlhood through representation, identity, and consumption* (Doctoral Dissertation). University of Georgia, Athens.

American Girl, LLC. (2008). American Girl website. August 31, 2008. Retrieved from http://www.americangirl.com

Anzaldúa, G. (1999). *Borderlands/La Frontera: The new mestiza* (2nd ed.). San Francisco, CA: Aunt Lute Books.

Barrera, R. (2008, July 16). Personal interview. Texas State University, San Marcos, TX.

Gonzales-Berry, E., & Maciel, D. (2000). The nineteenth century: Overview. In E. Gonzales-Berry & D. Maciel (Eds.), *The contested homeland: A Chicano history of New Mexico* (pp. 12–22). Albuquerque: University of New Mexico Press.

Grazian, D. (2008). Dynamic imagineering: The staging of urban nightlife. In D. Grazian (Ed.), *On the make: The hustle of urban nightlife* (pp. 29–62). Chicago: University of Chicago Press.

The Imagineers. (1996). *Imagineering: A behind the dreams look at making the magic real*. New York: Hyperion.

Jones, M., & LaPierre, Y. (1999). *1824 Josefina: Teacher's guide to six books about America's southwest frontier.* Middleton: Pleasant Company Publications.

Massey, D. (1994). *Space, place and gender.* Minneapolis: UP Minnesota.

Massey, D. (2005). *For space.* London: Sage Publications.

Medina, V. E. (2007). *Theorizing American girl* (Thesis). University of Missouri-Columbia.

Meléndez, G. (2000). Nuevo México by any other name: Creating a state from an ancestral homeland. In E. Gonzales-Berry & D. Maciel (Eds.), *The Contested homeland: A Chicano history of New Mexico* (pp. 143–68). Albuquerque: University of New Mexico Press.

Mignolo, W. D. (2000). *Local histories/global designs: Coloniality, subaltern knowledges, and border thinking.* Princeton: Princeton University Press.

Mills, C. (1993). Myths and meanings of gentrification. In James Duncan & David Ley (Eds.), *Place/Culture/Representation* (pp. 149–69). London: Routledge.

Mirabal, F. R. (2004). *Josefina: My Favorite New Mexican.* National Hispanic Cultural Center.

Pleasant Company. (1995). Summary of proposal: New Mexico series. Personal archives of Dr. Rosalinda Barrera. Texas State University, San Marcos, TX.

Rowland, P. (1995). Letter to Dr. Rosalinda Barrera. Personal archives of Dr. Rosalinda Barrera. Texas State University, San Marcos, TX.

Sandoval, C. (2000). *Methodology of the oppressed.* Minneapolis: University of Minnesota Press.

Soja, E. (1989). *Postmodern geographies: The reassertion of space in critical social theory.* London: Verso.

Spurr, D. (1997). New Mexico: Landscapes of the colonizing imagination. *SPELL: Swiss Papers in English Language and Literature, 10,* 13–35.

Steinberg, S. R., & Kincheloe, J. L. (2004). *Kinderculture: The Corporate Construction of Childhood.* 2nd ed. Boulder: Westview Press.

Tripp, V. (1997a). *Meet Josefina: An American girl (Book One).* New York: Scholastic.

Tripp, V. (1997b). *Josefina learns a lesson: A school story (Book Two).* Middleton: Pleasant Company Publications.

Tripp, V. (1997c). *Josefina's surprise: A Christmas story (Book Three).* Middleton: Pleasant Company Publications.

Tripp, V. (1998a). *Happy birthday, Josefina! (Book Four).* Middleton: Pleasant Company Publications.

Tripp, V. (1998b). *Josefina saves the day: A summer story (Book Five).* Middleton: Pleasant Company Publications.

Tripp, V. (1998c). *Changes for Josefina: A winter story (Book Six).* Middleton: Pleasant Company Publications.

Tripp, V. (2006). *Josefina's short story collection.* Middleton: Pleasant Company Publications.

Trujillo, P. M. (2008). *Gentefication: A spatial rhetorical analysis of differential landscapes in northern new mexican literature and social space* (Order No. 3337157). Available from ProQuest Dissertations & Theses Global: The Humanities and Social Sciences Collection. (288065301). Retrieved from https://search.proquest.com/docview/288065301?accountid=10349

Chapter 3

A Bone to Pick: Día de los Muertos in Children's Literature

Roxana Loza and Tanya González[1]

The Jorge R. Gutierrez-directed 2014 film *The Book of Life* is a beautifully rendered love story set against the backdrop of Mexico's Día de los Muertos celebration. The story follows the adventures and love triangle of friends Maria Posada (Zoë Saldana), Manolo Sanchez (Diego Luna), and Joaquin Mondragon (Channing Tatum).

Set in the fictional town of San Angel in Mexico, these childhood friends face family pressures and legacies as the two boys vie for Maria's love. When a wager between the ruler of the Land of the Remembered, La Muerte (Kate del Castillo), and the ruler of the Land of the Forgotten, Xibalba (Ron Perlman), leads to trickery, Manolo dies and must battle his way back to the Land of the Living with the help of his family to reunite with Maria.

The Book of Life is the first mainstream film for children to prominently feature Día de los Muertos iconography, the most recognizable traits that are: *pan de muerto* (especially made sweet bread with dough shaped like bones decorating the top), *cempasúchil* (marigold), religious iconography of crosses and the *Virgen de Guadalupe*, *ofrenda* (the decorated altars lit with candles and full of photographs), and *calaveras de azúcar* (sugar skulls).

The perpetually festive setting of the Land of the Remembered vividly illustrates a vibrant life after death. There are huge balloons, abundant food— "all you can eat *churros*" (Del Toro & Gutierrez, 2014)—fireworks, *papel picado* decorations hanging from the streets, *piñatas*, and colorful, elaborately decorated parade floats. Other films have incorporated an underworld, but none specifically using the unique Mexican aesthetics of this holiday.[2] In a way, the Día de los Muertos details signify authenticity to insider culture audiences already familiar with the holiday.

However, the film's mise-en-scene also reproduces what Michelle Habell-Pallán describes as a "Spanish Heritage Fantasy" that makes Mexican culture palatable as part of a Spanish tradition to mainstream audiences. The iconicity of Día de los Muertos, in cultural representations and celebrations at large, maintains this evocation of Spanish heritage in the depictions of mission and mission revival architecture; costumes evoking nineteenth-century "Spanish aristocrats and their haciendas" (Habell-Pallán 16); bullfighting; colonial-era military; and the centrality of the Catholic mission.

While *The Book of Life* combats some of these fantasies with feminist plot devices (a "señorita" female lead who is educated, independent, and just as capable as her male counterparts, and a "bullfighter" male lead who overcomes heteropatriarchy to become an artist), the structure of the film as a tour into Mexican culture through the "discovery" of an ancient museum artifact sets up a neocolonial experience of Día de los Muertos that privileges non-Latin@s as an ideal audience.

The filmmakers, interested in challenging stereotypes and bringing Día de los Muertos to the mainstream (J. Gutierrez, personal communication, May 27, 2016), framed the story as a lesson in Latin@ culture. In *The Book of Life*, a group of detention kids hear the story of Manolo, Joaquin, and Maria and learn about Día de los Muertos from a museum tour guide. The detention kids are quickly engrossed in the tale, and they become unlikely admirers of the "glorious beauty of Mexico" (Del Toro & Gutierrez, 2014).

Variety film reviewer Geoff Berkshire (2014) notices this narrative frame is used "to ensure every viewer has a window into the story." The use of "window" as a description of the function of the educational tour directly echoes a metaphor of multicultural education as a window and a mirror.

Rudine Sims Bishop, a scholar of African-American children's literature, coined this metaphor in her essay, "Mirrors, Windows, and Sliding Glass Doors" (1990). Bishop suggests that "historically, children from parallel cultures had been offered mainly books as windows into lives that were different from their own, and children from the dominant culture had been offered mainly fiction that mirrored their own lives. All children need both" (2012, p. 9).

In this case, *The Book of Life* offers "children from the dominant culture" a "window" into a Latin@ cultural practice, and Latin@ children a mirror in which they can see themselves. Nevertheless, *The Book of Life* also deliberately accommodates a Latin@ story for non-Latin@ viewers through this tour-guide frame, effectively othering the culture it seeks to promote. While the end of the film reveals Mary Beth, the tour guide, is actually an incarnation of La Muerte, the fact remains that within the diegetic world, the intended audience for the story is a group of non-Latin@ children.

Interestingly, most Día de los Muertos texts for children tend to reproduce this othering of Latin@ culture, even as they are produced and promoted as a means to foster multicultural education and understanding. In her article,

"In Search of the Ideal Reader for Nonfiction Children's Books about el Día de los Muertos," Denise Davila analyzes the use of nonfiction books about Día de los Muertos and argues that the content and form of the texts reinforce exclusionary pedagogical practices, all in the name of multiculturalism.

Thus the presentation of the content "is not ideologically neutral" (Davila, 2012, p. 16). In Davila's analysis, these nonfiction books "seem to authorize the exoticism of Mexican culture via sanitized content that is complicit with mainstream historical narratives" (p. 21). This kind of multiculturalism is, in fact, dangerous insofar as it fosters an education system that maintains inequality in the name of inclusion.

When texts such as these enter the classroom to provide diverse content, it demonstrates a lack of critical multiculturalism that "acknowledges the multiple histories among us; the dynamism, diversity, and fluidity of cultural experience; and unequal access to social power" (Botelho & Rudman, 2009, p. 5). Instead, these texts reinforce the status quo.

Davila observes that many of the nonfiction Día de los Muertos texts establish an ideal reader as a non-Latin@ unfamiliar with the holiday and an implied author that functions as a tour guide for such readers (2012, p. 23). Though the storyteller tends to be Latin@ in the fictional stories about Día de los Muertos, these texts invite the reader to view her or his family and traditional practice with the first-person plural "we," the voyeuristic element of tourism remains, as if the reader is being invited into a personal account that is not necessarily familiar.[3] Another of the story elements apparent in the fiction is the conflation of Día de los Muertos with Halloween.

For instance, in Bracegirdle and Bernatene's *The Dead Family Diaz* (2012) the author uses scary stories and fear as the principal conflict for the two protagonists—the dead Angelito and a living Pablo—versus the joy, celebration, and love that comes with reconnecting with the souls of the departed. These examples illustrate the way authors can use elements of Día de los Muertos in a colonizing and commodifying way.[4]

In contrast, Eric Gonzalez and Erich Haeger's bilingual picture book *Rosita y Conchita* (2010) operates within a decolonizing imaginary, a space where subjects can recognize a differential and multiple consciousness that fleshes out that which a fixation on colonial narratives makes invisible (Pérez, p. 7).[5] In *Rosita y Conchita*, we find a text that avoids marking an ideal reader or implied author; all readers are equally invited to share the sisters' story. Moreover, through its content, form, and production, this Chican@ picture book draws our attention to its potential as a teaching tool that avoids many of the colonizing and exoticizing moves present in other representations of Día de los Muertos. As such, *Rosita y Conchita* contributes to the body of Chican@ children's texts necessary in the current political and social climate that separates and others Mexican cultural heritage in the United States.

Because Día de los Muertos is "a time to remember and celebrate the lives of our loved ones who have passed away/un día para recordar y celebrar las vidas de nuestros parientes y amigos que han fallecido" (Gonzalez & Haeger, 2010, pp. 36, 37), the stories in picture books obviously deal with the loss of family and friends who have died.

The emphasis on celebration and remembrance, however, can sometimes mitigate the pain of loss. In this sense, many picture books and nonfiction books for children that deal with Día de los Muertos are made palatable as descriptions of a holiday. In her survey of Latin@ Children's literature, Mary Pat Brady writes, "The risks in packaging, commodifying, and containing difference in order to produce a marketable authenticity should be understood. . . . when a brand becomes fungible, its appropriation and rejuvenation as stereotype becomes far easier to manage" (p. 380).

Many of the depictions of the Día de los Muertos follow a visual schema that reproduces images of calaveras and festive "latinidad" without connecting these to meaningful narratives grappling with loss. Instead, the commodified and colonized prancing, dancing, and singing skeletons serve as empty signifiers of difference or are read through the lens of Halloween horror and fear. However, only *Rosita y Conchita* presents the perspectives of the living and the dead.[6]

Rosita y Conchita imbues a Día de los Muertos story with meaning as the book follows Conchita's efforts to remember and celebrate her twin sister, Rosita, who has died. Describing Conchita's construction of Rosita's altar, Gonzalez and Haeger (2010) write:

Together, they used to laugh and play,/Until one day little Rosita passed away./ So Conchita makes an altar for her sister,/So she can show her how much she missed her.
En este pueblito con su hermana jugó,/Hasta que un día, pobre Rosita murió./ Conchita le pone un altar a su hermana/Para que Rosita sepa cuanto la extraña. (4)

Here we have the parallels between "laugh and play" and "passed away" in English and, more poignantly in Spanish, between "jugó" and "murió," which signals that there will be a connection between playfulness and the idea of death.

Though it is not necessarily a plot point, these rhyming moments offer the sensibility that this holiday is used to communicate love and longing "So [Conchita] can show her how much she missed her"/"Para que Rosita sepa cuanto la extraña." As readers see Conchita's preparations and Rosita's many mishaps on her way back home, they understand the rationale for the holiday and for the sisters' contact. It also provides an emotional connection that establishes the conflict and tension in the story. If Conchita does not succeed in guiding her sister home, Rosita may not know her sister remembers and loves her. So the reader becomes invested in Conchita's success.

Rosita y Conchita works to flesh out the bones left by commodified representations of Día de los Muertos. Rather than present the story in the first person plural "we," a personal pronoun that can maintain an "othering" effect for the reader, Gonzalez and Haeger use third-person narration. This move reproduces the most common narrative point of view in fiction that just happens to be a traditional storytelling mode for children.

While it may seem like a distancing technique, the "once upon a time" structure ensures all readers—Latin@ and non-Laitn@ alike—are equally invited to listen to Rosita and Conchita's story. *Rosita y Conchita*'s invisible pane models the way storytelling is taught in the classroom. A "we" versus "you" (implied reader) narrative structure, though often meant as an inclusionary move, draws readers' attention to whether they are an insider or an outsider, and constantly reiterates their position relative to the text. These effects, reminders that this is a story about others, for children unfamiliar with Mexican traditions of Día de los Muertos effectively distance them from the story.

Conversely, Mexican and Mexican American children who identify with the narrative "we" might become aware that there is an implied "they" that finds their celebration strange or different. Thus *Rosita y Conchita*'s third person narration invites all readers to witness the sisters' love without emphasizing cultural differences that can interfere with a student's experience of the story.

Dramatic irony is another storytelling device that engages readers. The tension of the story is established when Rosita fears that she has been forgotten as Conchita systematically prepares an altar. From the beginning, readers know that Conchita is reaching out to her sister. But Rosita is "worried that her sister may have forgotten her lost little twin./Está muy preocupada de que de ella se van a olvidar" (Gonzalez & Haeger, 2010, p. 6). Conchita begins "to prepare an altar for her twin sister Rosita/a preparar un altar para su gemela Rosita" (Gonzalez & Haeger, 2010) on page three, but Rosita does not know until page eight. Thus, the brief, five-page suspense for Rosita draws readers into the story. The reader's omniscient perspective gives them an advantage and engages their attention.

Gonzalez and Haeger's text also engages readers through its strong Chican@ sensibility. Typically, Día de los Muertos texts tend to focus on a crossing over between the land of the living and the land of the dead, maintaining separate spheres through illustration. Gonzalez and Haeger's book offers a more fluid depiction of the border between life and death, connecting the characters through an adept use of bilingual text and illustrations. In this way, the authors "reimagine the social" and "imagine it differently than what the dominant imaginary offers" (Brady, p. 381). Their emphasis is on cultural mestizaje and presenting a narrative that gives equal time to each character.

Moreover, their use of color blurs the boundaries between the girls' worlds. According to artist and author Molly Bang (1991), "color's effect on us is very strong—stronger than that of other picture elements" (p. 74). Gonzalez and Haeger use bright, warm yellows, reds, oranges, and pinks in the scenes of the twins' home. The room where Conchita prepares her sister's altar is welcoming and suffused with light. Considering the content of death in the picture book, the illustrators' choice of colors for the underworld is very important.

They are already dealing with animated and stylized skeletons and since "black often symbolizes the unknown, and all of our fears associated with the unknown" (Bang, 1991, p. 68), they avoid activating these negative connotations in the scenes of the land of the dead. Gonzalez and Haeger opt instead to use varying shades of purple in the illustrations of the underworld. This mitigates associations with Halloween. The effect is much less scary while it still provides a contrast for the white of the skeletons.

In addition to the unthreatening color scheme, the visual representation of the dead themselves works to diminish fear and undermines stereotypes that would label the holiday morbid or grotesque. *Calaca* imagery is one of the most salient characteristics of Día de los Muertos. While *Rosita y Conchita* artwork relies heavily on this aesthetic, Gonzalez and Haeger make important modifications to the skeletons in order to make them more human. On the first page of the story, the main *plaza* of the land of the dead shows November 2nd festivities in full swing: a traditionally elegant *Catrina*, candles, *paper picado* decorations, fireworks, mariachis, sugar skulls, bread (here the image shows a *concha*, not the traditional *pan de muertos*), and a happy crowd enjoying the party.

The description of this scene is not unconventional; however, the variety of the skeletons is. Throughout the picture book characters range from a skinny *lotería Catrín*, complete with monocle, twirly moustache, coat, and bowtie, to a young girl with flowers in her hair and a pink crinolined dress to a squat, rotund mariachi. There are many shapes of heads, hairstyles, body types, heights, and garments that clearly distinguish each skeleton in the illustrations.

As the most important dead character in the story, Rosita's depiction is a powerful visual element. From the cover it is apparent that while Rosita is bone-white, she is not conventionally boney. Her arms are not segmented into humerus and ulna-radius; they are continuous, fleshed-out extremities that look like Conchita's except for the color. A round head frames her smiling face without jutting jawbones or prominently visible teeth. Readers' first glimpse of Rosita happens on a two-page spread.

emanates from her heart as do her efforts to create a beautiful altar to show her great love for her twin Rosita. The smell, and by extension the love, reaches Rosita's nose and mind. Her fear of being forgotten is calmed with this sign that Conchita remembers.

Día de los Muertos celebrations center on love, but also on memories. The creators of this picture book visually display the interconnectedness of the heart and mind while they emphasize the close connection of the sisters. This visually signals how the bilingual elements work in the text. Both English and Spanish are cognitively connected through the care taken with each language in the production of a meaningful, substantive language.

The textual and visual bridging of the world of the living and the world of the dead in *Rosita y Conchita* highlights the permeability of their borders. Many Día de los Muertos elements, "Cuando los portales al otro mundo quedan abiertos" (Gonzalez & Haeger, 2010, p. 2), hinge on this annual opening of the worlds. In addition to complicating the conceptualization of Spanish and English as separate spheres, it joins the living and dead through visual cues present in the illustrations.

The endpapers show mirror images of the world of the living and the world of the dead. The front one is of Pueblo City during the day and the back one is of "the land of those now gone/el mundo de los muertos" at night (Gonzalez & Haeger, 2010, p. 5). The mirrored setting undermines the idea that life after death is unfamiliar and frightening. Rosita might be alone wandering the street of the land of the dead, but she is not walking in a strange, unknown location.

More significantly, the visual mirroring of the sisters blurs the lines even further. Rosita and Conchita are identical twin sisters. There is a color photograph in a frame at the top of the altar visible six times in the story that shows both girls. Their appearance, in life and in death, mirrors each other. Conchita wears a pink dress with small, light pink shells on it and on her hair. Rosita wears a purple dress with small, red roses on it and on her hair (Gonzalez & Haeger, 2010, p. 4). In the scenes detailing the chocolate chip enchiladas, the illustrations show Conchita's tongue sticking out at the right corner of her mouth as she sees the delicious food (Gonzalez & Haeger, 2010, p. 7).

On the following page, when the smell reaches Rosita her tongue is positioned exactly like her sister's on the previous page (Gonzalez & Haeger, 2010, p. 8). The illustrations show Conchita's dance moves with her elbows and one knee bent (Gonzalez & Haeger, 2010, p. 11). Later, as Rosita runs to follow the music her elbows and knee are bent as well (Gonzalez & Haeger, 2010, p. 13). Next to the gramophone, Conchita's smiling mouth is slightly off-center to the right and a bit of her tongue is visible (Gonzalez & Haeger, 2010, p. 11). On the following page as Rosita is sitting under the bridge, her smile and tongue are similar to her sister's (Gonzalez & Haeger, 2010, p. 12).

However, the illustrations manage repetition and mirroring of images without exact replication.

Rosita and Conchita are almost identical, but Conchita has one ponytail while Rosita has two. Even when both are smiling similarly, Conchita has teeth while Rosita does not and her mouth is surrounded by little hash marks. The twins share many characteristics, but each has visual markers that differentiate them and signal their uniqueness. The visual doubling of the girls, their movements, their towns, and even their chocolate chip enchiladas, highlights the parallels between the living and the dead. Thus, both the text and illustrations in *Rosita y Conchita* blur the boundaries that separate the sisters.

The artwork and the bilingual text also work to undermine the perception of "cultural borders" in our society. While the creators do not modify the Spanish content of the picture book to make it accessible to non-Spanish-speaking readers, the high quality of both languages invites American readers of all backgrounds to experience the book. The rhymes, in Spanish and in English, are meaningful and carry the story. Although it maintains conventions of English and Spanish order on the page, this picture book works to equalize the power imbalance by resisting the privilege of English.

While *Rosita y Conchita* follows the traditional placement of text to show English at the top, Spanish below or English left, Spanish right which allows the English sections to benefit from primacy, as the title page indicates, Eric Gonzalez created the book and is credited with the Spanish text. Thus, the Spanish was written first. While the authors considered both languages—and the coauthorship signals that they treated them equally—the significance of conceiving of the Spanish first is that the reader of Spanish was not an afterthought.

Spanish speakers were not excluded from the position of ideal reader. All readers, Spanish and English speakers, were attended to in this story. Despite the final placement on the page, attention to the production of the book proper mitigates the significance of the English first positioning.

The equal value of Mexican and American cultures is not only apparent in the language; it is also visually and textually demonstrated through food. The four carnival food carts with tacos, churros, bacon-wrapped hotdogs, and burgers (Gonzalez & Haeger, 2010, p. 9) inhabit a shared space. These signifiers of culture do not fall under Stanley Fish's definition of boutique multiculturalism that only engages with difference superficially (qtd. in Dudek, 2011, p. 156) because visually they coexist in the same space while each retains its individual identity.

This is another way the story validates both English- and Spanish-speaking readers' experience. On the other hand, the chocolate chip enchiladas (Gonzalez & Haeger, 2010, p. 7) work as an example of mestizaje, a fusion of the cultures that embody a Chican@ role that borrows from Mexican and

American culture to produce something new and unique. *Rosita and Conchita* offers these two perspectives that avoid colorblind strategies that erase difference.

These examples of a decolonial imaginary makes the use of *Rosita y Conchita* in a classroom a powerful experience. As a classroom resource, this picture book contains literacy components such as rhyming, setting, characters, theme, sensory details, retelling, problem solving, and prediction and inferencing based on images and/or text. These skills, useful in critical explorations of literature, are introduced as early as Pre-K and Kindergarten.

CTA California Read's endorsement of *Rosita y Conchita* recommends it for grades 1–2; however, the richness of this text makes it useful in all elementary school grade levels since the teacher can help students gain literacy and secondary language acquisition.

The focus on rhyming makes it grade-appropriate for young English-speaking students who are beginning to read and Spanish-speaking students who are learning English as it is read aloud by an adult and relies on aural skills. The rhyming scheme, meaningful in Spanish and in English, helps reinforce one of the earliest stages in the phonological awareness continuum.

A read-aloud book in earlier grades, as students become independent readers and do not rely on word families to decode, the advanced vocabulary such as "estruendo" (Gonzalez & Haeger, 2010, p. 14) or "stranded" (Gonzalez & Haeger, 2010, p. 10) challenges them. *Rosita y Conchita* lends itself to building units and the use of whole language.

In retelling a story, students begin in broad categories of beginning, middle, and end. One effective retelling strategy can be to have students combine simple drawings with ideas from the text. In the back of *Rosita y Conchita*, there is a "How to Draw Rosita" segment with steps. If a class applies this to create Rosita and Conchita Popsicle stick puppets, they can practice oral retelling skills with a partner or at a literacy station. The narrative pattern lends itself to retelling as young students recall the details of the story.

An independent, written retelling activity can also build from the drawing activity as students draw scenes from the picture book and combine them with simple sentences and a word bank to describe the scenes they depicted. Through retellings and reenactments, students can figure out the main idea of the story. In *Rosita y Conchita*, the prominence of the theme of love makes this a great text to illustrate the concept of main idea or theme. Guiding students, teachers can demonstrate and help them understand that the most important idea in the story is love relying on the visual cues of hearts and hugging.

Rosita y Conchita's five sections centered on one of the senses provide a predictable structure. Each of the four first sections (smell/taste, music and sounds, sight with candles, and sight with *cempasúchil*) has a recognizable structural pattern of rising and falling action that allows readers to make reasonable predictions. Rosita begins dejectedly feeling discouraged, then Conchita's efforts restore her hope, she sets out to find her way back to the living, then her advance is thwarted with some obstacle that leaves her feeling low again.

Very young children can guess what comes next after the pattern is repeated a few times. In addition to the narrative pattern, the picture book contains explicit elements of problem-solving strategies as Conchita finds new ways to guide Rosita back. Teachers can encourage students to draw personal connections to the text though activities.

As students think of a relative's favorite food, or what clues would they give a sibling or a friend to lead them home, or "all about me" lessons where they explain how Conchita could lead them home, they are directly engaging with the story and making it relevant to their lives. This is where meaningful social studies skills can be addressed as a class learns about local and international holidays, explores how their families observe celebrations, and discovers how classmates' families commemorate important dates.

Also, the centrality of the sensory details in this picture book connects their reading to lessons about scientific observation using the five senses. The overview of the senses in *Rosita y Conchita* is detailed and seamlessly woven into the story's plot, and the cultural content is accessible to all readers without relying on stereotypes to ensure understanding.

As Davila suggests, "In the end, when children's writers, illustrators, and publishers position readers as mainstream American tourists, they undermine the objectives for fostering a pluralistic society" (2012, p. 24). *Rosita y Conchita* provides educators and readers a quality story that avoids stereotypes and unequal treatments of readers.

Because teachers and librarians are often mediators of the content that reaches children, this highlights the need for classroom resources to avoid perpetuating existing hierarchies of power that disenfranchise Mexicans, Chican@s, and others who celebrate *Día de los Muertos*. Perhaps *Rosita y Conchita* can provide a trail for other Chican@ authors and illustrators to follow toward fostering cultural pluralism through other tales of death, life, persistence, and love in children's literature.

NOTES

1. The authors would like to thank Alejandra Valadez for research assistance; Phil Nel, Anne Phillips, and Joe Sutliff Sanders for assistance with terminology; and Lorena Gauthereau for insightful comments on drafts of this essay.

2. See director Tim Burton's oeuvre, particularly *The Nightmare Before Christmas* (1993) and *Corpse Bride* (2005).

3. For example, Thong & Ballesteros' *Día de los Muertos* (2015), Barner's *The Day of the Dead* (2010), and Levy & Lopez's *I Remember Abuelito: A Day of the Dead Story* (2007).

4. In 2013, Disney tried to trademark "Día de los Muertos" in anticipation of their forthcoming Day of the Dead film *Coco* (2017). Following severe criticism from the Latin@ community, Disney withdrew the application and incorporated Latina/o consultants into the production staff.

5. Pérez's explanation of the decolonial imaginary includes the following: "The oppressed as colonial other becomes the liminal identity, partially seen yet unspoken, vibrant and in motion, overshadowed by the construction of coloniality, where the decolonial imaginary moves and lives. One is not simply oppressed or victimized; nor is one only oppressor or victimizer. Rather, one negotiates within the imaginary to a decolonizing otherness where all identities are at work in one way or another" (p. 7).

6. Other texts commemorate the death of a family member (an uncle or a grandparent) and a child trying to remember and make contact. See, for instance, Levy & Lopez's *I Remember Abuelito: A Day of the Dead Story* (2013), Thong & Ballesteros' *Día de los Muertos* (2015), Goldman & Chapman's *Uncle Monarch* (2008), etc.

REFERENCES

Bang, M. (1991). *Picture This: Perception and Composition*. New York: Little, Brown and Company.

Bang, M. (2000). *Picture this: How pictures work*. New York: SeaStar Books.

Barner, B. (2010). *The day of the dead El Dia de los Muertos*. New York: Holiday House.

Berkshire, G. (2014, October 11). Film review: 'The Book of Life.' *Variety*. Retrieved from http://variety.com/2014/film/reviews/film-review-the-book-of-life-1201326270/

Bishop, R. S. (2012). Reflections on the development of African American children's literature. *Journal of Children's Literature, 38*(2), 5–13. Retrieved from http://www.childrensliteratureassembly.org/docs/38-2-Bishop.pdf

Botelho, M. J., & Rudman, M. K. (2009). *Critical multicultural analysis of children's literature: Mirrors, windows, and doors*. New York: Routledge.

Bracegirdle, P. (2012). *The dead family diaz* (B. Bernatene, Illus.). New York: Dial Books.

Brady, M. P. (2012). Children's literature. In S. Bost & F. R. Aparicio (Eds.), *Routledge companion to Latino/a literature* (1st ed., pp. 375–82). New York: Routledge.

Davila, D. (2012). In search of the ideal reader for nonfiction children's books about el día de los muertos. *Journal of Children's Literature, 38*(1), 16–26. Retrieved from http://search.proquest.com.er.lib.k-state.edu/docview/1266034891?accountid=11789

Del Toro, G., Booker, B., Berger, A. D., Schulze, C. (Producers), & Gutierrez, J. (Director). (2014). *The book of life* [Motion Picture]. Los Angeles, CA: Twentieth Century Fox & Reel FX Productions.

Del Toro, G. (Producer), & Gutierrez, J. (Director). *The Book of Life* [Motion picture]. United States: 20th Century Fox.

Dudek, D. (2011). Multicultural. In P. Nel & L. Paul (Eds.), *Keywords for children's literature* (1st ed., pp. 155–60). New York: New York UP.

Goldman, J. (2008). *Uncle monarch*. (R. K. Moreno, Illus.). Honesdale, PA: Boyds Mills Press.

Gonzalez, E., & Haeger, E. (2010). *Rosita y Conchita*. Austin, TX: Muertoons Publishing.

Habell-Pallán, M. (2005). *Loca motion: The travels of Chicana and Latina popular culture*. New York: NYU Press.

Levy, J. (2007). *I remember Abuelito: A day of the dead story* (L. Lopez, Illus.). Morton Grove, IL: Albert Whitman & Company.

Luenn, N. (1998). *A gift for Abuelita*: Celebrating the day of the dead (R. Chapman, Illus.). Flagstaff: Luna Rising Books.

Pérez, E. (1999). *The decolonial imaginary: Writing Chicanas into history*. Bloomington: Indiana UP.

Thong, R. (2015). *Dia de los Muertos* (C. Ballesteros, Illus.). Chicago: Albert Whitman & Company.

Chapter 4

Águila: Personal Reflections on Reading Chicanx Picture Books from the Inside Out

Lettycia Terrones

Reading and thinking critically about Latinx picture books, especially those created by authors and illustrators of Mexican and Mexican American cultural heritage, is a personal and political imperative to me as a Chicana feminist and as a librarian educator. Picture books whose visual narratives communicate accurate and culturally responsive representations of the Mexican American and Chicanx experience have the capacity to counter the effects of racism and marginalization.

Indeed, as children's literature scholar Rudine Sims Bishop argues, multicultural children's literature moves forward the function of storytelling to transmit moral and cultural values (Bishop, 2003).

For children, whose stories are not often told or included in institutional spaces such as classrooms and library storytimes, the act of storytelling with multicultural picture books contributes to the work of transforming the corrosive effects of racism and marginalization because they affirm our voices and knowledges as Native and People of Color. The picture book, in particular, opens a necessary praxis between reader (typically an adult) and listener (child). Chicanx picture books enrich this praxis and space for cultural literacy because they enact and transmit unique epistemologies though language, iconography, cadence, and history.

Chicanx picture books, as those explored in this chapter, indeed afford a praxis that supports the cultural wealth of our people. Affirming this rich cultural wealth at a young age via picture books has the potential to positively impact how marginalized children conceive of themselves and their unique experiences as assets. Moreover, as critical educators, using Chicanx picture books can support our efforts in developing transformative and culturally relevant pedagogies.

This chapter offers an approach for weaving children's literature scholarship and personal reflection about how Chicanx picture book illustrations function alongside textual narratives to communicate stories and put into play expressions of cultural knowledge practices that express Chicanx experiences. Positioning myself as a Chicana feminist in this analysis is intentional. My critique of how Chicanx aesthetics operate in picture books emerges from my cultural insiderness. Moreover, my critique expresses my agency as an advocate for transformative pedagogy.

To set the context for this methodology, I first describe my experience as a young reader, and my present role as an educator librarian. I use this personal description as a springboard to discuss Chicanx picture book as organized into the following categories: Familia, Neighborhood, In Lak'Ech, Artists, and Chicanx Sensibilities.

YOUNG READER AND EDUCATOR LIBRARIAN

The concept of Mirrors and Windows in diverse and multicultural youth literature continues to inform children's literature research, advocacy, and publishing. First theorized by Rudine Sims Bishop in a 1990 essay entitled, "Mirrors, Windows, and Sliding Glass Doors," the concept articulates how culturally responsive children's literature has the power to reflect authentic experiences of marginalized people, while also serving to connect dominate culture children (and adults) to these realities and experiences that are so often made invisible by the social and personal spaces we inhabit.

As a person of color, I have a deep appreciation for the theoretical work advanced by Bishop's scholarship, especially because as a child, I cannot remember having read one book with a character or story that reflected my own sociocultural experience. In fact, my favorite book in kindergarten was Tomie De Paola's *Nana Upstairs & Nana Downstairs*. One of the reasons why I loved this book so much was because my mother often took me along with her to care for my great-grandmother Altagracia. I remember being especially drawn to the illustration showing Nana Upstairs tied and propped up to a chair; intently looking at this drawing of Nana Upstairs and Tommy tied up and sharing candy, I imagined it was me and Altagracia.

The facing illustration shows Nana Upstairs' vanity table—a box filled with mysterious trinkets, a powder container, and a brush. Altagracia kept the same things on her todcador! Later, when Altagracia died, *Nana Upstairs & Nana Downstairs* provided me much solace because it deals directly with death and its corresponding emotions from a child's eyes. This book was a window for me. Its illustrations resonated with me even though I did not come from a white middle-class family whose great and grandparents lived in a two-story house.

Bishop's insight into how children's literature operates is accurate to my own experience as a young reader. She writes: "Literature transforms human experience and reflects it back to us, and in that reflection we see our own lives and experience as part of the larger human experience" (Bishop, 1990, p. 1). As a child of working-class undocumented Mexican immigrants, I slipped through countless glass doors in East Coast suburbs, surreptitiously making friends with white girls in Judy Blume's books.

Years later in high school, I read Rudolfo Anaya's *Bless Me, Ultima*, and finally saw part of myself reflected in the literary mirror. I hold on to my memory of reading the lunch scene in *Bless Me, Ultima*, when Tony, at his first day of school, opens "a small jar of hot beans and some good, green chile wrapped in tortillas" that his mother had packed (Anaya, 1972, p. 54). It was a moment of affirmation and thrilling recognition, and one I would later share with my high school students in South Central Los Angeles, who like me, had similar reactions.

My students, being mostly Mexican and Central American youth, also saw themselves reflected in Anaya's mirror. They loved *Bless Me, Ultima*, because, like me, they saw themselves mirrored back in the text.

María E. Fránquiz, Carmen Martínez-Roldán, and Carmen I. Mercado's (2011) research describes the process forged by Latina and immigrant preservice teachers in developing "identities of *literary belonging*" to enrich their classrooms. In addition to culturally authentic children's literature, the preservice teachers in this study tap into their own family stories, memorias, and personal archives to uncover and reclaim the rich hidden literacies they possess—literacies which, because they exist in nontraditional educational spaces such as the home and among comadres, are rendered invisible.

Fránquiz et al. write: "Latina students in developing consciousness of a new bilingual teacher identity (in Spanish, a *maestra* identity)" must challenge dominate discourses of assimilation in order to "build a positive sense of self in relation to ethnicity, race, class, and gender" (p. 111). This critical pedagogy approach in reclaiming our marginalized voices by challenging dominate discourses has also been the work of Native American and People of Color librarians.

Indeed, the politics of (in)visibility of underrepresented voice in children's literature publishing is actively challenged by book award prizes, especially as it pertains to the history and advocacy of multicultural children's literature. Established in 1996, and named after the first Latina librarian of the New York Public Library, the Pura Belpré Award celebrates excellence in Latinx children's literature. Its significance cannot be understated. Pura Belpé, in addition to authoring numerous tales of Puerto Rican folklore, also innovated bilingual storytime practices that remain foundational to library services for children.

Starting in the 1920s, Belpré introduced Spanish-English storytimes, inviting and creating spaces for brown, Black, and Afro-Latino children, and advocating library service to the Spanish-speaking community of East Harlem, New York. Belpré's leadership in disrupting dominant discourses to challenge definitions of traditional library practices and library users employed a Mirrors and Windows approach. Belpré gave voice to her own linguistic and cultural heritage, and enriched the storied walls of the New York Public Library through her critical praxis via critical literacy approaches, as librarian.

Belpré's legacy and subsequent influence on Latinx children's literature as disrupting dominant discourses supports the principles of critical literacy. Sluys, Lewison, and Flint (2006) note the work of educator Linda Christensen in defining critical literacy as classroom discourses that are "grounded in students' lives, always connected to larger contexts, and work that invites students to be filled with hope as they work toward creating the world in which they want to live" (p. 199).

The transformative pedagogy of Belpré approach to library service is in turn reflective of Gloria J. Ladson-Billings' (1995) description of culturally relevant pedagogies where "teachers [and librarians make] conscious decisions to be part of the community from which the students come" (p. 479). As a Chicanx feminist educator librarian, these transformative methodologies offer a roadmap for critically reading Chicanx picture books as cultural productions that affirm our cultural knowledge and heritage, while serving as vehicles for enriching our visual and critical literacy.

FAMILIA

In his book, *Writing with Pictures*, Uri Shulevitz (1985) writes: "A picture book is read to the very young child who doesn't know how to read yet; consequently, the child sees the pictures and hears the words directly, without having to deal with the intermediate step of reading the printed word" (p. 16). As critical educators, how can we nurture this shared literacy practice to support second-language assets of bilingual children.

Tara Yosso (2005) writes how for students of color, "culture is frequently represented symbolically through language and can encompass identities around immigration status, gender, phenotype, sexuality and region, as well as race and ethnicity" (p. 76). Yosso's analysis is important in the context of the act of picture book reading because it opens a space for dual-language adults to affirm cultural capital and in turn transmit this asset to their child.

Educators play an important role in cultivating spaces for this type of pedagogical transmission, especially if they capitalize on the symbiotic interaction between adult and child necessitated by picture books. Picture books that communicate accurate portrayals of Chicanx cultural experiences can facilitate this praxis.

Carmen Lomas Garza's picture books *In my Family* and *Family Pictures* are classic examples that lend themselves well to early literacy practices that invite Mexican/Chicanx parents to participate in affirming the "communication, practices and learning that occur in the home and community," what Dolores Delgado Bernal (2001) calls *pedagogies of the home*.

Garza's picture books illustrate how Chicanx families do life. They capture special family events such as *tamaladas*, *quinceañeras*, the apparition of the *Virgen de Guadalupe* in the neighborhood, as wells ordinary everyday occurrences like hanging out in grandma's *cuarto*. The constant in Garza's visual narrative is family. Her illustrations capture and pass on cultural traditions and values typical of Mexican and Chicanx families.

Garza describes one of the ways her art is necessarily connected to family: "Every time I paint, it serves a purpose—to bring about pride in our Mexican American culture. When I was growing up, a lot of us were punished for speaking Spanish. We were punished for being who we were, and we were made to feel ashamed of our culture. That was very wrong. My art is a way of healing these wounds" (Garza, 1996, n.p.).

Garza's illustrations in *Empanadas* show us the act of family linguistic capital at work. The Garza's keeps alive their family history through the act of making food together. Garza's rendering of this cultural practice in a picture book in turn normalizes family literacies that fall outside traditionally recognized knowledge spaces such as the school.

One of the salient appeals of Jose Lozano's bilingual picture book *Little Chanclas* lies in its cultural insider perspective. Lozano's narrative pops with onomatopoeia and inventive Spanglish/Chicanx words in this story about a little girl and her chanclas. Lozano's visual narrative is alive with vibrant colors, and the cadence of family voices and noises emerges from the pages. Like Garza, Lozano's picture book celebrates how Chicanx do life.

There is a beauty to Lozano's use of space that affirms familial capital. The compactness in Lozano's illustrations push family, home, and gathering space together. And yes, as evidenced by the expanse of green in the backyard before the family parrillada, there is enough space for everybody, and everything fits.

NEIGHBORHOOD

Susan Guevara employs a similar aesthetic in her illustrations for *Chato and the Party Animals*. Guevara writes how her inspiration for the renderings of Boyle Heights, a working-class Mexican neighborhood in East Los Angeles, on which she modeled her illustrations for *Chato and the Party* emerged from walking around to "record the detail of the neighborhoods, the slouch of a vendor, the bounce of a child, the duty of a mother" (Guevara, 2003, p. 56).

When I first encountered *Chato and the Party Animals* as a graduate student in library school, I immediately connected with the visual feast and accuracy of Guevara's illustrations. I recognized this as my very own neighborhood. Specific details, such as the We are Not a Minority! and Virgen de Guadalupe murals, reflect the community literacies and cultural histories.

Guevara's illustrations are filled with representations of cultural productions and art aesthetics nascent to the Chicanx experience and to the Chicano Movement. She reflects the Chicanx barrio as a space that contains, produces, and inspires cultural productions comprised of cultural ingredients that make up Chicanx heritages.

In Lak'Ech, Tu Eres Mi Otro Yo

In Lak'Ech is a Mayan precept that expresses the sentiment: "Tú eres mi otro yo./You are my other me." In Lak'Ech affirms a necessary connection between education and the community's well-being.

I am reminded of *In Lak'Ech* when reading Tonatiuh's picture book *Pancho Rabbit and the Coyote: A Migrant's Tale*, which brings to life a migration journey to El Norte. Numerous curriculum guides use *Pancho Rabbit* to engage in critical literacy practices in their classrooms to humanize the authentic experiences of migration faced by children all over the world.

Tonatiuh, in his author's note for *Pancho Rabbit*, supports this. He writes: "We seldom see the dangerous journey immigrant go through to reach the U.S. and the longing that their families feel from them back home. It is my desire that *Pancho Rabbit and the Coyote: A Migrant's Tale* captures some of that sentiment . . . I hope this book will help teachers, librarians, and parents spark conversations with young people about this critical issue" (Tonatiuh, 2013, n.p.). In this way, Tonatiuh enacts the cultural practice of *In Lak'Ech* by creating a work of art that can be used to support the struggle for justice and dignity for Latino, and all other, immigrants.

Tonatiuh's bravery in the social commentary against government corruption at the expense of human lives is also a form of *In Lak'Ech*. His illustrations capture truthful scenes experienced in border crossings, and they transcend geographies, as we are reminded in news images of Syrian children refugees that harken to those illustrated in Pancho Rabbit's journey.

MEXICAN ARTISTS

At the 2016 Frances Clarke Sayers Lecture at UCLA, Yuyi Morales spoke of the healing and restorative power that art can bring to both artist and audience. At a dinner prior to the Sayers Lecture I had the opportunity to ask Morales about her referencing of Frida Kahlo's 1946 painting *La venadita (little deer)* in her picture book *Viva Frida*. Kahlo's painting shows a wounded deer impaled by spears yet standing still in a forest wood. Kahlo adds her self-portrait as the face of the deer.

Morales spoke about referencing this particular painting as a reminder of how the physical and creative act of art illuminates healing and perseverance (personal communication, May 14, 2016). Morales went on to describe that for Kahlo, her life-long struggle with her physically fractured body informed the subject of her art. In her presentation at the Frances Clarke Sayers Lecture, Morales described to the audience the inspiration and reliance Kahlo took on when she declared: "Pies, para qué los quiero si tengo alas pa' volar? Feet, why do I want them if I have wings to fly?" (Frida Kahlo, as cited in Zamora, Kahlo, & Smith, 1990, p. 126).

Morales' aesthetic choices in *Viva Frida* tap into Mexican artistic lineages. Alma Flor Ada (2003) writes about the impact that picture book illustrators can have on developing students' aesthetic sensibilities. She suggests that picture book illustration offers an important gateway for children to learn about the immense contributions that Latin American artists have had on the history of art. She adds: "The desire to inform [children] and to give them a message that they too can find a way to contribute to the world is a strong motivator to create books sharing the richness of the Hispanic culture" (p. 54).

Picture books, such as *Frida*, illustrated by Ana Juan, and *Funny Bones: Posada and His Day of the Dead Calaveras* by Duncan Tonatiuh, champion this aim by expanding children's visual literacy by referencing the works and creative processes of renowned Mexican artists.

In her illustrations for *Frida*, Juan combines visual references to the work of Frida Kahlo with that of surrealist master, Remedios Varos, who lived in Mexico for many years and was a contemporary of Kahlo. In this panel, Juan harmonizes Kahlo's 1954 painting *Viva La Vida (Watermelons)*, as well as Varo's 1957 painting *Creación de las* Aves (*Creation of the Birds*), which shows a woman life-weaver at her workstation or lab as she channels the sunlight to bring to life to magical and wondrous birds.

Similarly, Tonatiuh, in his illustrations for *Funny Bones: Posada and His Day of the Dead Calaveras*, shows José Guadalupe Posada, the iconic Mexican artist, at his work station as he creates the calavera designs that will represent Día de los Muertos iconography. When children (and adults, for that matter) wonder why Mexican *Day of the Dead* skulls and skeletons have a certain look, they can look to Tonatiuh's picture book to learn about Posada and how he first rendered these *calaveras* using print-making techniques.

Tonatiuh's picture book also delves into Posada's creation of "literary calaveras," or journalistic broadsides that were widely popular for their subversive political and social commentary as well as their accessibility to nontraditional readers. Tonatiuh gives life to Posada's cultural contributions in a picture book that is at once a biography of the artist, as well as an exploration into Mexican sensibilities toward life, death, and impermanence.

Tonatiuh interweaves his signature codex-style drawings and digital collage with Posada's own *calavera* prints, to place this story within the larger Mexican historical narrative, tracing the influence of technology, revolution, and the continued cultural significance of the Day of the Dead holiday. Tonatiuh's picture book is an exploration into one of Mexico's greatest artists and the iconography that is central to the celebration of el Día de los Muertos.

SENSIBILITIES

Rasquache is both an act and a description of sensibility or attitude. It describes a resilient attitude where one can make something from nothing. Amalia Mesa-Bains (1999) describes it in this way: "In rasquachismo, one has a stance that is both defiant and inventive. Aesthetic expression comes from discards, fragments, even recycled every day materials such as tires, broken plates, plastic containers, which are recombined with elaborate and bold display" (p. 157).

Spanglish picture book *Little Roja Riding Hood*, illustrated by Susan Guevara, expresses a rasquache "aesthetic bravado." Her illustrations employ a variety of Chicanx cultural iconography, making this well-known tale into a purely Chicanx cuento. Guevara weaves in traditional fairytale images, such as the Three Blind Mice, and winged gold-spinning fairies, along with visual clues that emphasize street attitudes that resonate with Chicanx art and street sensibilities. In this illustration, Guevara uses a listón or ribbon motif (visually referencing both Kahlo's use of ribbons to add descriptive titles to her paintings, as well as Chicano lettering often found in graffiti and tattoos) as a talisman and warning from the magpies to the Lobo: "Vete" (go away!).

Elements of Guevara's artistic style found in the *Chato* series blend into this picture book as well. The Lobo wears a bandana and a skull necklace, and "kicksback" against the tree in a chilled out relax stance that conveys street attitude. Guevara's rendering of Little Roja defies the gender stereotypes typically ascribed to Red Riding Hood as being naïve and vulnerable. Guevara's Little Roja is defiant and smart.

Attitudes and stances often seen as negative or uncooperative become examples of resiliency and a burlón jesting in Guevara's visual narrative. Using visual cues from Mexican and Chicanx households, Guevara communicates a visual sass throughout the story. Abue, for instance, uses Saint Jude statue as protection against Lobo. Similarly, Little Roja's mom fills her house with literary novels and *fotonovelas* alike. Guevara's illustration provide a feast for the discerning eye, with many rewards for Chicnax insiders who will see the objects commonly found in our homes, from *santos* on the walls to aluminum framed mirrors, to laptops for writing manuscripts.

Morales' picture book *Niño Wrestles the World* (2013) also brings to life the spark and wit and flavor of the type of language assets that Yosso (2005) describes as being specific to Latinos, where, as children they "often have been engaged participants in a storytelling tradition, that may include listening to and recounting oral histories, parables, stories (cuentos) and proverbs (dichos). This repertoire of storytelling skills may include memorization, attention to detail, dramatic pauses, comedic timing, facial affect, vocal tone, volume, rhythm and rhyme" (pp. 78–9).

Morales' *Niño*, indeed, is full of language cultural insider terms and tropes inherent to the Chicanx experience. Many of the major players found in Mexican storytelling and folklore make an appearance as Niño's adversaries in his Lucha Libre or wrestling battle: La Llorona (the Weeping Woman); Las Momias de Guanajuato, Los Ovnis (extraterrestrials); La Cabeza Olmeca (iconic Olmec stone sculptures); and El Chamuco (the Devil) challenge and are defeated by Niño.

Morales' language capital works with her choice in visual narrative to effect what picture books do best in using pictures to tell a story. In this image from *Niño Wrestles the* World, the text "too terrifying for him" is preceded by a turn of the page, that starts the sentence, "There is no doubt, no opponent is . . . [flip the page] . . . too terrifying for him" (Morales, 2013, n.p.). Not even El Chamuco, the DEVIL, can scare Niño. The irony works beautifully. Chamuco is sinisterly tempting Niño with an innocent popsicle, but Niño has an expression of confidence and risk-taking. He's up for the challenge!

The two succeeding panels that follow this image are filled with uniquely Mexican interjections: "¡ajúa!" (yippie) and "¡recórcholis!" (dagnabbit, roughly). The reader does not necessarily have to share this cultural heritage and "insiderness" to appreciate the vibrancy and pace of this picture book. Moreover, the text and visual narrative invite the reader to participate in the telling of the story by articulating these interjections. The rasquache sensibility of *Nino Wrestle the World* is found in Morales' ability to bring to the children's literature world the very stories and words that Chicanx children grow up with as part of their linguistic capital at home.

The stories and images that fill our homes, such as *cuentos* about La Llorona or Las Momias de Guanajuato, and the ways to outwit tricksters like las calaveras and los Ovnis, and celebrations of Mexico's rich heritage of renowned artists like Frida Kahlo, are all blended into Morales' storytelling. She holds up a mirror to show Chicanx children that our stories count and have place in literary spaces. The resilient stance that Morales' stories bring allows us to see our humanity.

CONCLUSION

Ada (2003) reminds us that "[e]verything that goes on in the classroom [and libraries spaces] reflects the teacher's approach to education" (p. 4). Educators invested in supporting the literacy and educational development of children through culturally responsive pedagogies can use Chicanx children's literature to advance these efforts. One's positionality as a Chicanx cultural insider is not a prerequisite to using Chicanx children's literature as a means to support transformative and transgressive critical teaching approaches to foster self-efficacy through the articulation of students' cultural capital.

It is necessary, however, to understand that literacy extends beyond decoding words, and is "rather anticipated by and extending into knowledge of the world. Reading the world precedes reading the word, and the subsequent reading of the word cannot dispense with continually reading the world" (Freire & Slover, 1983, p. 5).

REFERENCES

Ada, A. (2003). *A magical encounter: Latino children's literature in the classroom.* Boston: Allyn and Bacon.

Anaya, R. (1972). *Bless me, Ultima: A novel.* Berkeley, CA: Quinto Sol Publications.

Bernal, D. D. (2001). Learning and living pedagogies of the home: The mestiza consciousness of Chicana students. *International Journal of Qualitative Studies in Education, 14*(5), 623–39. doi:10.1080/09518390110059838

Bishop, R. S. (1990). Mirrors, windows, and sliding glass doors. *Perspectives: Choosing and Using Books for the Classroom*, 6(3), 1.

Bishop, R. S. (2003). Reframing the debate about cultural authenticity. In D. L. Fox & K. G. Short (Eds.), *Stories matter: The complexity of cultural authenticity in children's literature* (pp. 25–37). Urbana, IL: National Council of Teachers of English.

De Paola, T. (1973). *Nana upstairs & nana downstairs.* New York: Putnam.

Elya, S., & Guevara, S. (2014). *Little roja riding hood.* New York: G. P. Putnam's Sons.

Fránquiz, M. E., Martínez-Roldán, C., & Mercado, C. I. (2011). Teaching Latina/o children's literature in multicultural context: Theoretical and pedagogical possibilities. In A. S. Wolf (Ed.), *Handbook of research on children's and young adult literature* (pp. 108–20). New York: Routledge.

Freire, P., & Slover, L. (1983). The importance of the act of reading. *The Journal of Education, 165*(1), 5–11. Retrieved from http://www.jstor.org/stable/42772842

Garza, C. L. (1996). *In my family.* San Francisco: Children's Book Press.

Garza, C. L., Rohmer, H., & Zubizarreta-Ada, R. (1990). *Family pictures.* San Francisco: Children's Book Press.

Guevara, S. (2003). Authentic enough: Am I? Are you? Interpreting culture for children's literature. In D. L. Fox & K. G. Short (Eds.), *Stories matter: The complexity of cultural authenticity in children's literature* (pp. 50–60). Urbana, IL: National Council of Teachers of English.

Ladson-Billings, G. (1995). Toward a theory of culturally relevant pedagogy. *American Educational Research Journal, 32*(3), 465–91.

Mesa-Bains, A. (1999). "Domesticana": The sensibility of Chicana rasquache. *Aztlán: A Journal of Chicano Studies, 24*(2), 157–67.

Morales, Y. (2013). *Niño wrestles the world*. New York: Roaring Brook Press.

Morales, Y., personal communication (May 14, 2016).

Morales, Y., & O'Meara, T. (2014). *Viva frida*. New York: Roaring Brook Press.

Shulevitz, U. (1985). *Writing with pictures: How to write and illustrate children's books*. New York: Watson-Guptill Publications.

Sluys, K. V., Lewison, M., & Flint, A. S. (2006). Researching critical literacy: A critical study of analysis of classroom discourse. *Journal of Literacy Research, 38*(2), 197–233.

Tonatiuh, D. (2013). *Pancho rabbit and the coyote: A migrant's tale*. New York: Abrams Books for Young Readers.

Tonatiuh, D. (2015). *Funny bones: Posada and his day of the dead calaveras*. New York: Abrams Books for Young Readers.

Winter, J., & Juan, A. (2002). *Frida*. New York: Arthur A. Levine Books.

Yosso, T. J. (2005). Whose culture has capital? A critical race theory discussion of community cultural wealth. *Race Ethnicity and Education, 8*(1), 69–91. doi:10.1080/1361332052000341006

Zamora, M., Kahlo, F., & Smith, M. (1990). *Frida Kahlo: The brush of anguish*. San Francisco, CA: Chronicle Books.

Zeller, H. (2012, March 9). Art for the expo line: LA metro Lotería by Jose Lozano. *The source, transpiration news and views*. Retrieved from http://thesource.metro.net/2012/03/09/art-for-the-expo-line-la-metro-loteria-by-jose-lozano/

Section II

NEGOTIATING GENDER AND SEXUALITY

Chican@ children's and YA literature is reflective of the multivaried experiences, which are often awkward and confusing, of characters in the midst of their sexual and gender development. The chapters in this section trace such universal themes as masculinity, queerness, racial/ethnic identity formation, and complex familial relationships that shape the protagonists' lives as they navigate the world around them.

Beyond these thematic concerns, these chapters insist on the need to include children's and YA texts into larger disciplinary conversations that have tended to erase literature for younger audiences. Phillip Serrato's chapter, for example, reads Juan Felipe Herrera's middle-school novel in verse, *Downtown Boy*, through critical masculinity studies, and in a similar approach, Sonia Alejandra Rodríguez's analysis of the same text broaches the ideologically and politically complex trope of Chicanx fatherhood. Cecilia Aragón's discussion centers the formation of sexual identity within Chicanx children's literature, once again arguing for the inclusion of these texts within the field of sexuality and gender studies. Cristina Herrera's discussion of a commonly understood "rite of passage," the quinceañera, sheds light on contemporary Chicana YA literature's critical contributions on a subject that has inspired much ethnographic fieldwork.

For literary and education scholars alike, chapters in this section also illuminate the possibilities for using Chican@ children's and YA literature in K-12 classrooms. As student populations grow increasingly more diverse, educators must adopt texts that reflect the realities of young children of color, whose genders, ethnicities, languages, and socioeconomic backgrounds are rarely visible in course materials. To affirm children's lived experiences, Chican@ children's and YA literature must be an important component of the K-12 curriculum.

Chapter 5

A Portrait of the Artist as a Muchachito: Juan Felipe Herrera's *Downtown Boy* as a Poetic Springboard into Critical Masculinity Studies

Phillip Serrato

In "Reading Men Differently: Alternative Portrayals of Masculinity in Contemporary Young Adult Fiction," Thomas Bean and Helen Harper (2007) explore "the potential contribution young adult literature might make in engaging adolescents in examining and challenging rigid, singular, and essentialized views of masculinity produced and performed in our society" (pp. 12–13). Building upon the point that literature provides "powerful sites for student engagement" (p. 17), they propose, "The increasing number of young adult novels . . . that feature male characters reflecting on their masculinity . . . offers a critical space to take up discussions [of it]" (p. 26). Such an observation reflects ongoing interest in the capacity of children's and adolescent texts to facilitate interrogation of familiar gender definitions and expectations.

Inspired by the insights of feminism, gender studies, and queer theory, advocates for critical gender pedagogies have highlighted the ways that literature can—across all grade levels—enable student reflection on gender codifications, which they may take for granted yet feel pressured to embody. Literature thus emerges as a potential springboard into critical masculinity studies.

Juan Felipe Herrera's *Downtown Boy* (2005) is an award-winning, autobiographical verse novel fit for inclusion in a "transformative pedagogy that opens spaces for students to read against the grain of traditional masculinity" (Bean & Harper, 2007, p. 26). With its portrayal of ten-year-old Juanito Palomares negotiating peer pressure, an absent father, and a chronic sense of isolation and dislocation caused by the incessant moves of his family, this novel for middle-school readers provides a thought-provoking, emotionally palpable exploration of boyhood and masculinity.

Such work begins with Herrera situating Juanito at the center of a matrix of voices that attempt to suture him into different versions of masculinity. Owing to the utilization of first-person narration, readers have access to Juanito's subjectivity and so are privy to, and positioned to empathize with, the confused, scared, and lonely feelings that the boy experiences as he struggles to adjudicate the expectations and ideals that these assorted others impose on him.

At the same time, readers are invited to critically parse the conflicting messages that Juanito receives as well as the impact of these messages on him. In effect, rather than present masculinity as a self-secure state of being which boys automatically and comfortably inhabit, Herrera acknowledges the vulnerability of boys to competing influences and expectations. Boyhood thereby emerges as a fraught experience.

What is more, masculinity emerges as inconsistent and arbitrary vis-à-vis the conflicting touchstones and templates that Juanito receives from family and friends. In other words, masculinity is revealed—for Juanito and for readers—as contingent and constructed.

As *Downtown Boy* effectively deconstructs popular presumptions about masculinity and boys, it offers to validate different conflicts and anxieties which boy readers in particular may find themselves experiencing. All the while, it creates opportunities for "boys to see wider visions of how they and others can *be* in the world" (Dutro, 2003, p. 472). Admittedly, concerns do arise with regard to the central significance of Juanito's father, especially at the end of the novel.

As I explain toward the end of this chapter, whether readers choose to regard this aspect of the novel as a critical oversight that reinscribes patriarchal primacy or as a productive instance of narrative irony, illuminating conversations can be had regarding the representation of gender in literature. All told, *Downtown Boy* stands out as a potentially powerful focal point for critical discussions—in classrooms, youth reading groups, and other workshop settings—about gender socialization, identity formation, the arbitrary nature of masculinity, the politics of gender in literature, and the lived experiences of real boys.

RIDICULOUS VOICES

Downtown Boy opens *in medias res* with Juanito subjected to his cousin Chacho's desperate efforts to interpellate him into normative ideals of masculine toughness:

"Tonight, Juanito,"
my cousin Chacho tells me,

> "you're gonna knock out Sweet Pea Price
> at the Mission District Branch Boys Club
> on Alabama Street!
> You're gonna love boxing!
>
> "You're the new dog in town, Juanito!
> The tallest, slickest, and most of all—my *primo*,
> the toughest cat on Harrison Street!" (p. 5)

With these lines, readers immediately see another pressing Juanito into a common set of masculine expectations and behaviors. Exhortations such as "you're gonna knock out Sweet Pea Price" and "You're . . . the toughest cat on Harrison Street!" function as aggressive gambits deployed to get Juanito to conform to a type of toughness that Chacho, ventriloquizing normative gender values, fetishizes.

Notably, Chacho's repeated use of second-person pronouns—not to mention the number of exclamation points that punctuate his exhortations—renders him an overbearing presence in this scene. With every "you're" that Chacho dictates to Juanito, the latter finds himself told what he is going to do (knock out Sweet Pea Price), what he loves (boxing), and what he is (the toughest cat on Harrison Street). Quickly enough, the predominance of Chacho's voice in these lines allows a reader to appreciate the pressured situation in which Juanito finds himself. Juanito cannot even get in a word on his own behalf and so has no opportunity to express himself or otherwise fend off Chacho.

When Juanito begins to stammer, "I, I, uh, Chacho,/don't know about . . . box—" (p. 5), he finds himself cut off by his excited cousin. A few lines later, Chacho's hailing of Juanito comes together with his exclamation, "*Primo*, listen" (p. 6). In this deft rhetorical gesture, readers see Chacho attempt to turn Juanito into a passive auditor wholly receptive to his doctrine of masculine toughness.

Juanito's reluctance to submit to the dictates that his cousin proselytizes allows readers to contemplate disjunctures between popular discourses of masculinity and the actual nature of boys. In turn, popular discourses of masculinity emerge as unnatural expectations forced upon unprepared boys.[1] Such a disjuncture shows through succinctly when Juanito and Chacho arrive at the Boys Club. Chacho's forcefulness—and Juanito's reluctance—becomes apparent as Juanito narrates,

> I bump into the pool tables, shuffle
> through the gym doors. "This place smells like potatoes,
> vinegar, and socks, huh?" I whisper.
> "Stop dragging your feet!" Chacho says,
> pulling me forward. (p. 8)

In this scene, readers see Juanito feeling out of his element. If we take the "Boys Club" as a venue for gender socialization, Juanito's clumsy navigation of its physical space can be read as implying or reflecting his unpreparedness for navigating what amounts to an initiation into being a boy. Along these lines, the image of Chacho pulling an apparently recalcitrant Juanito forward into an unfamiliar situation literalizes Chacho—and the ideals he foists upon Juanito—as a force with which Juanito must reckon.

All of these early interactions between Chacho and Juanito—the pressuring, the pulling, the cajoling—create crucial opportunities for young readers, particularly under the guidance of careful teachers, to grasp the abstract concept of gender socialization. In many ways, in fact, *Downtown Boy* resembles the type of text for which Wayne Martino (1995) has argued for inclusion in literature curricula.

In "Deconstructing Masculinity in the English Classroom: A Site Reconstituting Gendered Subjectivity," Martino figures the English classroom "as a [sociopolitical] site for critical intervention in the form of challenging and dismantling gender-based ideologies." He goes on to posit that English classrooms should feature texts that "[open] up . . . a space . . . within which dominant versions of masculinity and their workings can be analysed, critiqued, and deconstructed."

Incidentally, Martino's praise for Michael Wilding's short story "The Altar of the Family" (1970) as "a useful starting point for teachers to explicate and make visible for their students the effects of [the] positioning of boys within . . . discourses [of masculinity]" applies just as well as to Herrera's *Downtown Boy*. Between the rhetorical and then physical coercion to which Chacho subjects Juanito, it becomes possible for young readers to conceptualize positionality as a variable in gender formation. By extension, and as occurs with "The Altar of the Family," *Downtown Boy* "open[s] up possibilities for encouraging students to reflect on their own positionality as gendered subjects" (Martino, 1995).[2]

Such critical implications and pedagogical possibilities multiply as an accumulation of other competing and conflicting voices challenge Juanito to meet diverse criteria for respectability. At the Boys Club, Coach Egan reinforces the ethos promulgated by Chacho by admonishing Juanito, "When I blow/this here sporty gold whistle,/there's no turning back. . . . You hit the floor with all you got, mister./Just make sure/it's all in your gloves/and not in your pants" (p. 14).

Shortly thereafter, Cousin Tito comes along to offer a touchstone for "cool" masculinity in the form of the Morgue Run, an endeavor that purportedly begins with one's illicit entry into the ventilation system of the local morgue and culminates with one keeping score of the number of spitballs he can, in the midst of an active autopsy, land inside an open cadaver.

Just when Juanito is convinced that the Morgue Run is the means to being a champ and not a chump, Edda, a local seventh-grader, enters Juanito's life to offer yet another perspective. According to Edda, hurling empty beer bottles into the interior of a nearby bar is "cooler than the old Morgue Run!" (p. 49).

Through the likes of Chacho, Coach Egan, Tito, and Edda, readers see Juanito receive messages that not only progressively trample each other, but ultimately prove empty. On one level, this emptiness comes across via ironization of the speakers themselves. For example, before the boxing match, Juanito observes of his cousin,

> Cousin Chacho counts down and bounces his shiny head
> back and forth, grins and punches out air from his nostrils
> like he's a tiny bull; then he slicks back the Vaseline goop
> on his hair that he poured on this morning . . .
> . . .
> . . . Now he presses back the
> gooey stuff on his head. *Heh-heh*, his head looks like a goose. (p. 12)

As Juanito contemplates his cousin more closely, he begins to see the boy as fundamentally ridiculous and distinctly unimpressive. Meanwhile, Coach Egan and his investment in his little whistle end up seeming rather inane. By the time Juanito refers to the Coach's preferred instrument of disciplinary enforcement as his "stupid gold whistle" (p. 15), the Coach's philosophy and performance of toughness turn out as hollow as his whistle.

With similarly deconstructive implications, Juanito observes that when Tito talks about the Morgue Run, he "strokes his invisible goatee" (p. 36). Whether one processes this goatee as a synecdoche for the cool, mature masculinity that Tito alleges to embody or specifically as a sort of phallic signifier, the fact is that this signifier on which he grounds his gender performance is invisible, and so a fiction, a fraud. This leaves Tito—and his value system—with compromised credibility. And while Edda dismissively and boldly proclaims, "The Morgue Run is for chumps!" (p. 48), Juanito's skepticism about the alternative that this seventh-grader proposes invites readers to regard him and his claim similarly.

In a word, all of the others who impose their masculine ideals on Juanito end up looking silly and unconvincing, which leaves the ideals that they espouse looking silly and unconvincing, too.

"BUT HE WASN'T THERE"

The absence of Juanito's father for much of the novel only exacerbates the incertitude that plagues the boy as he confronts competing discourses of masculinity. To the dismay of Juanito, Papi spends most of his time in Mexico, supposedly to drink the waters of healing springs to treat his diabetes. Late in the book, however, Juanito learns the truth: in Mexico, Papi has another set of children with whom he has been staying. At different points, especially when struggling to disentangle rival versions of masculinity, Juanito yearns for his father to return to provide the modeling and advice that he needs.

Contemplations such as, "I wish Papi was here./But he isn't" (p. 105), and "Papi said, 'Talk to me first,'/but he's not here; he's never here./He's walking around somewhere,/with a bucket in his hand searching/for water" (pp. 23–4), register Juanito's vulnerability. In times of uncertainty, Juanito can only summon bits of past counsel that, owing to temporal distance, barely seem real or relevant anymore.

Thus, when he finds himself involved in the theft of "raisin pies from a Langendorf's bread truck on Treat Street" (p. 15), he reminds himself of an occasion long ago when "Papi said, 'I better never catch you stealing'" (p. 15). And when Juanito has second thoughts about his bottle-throwing excursion with Edda, he muses, "Papi, you said, 'Don't get in trouble,' but/ this isn't trouble, is it?" (p. 52).

In these instances in which Juanito is caught in a critical juncture in his personal development, readers see him attempt to conjure up paternal authority and guidance. Of course, such efforts at recovering Papi's presence only underscore the man's absence. Every time, phantasmic paternal presence comes up profoundly short of what Juanito feels that he needs. Juanito may carry a repertoire of some of Papi's sayings, but he requires someone present who can elaborate on the difference between right and wrong in specific situations.

Most clearly this comes across when Juanito wonders whether tossing beer bottles into a bar does or does not count as trouble. Obviously, the critique of the absent father arises in this instance with Juanito asking for advice from a man who is not around. With some close reading, however, young readers can realize that the layout of this section of text further conveys Juanito's predicament and so amplifies the critique being delivered:

> Papi, you said, "Don't get in trouble," but
> this isn't trouble, is it?
>
> *Whooosh!* (p. 52)

Beneath Juanito's question appears a skipped line followed by the "*Whooosh!*" of the beer bottle that he ends up throwing. The blank line here indicates the silence that meets Juanito's request for clarification. In fact, through the blank line Papi himself emerges as nothing more than an empty space or void in Juanito's life. With no response—with no Papi to counsel him—Juanito ends up following the lead of a surrogate mentor such as Edda, resulting in the "*Whooosh!*"

As the novel progresses, readers discern the divided feelings that Juanito harbors toward his father as a result of his father's absence. Sometimes Juanito clings to (and thus sustains) the paternal imago. For this reason, when he thinks about his family's travels, he warmly recalls, "Papi/calls the Greyhound station *El Perro*, the hound" (p. 15).

On another occasion, when Juanito and a new friend, Georgey Wong, go to Fisherman's Wharf to capture crabs, Juanito invokes Papi's mantra about the preciousness of water, thinking to himself, "Papi would love this ocean./ If he was here. Water is precious" (p. 91). In the former moment, Juanito admires his father's (supposed) mastery of the symbolic order vis-à-vis the man's capacity to name. For Juanito, his father's capacity to perform such naming accrues for him patriarchal respectability—in fact, phallogocentric primacy—by attesting to a dexterous ability to put worldly knowledge into wittily crafted language.

Phallogocentric reverence continues in the second instance when Juanito's experience of the ocean culminates with his recitation of his father's ostensibly wise words. When he lingers on the thought, "Water is precious," we see Juanito turning to Papi and Papi's words to process a veritably sublime experience of the ocean.[3] In the process, Papi essentially assumes the status of a sage.

Similar dynamics play out when Papi returns and readers see Juanito act out a desire to submit to paternal authority and wisdom. Recurrently, Juanito regards Papi as a venerable source of insight. In one instance, the family is walking down the street when Papi finds a piece of leather on the sidewalk. Juanito narrates that "Papi says proudly," "When my heels wear out, I'll hammer/pieces of this leather into the sole of [my] shoe./You gotta use your *cabeza*, Chico./But never forget your *corazón*—your heart" (p. 141). Resourcefulness as well as a seemingly infinite aptitude for dispensing nuggets of profound philosophy come together in these lines and leave Juanito enchanted. In another instance, Papi strikes Juanito even more impressively:

> . . .[Papi] takes out
> his Baptist Bible and places it by the bed.
> He reads a few pages to himself. Closes
> the thick book. Recites in a whispery voice.
>
> "*Come tu pan con gozo,
> y vivirás!*
> Eat your loaf of bread with joy,
> and you shall live!"
>
> Papi likes to say things like that,
> I don't know if it's poetry or Bible sayings. (p. 121)

For Juanito, Papi's words basically amount to poetry and Bible sayings, such is the extent to which he cherishes the man and believes in his genius and insight. Or, at least such is what he wants/needs to believe his father is capable of.

Importantly, there is a pathos to Juanito's invocations of the paternal imago and his ongoing enthrallment to phallogocentric primacy. This pathos arises as his mourning of his absent father shows signs of modulating into melancholia. Of course, apropos for thinking about Juanito in this regard is Judith Butler's (1997) oft-cited discussion of mourning and melancholia.

In *The Psychic Power of Life*, Butler builds on Sigmund Freud's "Mourning and Melancholia" (1917) and *The Ego and the Id* (1923) and explores the idea that "*ambivalence may well be a result of loss*, that the loss of an object precipitates an ambivalence toward it as part of the process of letting it go" (p. 174). She subsequently posits, "If so, then melancholia, defined as the ambivalent reaction to loss, may be coextensive with loss, so that mourning is subsumed in melancholia" (p. 174).

In the case of Juanito, Papi can be regarded as a lost object, and it is this experience of loss that engenders more than just a wish for his return; it also engenders what might be deemed, in Butler's terms, ambivalence. After all, while the boy on numerous occasions faithfully expresses reverence toward his father and poignantly wishes for his father's return, on other occasions more resentful feelings come across.

Thoughts such as "Don't even know if/Papi will come back/in a month or a year. He never says" (p. 24), "Where is he?/When will he come home?" (p. 30), and "He's a stranger and a papi at the same time" (p. 110) all bespeak a recriminating dimension to Juanito's feelings and betray a distinct ambivalence on his part. In fact, in the aforementioned passage "Papi would love this ocean./If he was here. Water is precious," ambivalence appears within the span of two short lines. Juanito alternates from missing his father ("Papi would love this ocean") to reproaching him ("If he was here") to displaying phallogocentric enthrallment ("Water is precious").

Also applicable to Juanito's relationship with his father is Butler's explanation that "Melancholia describes a process by which an originally external object is lost, or an ideal is lost, and the refusal to break the attachment to such an object or ideal leads to the withdrawal of the object into the ego, the replacement of the object by the ego, and the setting up of an inner world in which a critical agency is split off from the ego and proceeds to take the ego as its object" (p. 179).

Every incantation of Papi's counsel manifests Juanito's "refusal to break" his attachment to his lost Papi and suggests "the withdrawal of the [lost] object into the ego." Granted, young readers might not be expected to follow the dynamics put forth by Butler in Butler's exact terms. But they can be led into and through an understanding of the broader strokes of Juanito's ambivalence for the sake of a fuller understanding of the nature and implications of his relationship with his father.

Indeed, an understanding of Juanito's ambivalence renders his willful submission to paternal primacy—which includes the corollary repression of his father's shortcomings—not just poignant, but fodder for discussion about the role of fathers in the lives of their sons, fathers' responsibilities to their families, and the existence of patriarchal primacy in the first place.

"AY! I WISH FELIPE WAS HERE"

As much as *Downtown Boy* features elements that render it a powerful introduction to critical masculinity studies, the disproportionate narrative energy accorded to Papi compared to Mami yields mixed results. Most obviously, the novel's focus on a male protagonist and his relationship with his father—admittedly akin to this chapter's focus on matters pertaining to boys and boyhood—threatens to reinscribe the centrality of men and masculinity. For this reason, it is not uncommon for masculinity studies scholarship to acknowledge the risks inherent in such projects and to provide a defense for fixing attention on men and masculinity.[4]

That said, the status of Juanito's mother in the course of *Downtown Boy* complicates evaluation of the novel. After all, if Juanito seeks counsel or some rules and guidelines to which to submit, his mother is with him, fully capable of serving in such a capacity. In many ways, however, Mami comes across as an ineffective and marginalized figure. When she and Juanito first move to San Francisco, she pleads with Juanito, "No rough stuff" (p. 19). As the distance between them subsequently increases and her influence over him becomes increasingly tenuous, she attempts to get more forceful.

> After the bottle-throwing incident, she scolds Juanito,
> I told you more than once, Juanito,
> No play rough. But you don't listen to me.
> I don't know what is happening to you.
> Ever since we came to San Pancho, you don't talk,
> you don't listen! (p. 53)

While the novel may be autobiographical in nature, and while this may (or may not) account for details such as Mami's broken English, within the diegesis her speech style is noticeable and colors her characterization. One implication is that in contrast to Papi's supposed (though ultimately ironized) mastery of the symbolic order, Mami has a noticeably fractured relationship to the symbolic order.

This form of disempowerment, or diminution, plays into her ineffectiveness with Juanito and potentially into the reader's estimation of her. Her ineffectiveness comes across even more conspicuously as she gets ever more desperate in her efforts: "You know," she declares at one point, "if you lie to your mother,/that is enough to ruin the rest of your life and your soul/will rot and end up wandering in Purgatory when you die" (p. 54). Try as she may, Mami's anxious efforts at laying out a Law of the Mother go unheeded. She eventually resorts to citing (and deferring to) paternal logos by saying, "No more rough play, eh? Your Papi said, eh?" (p. 54).

The uneven status of paternal and maternal authority causes concern due to its potentially patriarchal implications. On a narrative level, the novel's preoccupation with the importance of the father in the life of a Chicano boy seems to entail, or turn on, the concomitant marginalization and devaluation of his mother. By the end of *Downtown Boy*, though, Herrera does somewhat—though not wholly satisfactorily—redress such unequal gender implications by deflating the primacy of the father at the same time that he creates space for appreciation for Mami.

The deconstruction of patriarchal primacy is set up through different observations that Juanito makes in the course of the novel, such as "Open up the toolbox Papi gave me./Never noticed how scratched/and small it is" (p. 38) and, during a family outing to the beach, "Papi walks into the water,/well, just a little, up to his ankles" (p. 197). In both instances, Papi—or Juanito's estimation of him—undergoes an unflattering recalibration.

Late in the novel, the reduction of Papi is literally and symbolically completed when a sequence of diabetes-related events results in the amputation of both of his legs.[5] After his amputations Papi may continue to dole out advice like "You got to work with what you got, Son!/Never give up!" (p. 228), but such proclamations end up ironized not only by Papi's incapacitated state, but especially by the fact that the amputations are a result of his stubborn refusal to get proper medical care.

As Papi's irresponsibility with his own health becomes a more prominent issue, Juanito becomes emboldened to call the man out for his irresponsibility as a father. Thus, amidst the later portion of the novel, we see Juanito think to himself while recalling a school incident,

> Papi always told me not to make trouble.
> Told me to tell him
> when something was wrong. But,
> but he wasn't there; he was away like always. (p. 249)

A Portrait of the Artist as a Muchachito 71

His resentment (or, in Butler's account of melancholia, rage) eventually boils over when, in a passage rich with symbolic significance, he finally speaks up to Papi:

> "It was your fault
> we had to leave!" I yell out.
> . . .
> "You told me that if I
> got in trouble you'd be there," I tell him.
>
> "Uh-huh."
> Papi pulls the blade across his cheek.
> . . .
> "But you weren't there!"
> "Where, Son?"
> "You weren't at the *traila*
> when the green van came!
> You were with [your other children]!"
>
> "Juan, don't raise your voice
> at your *papi*!" Mami says.
> . . .
> "Well, Son, I—
> Ouch!"
> Papi scrapes his nose
> and a little blood trickles into his soapy beard. (p. 265).

Between Juanito's indictment of his father, the symbolic castration of the man vis-à-vis his amputations, and, finally, the image of him bleeding—which aligns him with nonpatriarchal abjectness—Papi emerges an unraveled patriarch.

Alongside this Oedipal-ish shakeup of the legitimacy of the patriarchal organization of Juanito's family, Juanito's regard for Mami evolves. "She's always/reading little things, always showing me/the newspaper. She's a better teacher/than Mrs. Sniffins" (p. 135), he observes one day. On another occasion he realizes—with the unsophisticated criteria expected of a ten-year-old child—that Papi is not the only member of the family who can gracefully navigate the public sphere and its symbolic order:

> Papi knows all the places;
> he's a super walker.
> If Papi had a driving license,
> he could be a taxi driver.

> Mami, too. She could drive the Kensington #11
> to the Frosty shop before dropping me off
> at Burbank elementary. (p. 162)

By the time he overhears Mami one day talking to herself in the kitchen, muttering, "*Why does he always leave?*" "*He said he would stay with me to raise Juanito,*" and "*I must be strong, like my* mama grande *Juanita,/who raised all eight of us in Juárez*" (p. 178), her strength, in the face of her challenging situation, is clearer for Juanito as well as the reader.

By the conclusion of the novel, however, questions reintensify as to whether it ends up reinscribing patriarchal centrality or offers a savvy complication of Juanito's subjectivity and identity formation. The final pages feature Juanito stitching together a flood of thoughts and memories that acknowledge not just his own experiences, but the hardships and hurt that haunt different family members.

Written in a freer form of verse in which words—and, thus, thoughts and emotions—uninhibitedly spill over the page, the closing section presents a stream of Juanito's consciousness that expresses his cosmic understanding of the pathos of life. "Precious Papi,/precious Mami,/precious every moment—/precious, like water" (p. 293), Juanito resolves in the final lines of the novel. Notably, this sort of final note is a dramatic swerve from the novel's opening notes.

Whereas the novel begins in a boxing ring with an injunction to embody a violent, competitive brand of masculinity, it closes with a beautiful example of intrapersonal expression and interpersonal compassion. Indeed, the freedom of expression on these last pages—on the part of Juanito and Herrera—embodies the inspiring idea that, like poetry, masculinity and the identities and subjectivities of boys do not have to be constrained by convention.

On the one hand, Juanito at the end of *Downtown Boy* resembles the boy at the end of Tomás Rivera's (1971/1991) *. . . y no se lo tragó la tierra*. At the conclusion of Rivera's classic novel, the unnamed child articulates a newly realized compassion that emanates from a breakthrough capacity to appreciate the struggles and existential hardships that the people of his community must endure.

As a rush of communal memories and insights come together in his mind, the boy thinks to himself, "I would like to see all of the people together. And then, if I had great big arms, I could embrace them all. I wish I could talk to all of them again, but all of them together" (p. 219). Carlos Gallego (2014) posits that at this point Rivera's boy arrives at a "useful map of the social totality, which yields a newfound knowledge that inspires a 'thrill' in [him]" (p. 32).

For Juanito, a similar cognitive summation occurs, but rather than prompting a "thrill" in him, the assorted memories from the year which *Downtown*

Boy covers—a temporal frame which parallels the "lost year" that Rivera's boy tries to recover—produces what might be read as saudade. In this manner, the sensitivity, sensibility, and fluidity that distinguishes Juanito's subjectivity in the final pages could be seen as indexing a broadened, enlightened, and evolving perspective capable of, among other things, cherishing both Papi and Mami.

On the other hand, Juanito's "precious, like water" recitation at the end of *Downtown Boy* leaves him resembling Stephen Dedalus at the end of James Joyce's (1916/1976) *A Portrait of the Artist as a Young Man*. As occurs in *Downtown Boy*, *A Portrait of the Artist as a Young Man* explores the formation of a boy's identity and subjectivity by following Stephen Dedalus' efforts to "create proudly out of the freedom and power of his soul . . . a living thing, new and soaring and beautiful, impalpable, imperishable" (p. 170).

As the novel progresses, Stephen's efforts to assert an autonomous identity prove impossible. He professes, "I will try to express myself in some mode of life or art as freely as I can and as wholly as I can" (p. 247), but never manages to extricate himself from the sway or even the presence of the assorted ideologies and voices that have infiltrated and taken root within his subjectivity.

The same sort of infiltration and polyvalent subjectivity that appear in *A Portrait of the Artist* appear in *Downtown Boy* and could be said to have the same effect: the ironization of the formation of the individual self. On the last page of Joyce's work, in a journal entry for April 26, Stephen resolves, "Welcome, O life! I go to encounter for the millionth time the reality of experience and to forge in the smithy of my soul the uncreated conscience of my race" (p. 253). But then in the next and final entry, he writes, with ambiguous implications, "Old father, old artificer, stand me now and ever in good stead" (p. 253).

Among other things, it is intriguingly unclear whether Stephen is, in the final line, actually flexing creative autonomy by satirizing Catholic discourses such as "Holy Mary, mother of God, pray for us sinners, now and at the hour of our death." Or, given Cranly's earlier observation to Stephen, "It is a curious thing . . . how your mind is supersaturated with the religion in which you say you disbelieve" (p. 240), is Stephen in fact revealing his hopeless enthrallment to Catholic discourses, unable, as evidenced by the rhythms of the last line, to escape his subjectification to and by external influences?[6]

Along these lines, when Juanito reflects, "precious, like water," is he betraying his own hopeless enthrallment, in this case to phallogocentric primacy? After all, at the end of a chapter which features the novel's young protagonist expressing himself more freely, the reader sees Juanito come back to his father's familiar mantra, potentially bespeaking an inability on the part of the boy to transcend this particular influence.

If we take the final line of *Downtown Boy* at face value (i.e., not ironically), it can be seen as a nostalgic—perhaps melancholic—gesture on the part of Juanito and maybe even Herrera, one that memorializes an imperfect father and unintentionally or unwittingly perpetuates phallogocentric primacy. In turn, this line could be read as a critical oversight that shortcircuits the critical masculinity studies work that otherwise takes place in the novel. Alternatively, we can read the final line ironically, akin to reading Joyce's final line as satirizing Stephen's insistence on his autonomy.

Such a reading involves, though, a critical detachment from Juanito and realization of an enthrallment on his part that he himself does not realize. In this reading, Juanito may be able to articulate appreciation for "precious Papi" as well as "precious Mami," but his invocation of his father's patented simile to express this appreciation betrays an unsuspecting, tragic tethering of his subjectivity. Of course, and as occurs with *A Portrait of the Artist*, such narrative irony would be tremendously generative. A reader would be positioned to arrive at a powerful awareness of identity formation and the machinations of subjectivity.

CONCLUSION

Whether one regards the ending of *Downtown Boy* as unfortunately patriarchal or as a shrewd lesson on identity formation and the machinations of subjectivity, the fact remains that it enables unusually productive insights into and conversations about a host of issues. Regarding the conclusion, one upshot is that readers must vigilantly evaluate the implications of a text and be on the lookout for shortcomings that may arise.

Conversations thus might revolve around the politics of gender representations and, consequently, how and why literary criticism is important. From another angle, the ending of *Downtown Boy* lends itself to exercises in literary analysis. Thus, another set of conversations can revolve around topics such as phallogocentrism, enthrallment, and narrative irony. Either way—or, even better, both ways!—readers cannot help but emerge from Herrera's novel with different kinds of critical awareness and analytical acumen.

In his essay "Who the Boys Are: Thinking about Masculinity in Children's Fiction" (2002), Perry Nodelman points out the importance of developing in young readers critical awareness and analytical acumen about gender. He asserts, "The more aware of [matters of gender and gender relations] we work to become, the more we can help children to become aware of them also—and then to make more conscious commitments for or against them" (p. 17). A text like *Downtown Boy* can play a part in the development of such awareness.

In the process, it affords young readers an opportunity to consider identity and subjectivity and to contemplate, for example, "in what ways is 'I' defined, what constitutes the 'I,' and how is gender integral to the formation of 'I'?" (Wannamaker, p. 26). These and other sorts of questions prompted by Herrera's novel would prove empowering to young people who must learn not only how to parse the values, ideologies, and discourses that circulate in the world around them, but also figure out how they want to position themselves in relation to all of these influences.

NOTES

1. See Anderson (2009) for a discussion of the ways that "Much of what masculinity is predicated on is wholly *unnatural*" (p. 64). See Frosh, Phoenix, and Pattman (2001) for analyses of boys and their subjection to discourses of masculinity.

2. For a review of late-twentieth/early-twenty-first century Latino/a children's literature that facilitates student engagement with the subject of masculinity, see Serrato (2012).

3. The lyricism with which Herrera depicts Juanito's subjective perception of the ocean bespeaks the transcendental nature of this experience:

> The sun breaks into a thousand seashells on
> the waves rolling in from *whoknowswhere*
> rolling out to everywhere.
> They come in on little boats, like half moons,
> carved out of salty light. (p. 91)

Notably, passages such as this one invite discussion of the crucial role that more "aestheticized" types of books such as *Downtown Boy* can play in the development of all readers despite popular protestations that boys are "reluctant readers" who need to be lured into literature through allegedly "boy-friendly" fare.

4. See Traister (2000) for a discussion of the rise of American masculinity studies and the stakes involved in this kind of work. For multifaceted introductions to the study of masculinity in children's literature, see Stephens (2002) and Wannamaker (2008).

5. From the vantage point of disability studies, such a narrative strategy certainly requires problematization. For a discussion of physical impairment as "an opportunistic metaphorical device" (p. 47) used too often and too uncritically in literature, see Mitchell and Snyder (2000).

6. For an analysis of the different stakes involved in the last lines of *A Portrait of the Artist*, see Osteen (2003).

REFERENCES

Anderson, E. (2009). *Inclusive masculinity: The changing nature of masculinities*. New York: Routledge.
Bean, T., & Harper, H. (2007). Reading men differently: Alternative portrayals of masculinity in contemporary young adult fiction. *Reading Psychology, 28,* 11–30.

Butler, J. (1997). *The psychic life of power: Theories in subjection.* Stanford: Stanford University Press.

Dutro, E. (2003). "Us boys like to read football and boy stuff": Reading masculinities, performing boyhood. *Journal of Literacy Research, 34,* 465–500.

Frosh, S., Phoenix, A., & Pattman, R. (2002). *Young masculinities: Understanding boys in contemporary society.* New York, NY: Palgrave Macmillan.

Gallego, C. (2014). Topographies of resistance: Cognitive mapping in Chicano/a migrant literature. *Arizona Quarterly: A Journal of American Literature, Culture, and Theory, 70*(2), 21–53.

Herrera, J. F. (2005). *Downtown boy.* New York: Scholastic Press.

Joyce, J. (1976). *A portrait of the artist as a young man.* New York: Penguin Books.

Martino, W. (1995, June). Deconstructing masculinity in the English classroom: A site reconstituting gendered subjectivity. *Gender & Education, 7*(2), 205.

Mitchell, D. T., & Snyder, S. L. (2001). *Narrative prosthesis: Disability and the dependencies of discourse.* Ann Arbor: University of Michigan Press.

Nodelman, P. (2002). Who the boys are: Thinking about masculinity in children's fiction. *The New Advocate, 15*(1), 9–18.

Osteen, M. (2003). The great expectations of Stephen Dedalus. *James Joyce Quarterly, 41*(1/2), 169–83.

Rivera, T. (1971/1991). *. . . And the earth did not devour him.* In J. Olivares (Ed.), *Tomás Rivera: The complete works* (pp. 149–220). Houston, TX: Arte Publico Press.

Serrato, P. (2012). Transforming boys, transforming masculinity, transforming culture: Masculinity anew in Latino and Latina children's literature. In P. Noguera, A. Hurtado, & E. Fergus (Eds.), *Invisible no more: Understanding the disenfranchisement of Latino men and boys* (pp. 153–65). New York: Routledge.

Stephens, J. (Ed.). (2002). *Ways of being male: Representing masculinities in children's literature and film.* New York: Routledge.

Traister, B. (2000). Academic viagra: The rise of American masculinity studies. *American Quarterly, 52*(2), 274–304.

Wannamaker, A. (2008). *Boys in children's literature and popular culture: Masculinity, abjection, and the fictional child.* New York: Routledge.

Wilding, M. (1970). The altar of the family. *Southerly, 30*(4), 301–5.

Chapter 6

Not-So-Sweet *Quince*: Teenage Angst and Mother-Daughter Strife in Belinda Acosta's Young Adult Novel, *Damas, Dramas, and Ana Ruiz*

Cristina Herrera

"The Hispanic community is this very fractured community," he explains. "You have your Mexican Americans and your Puerto Ricans and your Cuban Americans. And the only thing that ties all these separate nationalities together—no, it's not Spanish," he says, anticipating what I might think, "in fact, many in the second and third generation don't even speak Spanish. What ties them together, the one single tie that binds all these cultures."

As he drumrolls toward his conclusion, I'm thinking that Will Cain learned something from growing up surrounded by a Hispanic community: a sense of drama.

is this tradition celebrated across the whole diverse group: the quinceañera. I mean, it is big! And the rest of America is starting to pay attention to it. (Alvarez, 2007, pp. 68–9)

In the above epigraph, acclaimed Latina writer Julia Alvarez documents an interview she conducted with Will Cain, founder of the magazine, *Quince Girl*, for her 2007 book, *Once Upon a Quinceañera*. Aside from Alvarez's obvious reference to the stereotype of Latin@s as possessing a "sense of drama," she captures an Anglo man's oversimplified sentiments regarding the quinceañera (a girl's fifteenth birthday, also referred to as a quince) as a "tradition" that connects the various Latin@ cultures. Alvarez's interviewee describes Latin@ culture as monolithic rather than varied and nuanced, and his assertion that the quinceañera is an increasingly globalized and capitalist phenomenon, seen in the casual uttering of the word "tradition," is ripe with contradictions and problematic implications.

If we take Cain's comments at face value, we would infer that Latin@ culture consists not of diverse and fluid languages, histories, and experiences; instead, Latin@s know how to party, and party big. But Cain does have a point, albeit a small one, when he proclaims that the quinceañera is "big," at least in terms of the general public's awareness of it.

Can we challenge this assertion, given the many references to fifteenth birthdays in popular culture, seen in films such as *Quinceañera* (2006), or in Chicana literature, perhaps most notably in the young adult (YA) writer Belinda Acosta's two-part "quinceañera club" book series, *Damas, Dramas, and Ana Ruiz* (2009) and *Sisters, Strangers, and Starting Over* (2010)?[1] We would be hard-pressed, indeed, to meet someone who had not at least remotely heard the word "quinceañera."[2]

Quinceañeras have also been the subject of important anthropological and ethnographic studies by Chicana scholars such as Karen Mary Dávalos and Norma E. Cantú, both of whom have documented this celebration as far more complex and contradictory than depicted in popular mainstream culture. In Karen Mary Dávalos' groundbreaking study, "*La Quinceañera*: Making Gender and Ethnic Identities," the author critiques what she calls the "public discourse" surrounding the quinceañera, visible in Cain's free use of "tradition." As she describes of the many conversations conducted with teenage girls, their mothers, and other family members:

> The field notes and transcriptions from the interviews include aspects of the *quinceañera* that are rarely mentioned in the public discourse. For example, young *mexicanas* spoke about the arguments they had with their parents over things such as the color of the dress, number of guests, or the location of the reception. This kind of parent-child conflict was missing in the public discourse. . . . In general, *mexicanas* discuss a wider range of issues surrounding the quinceañera than clergy and journalists. (1996, p. 114)

According to Dávalos, the public discourse typically defines the quinceañera according to the so-called customs, which include the common narrative of the quince as a young girl's transition into womanhood, or the necessity of a Catholic mass to mark this significant moment. Uncommon in these public accounts of the quince are intense negotiations of the festivities, arguments, and tensions that can arise between mothers and daughters, issues that leave an incomplete and simplified glimpse into the complexities surrounding the fifteenth birthday.

In fact, Chicana YA writer Belinda Acosta's 2009 novel, *Damas, Dramas, and Ana Ruiz*[3] addresses the many complicated layers of Cain's assertion of quinces as "traditional." The novel uses the planning of a Chicana's quinceañera as a backdrop to comment on the increasingly tense relationship between the protagonist of the title, Ana Ruiz, a thirty-eight-year-old Chicana mother who dreams of planning her daughter Carmen's fifteenth birthday celebration in the hopes that it will heal their damaged union.

While the overtly intrusive and sometimes snarky narrator comments on the futility of planning a birthday party to cure a troubled relationship that has disintegrated following the break-up of Ana's marriage to her husband, Esteban, Ana initially believes a quince can bond the maternal relationship. The text references the so-called traditional aspects of the quince, such as a father-daughter waltz, the cake, and of course, the dress, but the novel is far more interested in narrating moments and events leading up to the celebration, seldom seen in quince magazines or popular culture, as Dávalos argues.

This chapter will examine these moments in the novel, using Chicana feminist scholarship by Dávalos and Cantú as a theoretical foundation on which to place the analysis of this text. As this chapter claims, Acosta's YA novel exposes the underlying tensions between the Chicana mother and daughter characters to demystify the quince celebration. Rather than portray the quinceañera as a generalized or idealized "tradition" of a young girl's entrance into womanhood, the novel instead uncovers the mother-daughter strife caused by misunderstandings and disappointments resulting from a shift in the Ruiz family structure, which moves from the nuclear family to single-mother household.

Ana and Carmen do indeed reunite as loving mother and daughter, but Carmen learns the joys and heartbreaks of Chicana womanhood through the events leading up to and after her fifteenth birthday, and the party itself becomes a rather insignificant moment in the overall narrative. As this chapter suggests, both mother and daughter essentially "come of age" through their interactions with each other before the celebration. Like her daughter, Ana must negotiate her own views of mature Chicana womanhood in her transition from married woman to single mother.[4]

FROM NIÑA TO MUJER? QUINCEAÑERAS, "TRADITION," AND CHICANA RITES OF PASSAGE

In Karen Mary Dávalos' seminal ethnographic work on Chicana and Mexicana quinceañeras in Chicago, the Chicana scholar discourages readers from assuming her analysis will entail a discussion of apparently "traditional" aspects of fifteenth birthday celebrations. For Dávalos, what marks the quinceañera as a much more complicated event is how Chicanas and Mexicanas "construct themselves as historical and oppositional subjects" (1996, p. 103). Further, she advocates a discussion of "'tradition' as an open, and sometimes chaotic, terrain that is constantly reconfigured in everyday experience" (1996, p. 103).

This chapter heeds Dávalos' "third world feminist concern" (1996, p. 103) and does not suggest that Acosta's novel be read as a generalization of the quinceañera celebration; rather, the novel similarly cautions readers against reinforcing problematic views of gender and ethnicity that mark the fifteenth birthday celebration as a "natural" phenomenon without accounting for variations across family makeup, region, ethnicity, language, citizenship, and sexuality.

To better situate Chicana feminist contestations of the discourse surrounding la quinceañera, it is useful to offer a brief overview of books and studies that have affirmed problematic notions of this event. This chapter began with a quotation from Alvarez's book, and it bears mentioning the mainstream visibility of the quinceañera when a canonical writer is tasked with penning a book that reads partially as ethnography as well as a condensed memoir of her growing-up process in the United States.

The book refers to the quinceañera celebration as both a "tradition" (2007, p. 5) and "highly ritualized" (2007, p. 3) marking of a girl's passage to womanhood, yet what is rather striking are passages throughout the book that evoke critical, if not judgmental, views on the families she interviewed during the research process. In an early section of the book called "The sad state of Hispanic girls," which cites high rates of teen pregnancy and high school dropout numbers among Latinas, Alvarez laments, "If the situation is indeed this bad, shouldn't our community en masse and each of us individually rush to rescue our girls?" (2007, p. 22).

While Alvarez appears to be sincere in her concern over the "sad state of Hispanic girls," its placement in a book that purports to be about the quinceañera would suggest an underlying view that this event is, at best, frivolous, and at worst, a contributing factor in Latina teen pregnancy and educational achievement gaps. The writer's claim does little to challenge dominant racist, classist, and sexist misperceptions of Latinas as hyperfertile and uneducated; in fact, it reaffirms this stereotypical view. Take, for example, the following passage: "The quinceañera is like a rehearsal wedding without a groom, and it sends a clear message to the Latina girl: we expect you to get married, have children, and devote yourself to your family. It's no wonder that girls end up getting pregnant soon after celebrating their quinces" (2007, p. 56).

Alvarez's generalized assertion that Latin@s view the quinceañera in the same way, as preparation for eventual heterosexual coupledom, is further problematic for its accusation that many Latinas "end up getting pregnant" before they exchange said wedding vows. What does it mean for a Latina writer to exploit all-too-familiar stereotypes of Latina girls as sexually active, pregnant, and underachieving? Or, what does it mean for a Latina to insert these hypercritical sentiments in a quinceañera book?

It is unlikely that Alvarez had Latin@ readers in mind when authoring this book, despite her use of the pronouns "us" and "our," given that these statements fit quite comfortably within mainstream rhetoric. Undoubtedly, Alvarez attempts to provide a sociocultural context for understanding the quinceañera trend and its significance to Latin@ communities, but her apparent reluctance to examine moments of subjectivity and agency for Latina girls is deeply troubling. According to her "research," Latina teens are always already in need of rescue.

Sociological studies of the quinceañera have offered more sophisticated interpretations of this event. Some studies have examined Spanish language use in the preparation of the fifteenth birthday (Potowski & Gorman, 2011), kinship (Horowitz, 1993), ethnic and gender identity formation (Rodriguez, 2013; Napolitano, 1997), including the quince's role in studying globalized ideals of beauty and fashion (McCracken, 2014).

For the most part, however, these investigations have been performed by non-Chicana/Latina scholars, with the exceptions being two of the most significant contributions to theories on the quinceañera, those by Dávalos and Cantú. According to Cantú, celebrating the quince may be read as a subtle act of resisting assimilation, given that it "allows Chicanas to perform their cultural identity outside the realm of mainstream U.S. culture" (2002, p. 16). This sentiment situates the quince in stark contrast to the epigraph at the beginning of this chapter, which cites the founder of *Quince Girl* authoritatively claiming its transnational growth.

While we cannot underestimate the mainstream familiarity of the quinceañera, Chicana scholars such as Cantú insist on uncovering the subversive elements of the celebration that Cain (and for that matter, Alvarez) are unable, or reluctant, to acknowledge. As Cantú explains, the quince "functions as a coming-of-age ritual that offers the young woman a space to perform her emergence into adulthood and to contest and shape the expectations that the symbolic act implies" (2002, p. 18). These scholars suggest that "there are more to these customs than frivolity, materialism, and the romanticizing of colonial cultures and old-fashioned ideas of womanhood" (Rodriguez, 2013, p. 4).[5]

Although Alvarez claims that the quinceañera sends heteronormative messages to young girls about "proper" behavior that apparently lead to teen pregnancy, this chapter instead heeds Chicana feminist theorizing proposed by Dávalos and Cantú that encourages a "reading between the cracks," so to speak. Rather than romanticize material items such as the dress and shoes, or the supposed symbolism of preparing a young girl for heterosexual marriage, Acosta's novel, like Chicana feminist theorists Dávalos and Cantú propose, invites readers to witness young Carmen's coming-of-age that is negotiated through her many arguments and tense interactions with her mother, a woman who is herself learning what it means to be a single adult Chicana.

"Reading between the cracks" of the quinceañera planning allows moments of subjectivity and agency for both Chicana characters to emerge, a Chicana feminism in practice. By witnessing Ana's resilience and emotional growth alongside her daughter Carmen's, Acosta successfully turns the common perception of the quince on its head by suggesting that Chicanas are never too old or young to re-invent themselves.

MAMA DRAMA: MATERNAL STRIFE IN BELINDA ACOSTA'S QUINCEAÑERA CLUB NOVEL

While texts like Alvarez's reference the sky-high costs of planning a quinceañera, which serves as a shaming tactic to castigate working-class Latin@s for spending money unwisely, it must be noted that Acosta's novel features two educated, white-collar Chicana characters, the protagonist Ana and her best friend and comadre, Beatriz Sánchez-Milligan, both executive associates for administrators at a university in San Antonio, Texas.[6] Educated Chicana characters are hardly unique in Chicana literature, but this facet of two characters' identities in a YA novel, coupled with the novel's more complex depiction of the quinceañera, is a subtle but important element that should not be overlooked.

Moreover, Ana's white-collar career and her respected position within a privileged space such as a university functions as a critical gesture by Acosta to normalize Chicana educational and career aspirations. This element of featuring an educated Chicana character like Ana, who struggles to connect with her head-strong and resentful teenage daughter, also must be acknowledged as a useful tactic employed by the writer to reach a wide Chicana adolescent readership; that is, even young Chicanas not growing up in a relatively privileged household like the teenager Carmen may identify with this teenager's disillusionment with growing up, her parents' separation, and fights with her mother.

As we learn within the opening pages of the novel, the Ruiz family household has undergone a major shift following Ana's separation from her husband, Esteban, who committed an extramarital affair and fathered a child outside his marriage, facts that Ana at first withholds from her two children, Carmen and Diego.

Although the reasons behind the marriage's breakup are not divulged to readers until at least halfway through the novel, the wise-cracking narrator makes it very clear where Carmen stands: "Diego, the oldest, was sad and brave. He did his best to help around the house and look after his mother and sister, but Carmen—ay, Carmen!—that one wasn't making it easy. She was so sure that the reason her father left was all her mother's fault" (2009, p. 7).

Other intrusive narrative moments throughout the novel equally comment on Carmen's disrespectful behavior to her mother (pp. 177, 185), as if to caution teenage readers against this sort of acting out.

Beyond the narrator's warning to teenagers, however, the novel also shows the dangers of Carmen's refusal to believe that her father is culpable or capable of committing betrayal; in short, Carmen has to learn the hard way the painful consequences of idealizing her father and stubbornly blaming her mother. In Ana's decision to host a quinceañera, she hopes to bond with her daughter while also teaching Carmen not to identify too closely with a highly flawed man: "She had wanted this to be an event they planned, a way for them to grow close again, not another way for Carmen to be Daddy's Girl" (p. 87).

But perhaps most important in Ana's thoughts are the ways in which she initially contextualizes the quinceañera celebration as a romanticized maternal-daughterly experience, what she also refers to as "an old tradition" (p. 77). Significantly, Ana herself places much emphasis on the day of the event, not realizing until much later in the novel that she, like her understanding of the quinceañera, will evolve through these almost daily battles with Carmen.

Although the many arguments between Ana and Carmen are a result of Carmen's incorrectly placed blame and Ana's frustrations with her husband and daughter, the novel insists on exposing both Ruiz women's complicated emotions and simultaneous feelings of heartache and loss. Ana wants to shield Carmen from pain even as she attempts to teach her daughter to accept life's many challenges. As the narrator puts it, "She wished she could crawl inside her daughter's head and help her understand that the world was not painted in crayons. Ana didn't want to kill Carmen's image of her father, but this was too much" (p. 178).

This delicate balance in which Ana finds herself, namely, the desire to protect her daughter from the knowledge of her husband's betrayal while also wanting her to grasp the complexities of life, forms the crux of their ruptured bond.[7] But though it would seem that the text mainly conveys Ana's perspective, thereby privileging the maternal voice, the novel, in fact, also provides insight into Carmen's teenage angst and her attempts to make sense of such a dramatic shift in her family's dynamics. In one particularly intense argument that leads to Ana's sudden outburst, calling Carmen a "self-righteous little bitch" (p. 178), both mother and daughter voices are narrated by the speaker:

"I'm sorry I called you a bitch."
"You called me a *self-righteous* bitch," Carmen snapped.
"You *are* self-righteous!"
Carmen's mouth fell open.

"You are!" Ana insisted. "Ever since your father and I—you act like you're the only one with God on your side."
"Why are you talking to me like that?"
"Oye, chica, if you're going to throw chingazos, you better learn to take some punches."
"You're not supposed to talk to me that way," Carmen whined.
"And I'm not your personal punching bag!"
She wasn't trying to fight with her mother, but she wasn't trying to make up with her, either. She just wanted things to be normal. Pero, she wasn't sure what normal meant anymore. She didn't want to be treated like a little girl, but she had no idea, no real idea, what it meant to be treated like an adult. If hearing the truth about yourself was part of it, she didn't know if she liked it. (pp. 180–1)

This passage, and many others like it in the novel, reflects a wide range of maternal and daughterly emotions. Ana's outburst, while inappropriate, is not treated by the author as evidence of her "bad" mothering; instead, calling her daughter a rather ugly name reveals a moment of despair, desperation, and raw honesty.

Rather than encourage readers' judgment, the passage demands compassion and sensitivity for both Ana and Carmen, each of whom is trying to make sense of their current life situation. Carmen's own frustrations and confusion over her mother's behavior are equally evident, and in her inner lament, "she wasn't sure what normal meant anymore," the novel exposes a teenager's complex growing pains that are wrought with feelings of ambivalence.

The back-and-forth shouts at each other, I would suggest, demonstrate both women's emotional growth, although their inability to understand each other's pain and confusion is evident. The argument *is* communication, though painful, and it points to the novel's insistence on capturing these stressful moments leading up to Carmen's birthday. Further, Ana's and Carmen's coming-of-age process entails this articulation of pain to each other, not the planning of a quinceañera.

Ana's respective coming-of-age also requires an admission of her own disappointments over dreams deferred as a result of a young marriage and children. For though her separation from Esteban undoubtedly causes intense hurt, it also forces Ana to reflect on painful sacrifices she has made. Significantly, Ana acknowledges her relative privilege and education, but her outward financial and emotional stability mask her inner desires she has been at pains to keep buried: "Ana had it all . . . What they—including Carmen y Diego—didn't know is that it wasn't exactly the life Ana wanted. She had wanted to study art. She wanted to travel and see all the world's great museums . . . Ana would be the first one to say she had a good life. Pero it just wasn't the one she was waiting for" (p. 39).

Ana's secret desires that are revealed during the planning stages of her daughter's quinceañera point to the ways in which she must negotiate her own emotional and personal growth alongside Carmen's. Her marital separation and the resulting parental strife uncover Ana's ambivalence over the life decisions she has made. On the one hand, her middle-class, white-collar career grants her professional respect and the means to support her family; yet the novel also digs up Ana's regret over the decision to postpone her artistic aspirations and dreams of traveling the world.

By providing an outlet for Ana's frustrations and complicated emotions of regret and guilt, the novel humanizes the Chicana mother, refusing to castigate her for daring to admit that her life is not what she had imagined. The sympathetic treatment of a thirty-eight-year-old Chicana's innermost pain in a YA novel demonstrates to readers, adolescent or not, that hopes and dreams should not be a source of shame, and the text's ability to sensitively convey a grown woman's disappointments in a text intended for YA audiences cannot be underestimated.

While the novel documents the mother-daughter strife that has recently plagued both women's lives, the text also accounts for their simultaneous rethinking and refashioning of the quinceañera event. For Carmen, the event is initially thought of as a burdensome (not to mention boring) obligation to please her demanding mother (p. 77). Further, Carmen only feigns excitement over the celebration's planning by plotting "to make her father's part in the quinceañera bigger" (p. 88). Ana, on the other hand, at first emphasizes what Dávalos has called the public discourse's understanding of the birthday—picking out a dress, choosing a reception location, and deciding on a cake—assuming these "fun" activities will unite her with her daughter:

> It had been a long time since Ana had any conversation with Carmen, and she was beginning to think it would never happen again. She had wanted the quinceañera to be a time to bond and become close again. Now, although things seemed to be coming together, it seemed like a way for Carmen to avoid talking to Ana about anything outside the quinceañera; the whole thing was feeling more and more like a giant to-do list. (p. 247)

Most telling in these lines are the ways in which Carmen exploits the quinceañera as a distracting technique to avoid communication with her mother; what is more, Carmen performs the role of dutiful daughter by agreeing to allow Ana to host a birthday celebration while also hiding her underhanded attempts to overshadow Ana's role through Esteban. Ana's detection of her daughter's avoidance and her disappointment that the birthday is not what she had hoped, I would argue, are a result of her early misguided, even shortsighted understanding of the quinceañera as a generalized "tradition" (p. 77).

What also bears mentioning is Ana's assumption that Carmen would hold interest in a quinceañera, given the rather random mode in which she presents the idea to her daughter. When Ana shows Carmen an advertisement for a "quinceañera expo," we read Carmen's inner disgust: *"what makes you think I'd be interested in that old-fashioned thing?"* or what she was really dying to say, *"What makes you think I want to be like you?"* (p. 6, original italics).

Carmen's criticism of the quinceañera as "old-fashioned," of course, reveals more about her problematic views of her mother than the event itself. But significantly, her belief that the quinceañera reflects outdated "traditions" is symbolic of the novel's attempts to offer a more complex and subversive account of the event. We may also read Carmen's annoyance with this "old-fashioned" event as a rejection of what she perceives as Ana's efforts to mold her daughter into a "proper" Chicana young woman.

Although readers understand that Ana merely desires to host a birthday celebration to reconnect with Carmen, the teenager's subtle rejection of prescribed gender roles hints at the writer's use of the YA genre to provide her adolescent readers with multiple perspectives on an event that is wrought with much more fluidity and contradictions than may seem apparent.

Interestingly, however, Carmen decides to follow through with her mother's planned event, although it occurs the day after Ana at last divulges the details of Esteban's betrayals. Carmen is not only forced to listen to Ana's words, but she also learns of the depth of Esteban's secrets when she and her brother witness their father's grief surrounding the death of his stillborn child to another woman (p. 286). While Ana interprets her inability to spare her children's knowledge of these secrets as evidence of her "failure" (p. 287), this moment of reckoning for her children is significant for its role in shaping Carmen's development as a Chicana. Carmen's resilience demonstrates to Ana the liberating potential of heartache while showing the futility of believing that a mother can always shield her children from pain.

It is Carmen, in fact, who teaches Ana that she is capable of withstanding pain and recovering from it. Rather than accept Ana's pleas to cancel the event because of her fears that it will cause her daughter more emotional pain, Carmen chooses to celebrate her birthday, as she confides to Ana: "I was trying to figure out why you didn't say anything about all this before, why you let me think you had kicked 'Apá out, and how mean I was to you. I was so mean to you, 'Amá. I was *so* mean! All the things I said and did. I couldn't figure out why you didn't say anything" (p. 290). Carmen's apology to Ana reads as a condensed monologue, the novel granting a heartbroken young Chicana a voice.

But though Carmen's apology is filled with shame, when she adds, "You deserve a better daughter. . . . I need to be as good a daughter as you've been a mother" (p. 290), we must not read the binary terms of "good" and "bad" as the novel's castigation and judgment over Carmen's behavior. Instead, we must witness Carmen's maturity and grace, her admission of the pain she has caused Ana, a significant departure from earlier behavior.

When Carmen insists that Ana walk her in the church without her father at the start of the quinceañera ceremony (p. 297), she communicates to her father and extended family her acceptance of Ana's role as a single Chicana mother. If common accounts of the quinceañera cite the "tradition" of the father escorting his daughter down the aisle, Carmen's choice to rewrite this "tradition" reads as a Chicana feminist coming-of-age. Further, this symbolic moment of Chicana feminist maternal bonding privileges the new single-mother family rather than the nuclear family unit of her past.

Carmen's acceptance of the maternal bond, along with her growing maturity, coincides with Ana's own new feminist coming-of-age. While observing Carmen and her friends dress up for the celebration, Ana's reimagining of her daughter's important day is clear: "There were good things about being a woman, but being a woman wasn't about wearing high heels or getting to wear lipstick, or staying up past midnight, though that's what she suspected most of these girls thought it meant" (p. 292). As a wiser Chicana who has suffered a husband's infidelity and temporary estrangement from her only daughter, Ana critically casts off these so-called traditional elements of the quinceañera, astutely commenting on the irony of using such trivial items as makeup and high heels as markers of maturity.

Further, Ana tells her comadre, Beatriz, that through Carmen's quinceañera, she is "celebrating survival" (p. 293). Her daughter's coming-of-age is indeed cause for celebration, but the reference to her survival marks her recognition of her own personal and emotional growth, this newfound resilience to withstand life-altering events. Identifying as a survivor is both an acknowledgement of her suffering and a reminder of the strength she exhibited to combat such turmoil. Moreover, Ana acknowledges that Carmen's festivities warrants a celebration of her own, marking her transition from married woman to single, independent Chicana mother.

CONCLUSION

Belinda Acosta's YA novel, though referred to as part of a "quinceañera club" book series, spends few pages narrating Carmen's birthday fiesta. Even more intriguing in Acosta's playful, though brief account of the big day as "a blur" that involves the cake almost toppling over, a torn dress, and an accidental black eye (p. 296), is the concluding paragraph, which describes Ana's "drama" (p. 298) in the future: global travel, fun, even no strings-attached sex with a foreigner in Paris.

The writer's decision to end the novel with a peek into Ana's future points to the texts' subversive and critical treatment of the quinceañera to demystify this celebration, shattering readers' preconceived notions. What matters is not how the quince turned out, but how Ana and Carmen learn from each other in their respective journeys of Chicana adolescence and mature womanhood. Essentially, Acosta is suggesting that readers should look elsewhere if they are expecting an affirmation of these public ideals of the quince.

Chicana feminist scholarship by Karen Mary Dávalos and Norma E. Cantú has offered significant reconfigurations of the quinceañera by pointing to the complex negotiations of gender and racial identities that are typically ignored in mainstream accounts of this birthday. Unlike the general public's understanding of the quince and apparent "traditional" aspects, Chicana feminist scholarship excavates crucial moments of identity formation through moments hidden within the cracks. Likewise, Belinda Acosta's *Damas, Dramas, and Ana Ruiz* narrates intense arguments between Ana and her daughter, Carmen, to problematize how we narrate and understand the fifteenth birthday.

Rather than provide details of the celebration, the novel instead is far more interested in highlighting the complex coming-of-age of both Chicana characters that occurs through these daily battles. What Carmen learns about Chicana womanhood has little to do with symbolic items, such as lipstick or heels; rather, she learns first-hand the painful consequences of idolizing a flawed father and the dangers of pushing against a maternal ally. Ana, too, comes into her mature Chicana womanhood by at last freeing herself from a doomed marriage and accepting her new identity as a single adult. In their reunion as mother and daughter, Ana and Carmen enact a simultaneous Chicana feminist coming-of-age, giving new meaning to the sweet fifteen.

NOTES

1. I would be remiss if I did not also mention TLC's short-lived series, *Sweet 15: Quinceañera*, which had not been renewed for a second series, at the time of this writing. The epigraph's reference to *Quince Girl* magazine and Julia Alvarez's own book on this event further demonstrates the mainstream visibility of this occasion.

2. Acosta's novel is not the only Chicana YA text that features a quinceañera storyline. Malín Alegría's 2006 novel, *Estrella's Quinceañera*, as the title suggests, traces a young Chicana's frustrations with turning fifteen, assimilation, her family's economic difficulties, and identity-formation. Yet whereas Acosta's text quite deliberately avoids detailed insight into the character's birthday celebration to challenge this event as integral to Carmen's coming-of-age, Alegría's novel spends much time narrating the quince. Further, the novel suggests that the event itself is fundamental to the young protagonist's Chicana identity. While I do not engage in an analysis of this

novel, it is useful to note the prevalence of quinceañera themes in Chicana literature and the varied ways in which writers present them.

3. I will heretofore refer to this novel as *Damas*.

4. See my 2014 study, *Contemporary Chicana Literature: (Re)Writing the Maternal Script*, for an in-depth discussion of mother–daughter strife and bonding in Chicana literature.

5. Indeed, scholar Annette Portillo's brilliant 2011 analysis of Cantú's seminal work, *Canícula*, documents Cantú's "literary quinceañera" held in 2010 to celebrate the fifteenth anniversary of the book's publication to demonstrate Cantú's critical theorizing of this event; in Cantú's case, the fifteenth birthday celebration is in honor of a book rather than a person. In an online blog essay, scholar Sonia BasSheva Mañjon further subverts the gendered "tradition" of the quince by narrating the celebration she hosted for her sons. Full citation listed in references.

6. Readers may note the similarities between *Damas* and Alegría's *Estrella's Quinceañera*, published three years earlier. While Alegría's novel also unpacks the quinceañera discourse by narrating tense exchanges between mother and daughter, *Damas* offers insight into both women's frustrations with coming-of-age, unlike *Estrella's Quinceañera*. It is not my intent to dismiss Alegría's text, but it bears mentioning that the novel privileges the teenage daughter's perspective in contrast to Acosta's plot and narrative structure that acknowledges both women's points of view.

7. Beatriz is the protagonist in the second book in the series, *Sisters, Strangers, and Starting Over*.

REFERENCES

Acosta, Belinda. (2009). *Damas, dramas, and Ana Ruiz*. New York: Grand Central Publishing.

Alegría, Malín. (2006). *Estrella's quinceañera*. New York: Simon Pulse.

Alvarez, Julia. (2007). *Once upon a quinceañera: Coming of age in the USA*. New York: Plume.

Cantú, Norma E. (2002). Chicana life-cycle rituals. In Norma E. Cantú & Olga Nájera-Ramírez (Eds.), *Chicana traditions: Continuity and change* (pp. 15–34). Urbana and Chicago: University of Illinois Press.

Dávalos, Karen Mary. (1996). La *quinceañera:* Making gender and ethnic identities. *Frontiers: A Journal of Women Studies*, *16*(2/3), 101–27. Retrieved from http://www.jstor.org/stable/3346805

Herrera, Cristina. (2014). *Contemporary Chicana literature: (Re)writing the maternal script*. Amherst, NY: Cambria Press.

Horowitz, Ruth. (1993). The power of ritual in a Chicano community: A young woman's status and expanding family ties. *Marriage and Family Review*, *19*(3–4), 257–80. doi:10.13001J002

Mañjon, Sonia BasSheva. (2016, June 14). A quince for my boys: Celebrating 15 Latina style. Retrieved from https://library.osu.edu/blogs/mujerestalk/2016/06/

McCracken, Angela B. V. (2014). *The beauty trade: Youth, gender, and fashion globalization*. New York: Oxford University Press.

Napolitano, Valentina. (1997). Becoming a mujercita: Rituals, fiestas and religious discourses. *The Journal of the Royal Anthropological Institute*, 3(2), 279–96. Retrieved from http://www.jstor.org/stable/3035020

Portillo, Annette. (2011). Writing photomemories: Crossing borders, crossing genres in Norma E. Cantú's *Canícula: Snapshots of a Girlhood en la Frontera*. *Chicana/Latina Studies*, 11(1), 84–123.

Potowski, Kim, & Gorman, Lillian. (2011). Hybridized tradition, language use, and identity in the U.S. Latina *quinceañera* ritual. In Kim Potowski & Jason Rothman (Eds.), *Bilingual youth: Spanish in English-speaking societies* (pp. 57–87). Amsterdam: John Benjamins Publishing Company.

Rodriguez, Evelyn Ibatan. (2013). *Celebrating debutantes and quinceañeras: Coming of age in American ethnic communities*. Philadelphia, PA: Temple University Press.

Chapter 7

"You Wanna Be a Chump/or a Champ?": Constructions of Masculinity, Absent Fathers, and Conocimiento in Juan Felipe Herrera's *Downtown Boy*

Sonia Alejandra Rodríguez, PhD

Thirteen-year-old Andy Lopez died on October 22, 2013, in Santa Rosa, California, after being shot seven times by a policeman who suspected him of carrying an AK-47 when in reality Lopez was in possession of a toy replica. According to news article "Toy Guns, Deadly Consequences," when Deputy Erik Gelhaus asked Lopez to slowly turn around the toy replica moved and Gelhaus suspected Lopez was readying to shoot and instead Gelhaus shot first and proceeded to shoot seven more times.

The community of Santa Rosa marched and protested the injustice against Lopez and shone light on a larger issue of discrimination by the police against boys and men of color. While the Lopez family filed a federal civil rights suit, no charges were filed against Gelhaus.

Among many complicated issues, Lopez's murder demonstrates the precarity of black and brown lives in the United States. While the Lopez's family lawyer attempted to demonstrate that Gelhaus fired at Andy without a valid reasonable cause, Andy's deviant appearance and behavior in a town that is predominantly Chicanx[1] was enough to warrant his death.

In "'You Don't Know How Much He Meant': Deviancy, Death, and Devaluation," an essay about her cousin's death, Lisa Marie Cacho (2007) explains, "Young men of color are not very sympathetic subjects if they don't want to work 9–5 jobs, if they use their expendable income on recreational activities, or if they take risks with their lives" (p. 196). On October 22nd Lopez was on the street appearing seemingly unproductive, which made him an unsympathetic subject and, therefore, vulnerable to be read as suspicious and criminal.

Lopez may have unknowingly taken a risk with his life by walking around with a toy replica of an AK-47; however, he took a risk every day by simply existing and inhabiting public space. The photo that circulated in the media, and that was used at his memorial, was of Lopez wearing a black sweatshirt and black beanie with a diamond stud earring on each earlobe. Although Lopez's attire is typical of youth of color culture, it has also been misappropriated as a signifier for criminality.

The media coverage of the shooting focused on the toy gun, on why Lopez carried it out in public in the first place, and on how Gelhaus could have shot a child that carried only a toy gun. Lateef Mungin argues in the CNN article "Deputy kills 13-year-old carrying fake riffle" that Lopez was possibly on his way to play and show off the weapon replica to a friend.

Another newspaper claimed that Gelhaus fired because that is what his police training dictated he do in these types of situations. The media coverage portrayed Lopez's death as an accident that could not have been prevented. In this way, the media underplays the racial politics at work that cost Lopez his life. Lopez died not because of the toy replica alone but because he was a brown youth on the street presumed to be up to "no good."

The history of violence that black and brown young men have experienced in the United States suggests that if Lopez had not been killed at age thirteen it is very likely that his life would have been threatened at a later time. Unfortunately, there many more stories like Andy Lopez's. Given the constant threat under which young men of color live it is important to discuss the ways in which they construct their masculinity, the roles that healing can play in their lives, and how Chicanx children's and young adult literature can address these issues.

Through an examination of Juan Felipe Herrera's *Downtown Boy* (2005) I examine the ways that Juanito's father's absence informs his understanding of masculinity and also impacts what Gloria Anzaldúa theorizes as a "conocimiento" process. Herrera's text complicates representations of absent fathers by pausing to examine the causes of their absence. This particular attention to fathers is significant because it presents an opportunity to also understand the systemic oppressions that make it difficult for fathers to parent.

Herrera creates a narrative that investigates the possibilities and limitations of Chicanx masculinity. Throughout this chapter I demonstrate how reading Chicanx children's and young adult literature, like *Downtown Boy*, with Anzaldúa's conceptualization of conocimiento as a lens provides a theoretical and practical application that can be used in the lives of Chicanx children and young adults.

Phillip Serrato (2012) argues in his foundational essay "Transforming Boys, Transforming Masculinity, Transforming Culture: Masculinity Anew in Latino and Latina Children's Literature" for a practical application of

Chicanx children's and young adult texts in the lives of Chicanx boys. Serrato suggests:

> Perhaps above all else, this literature invites boy readers in particular to think about the examples of masculinity surrounding them, to reflect upon the pressures that they themselves have faced or will face as they grow up, and to figure out what kinds of men they want to become. (pp. 154–5)

Serrato's vision for the potential that Chicanx children's literature offers Chicanx boys is one that speaks to their very livelihood. In this way, this literature gives Chicanx children and youth an opportunity to examine different representations and use those to develop their own sense of self.

Serrato further explains that while plenty skepticism exists on the reality that books like these will be accessed by the children that need them or that these books could even stand a chance against the bombardment of negative messages that children receive from society and the media there still remains hope for an opportunity to change existing ways of knowing. In other words, Serrato demonstrate the need for a lens, or space, that understands Chicanx boys as having the potential for healing and in turn challenge that way society devalues them. Through Juanito, Herrera engages in a dialogue where the lives of Chicanx boys are valuable and worth saving.

A theoretical understanding of Chicanx children's and young adult literature as having the potential to serve as a tool for healing stems from Gloria Anzaldúa's (2002) essay, "now let us shift . . . the path of conocimiento . . . inner work, public acts." In this semi-autobiographical essay she explains conocimiento as "that aspect of consciousness urging you to act on the knowledge gained" (p. 577).

She also calls this an "aja" moment like that of an epiphany—a realization of sorts that forces us to take action. Knowledge in this way can serve as a catalyst for transformation. Conocimiento is a process that allows us to go from desconocimiento—the state of unknowing where we unquestionably accept the status quo—through stages that allow us to know differently and therein create possibilities for social change.

In this way, conocimiento is used as a means to use knowledge for the purposes of healing. This chapter proposes "conocimiento narratives" in Chicanx children's and young adult literature as an attempt to address the wounds that have no foreseeable end that continue to plague the existence of Chicanx children in the United States. Through conocimiento narratives this chapter offers a way for Chicanx children to process the violence they witness and the experience at home, in their communities, and as subjects of the US nation, and to transform that knowledge into one that can shift their realities.

Anzaldúa (2002) explains that there are seven stages of conocimiento through which we navigate in our search for transformative knowledges. The first stage of conocimiento is el *arrebato*, the rupture—the moment that forces you to question your reality, in conocimiento narratives those moments often time have to do with immigration, sexuality, the prison industrial complex, mental health, and the like.

The second stage is *nepantla*, the in-between spaces; the third stage is the Coatlicue state, the depths of "despair, self-loathing, and hopelessness" (p. 545) or depression; the fourth stage is a call for action—or the moment you decide to do something; the fifth stage is putting Coyolxauhqui[2] together by writing "personal and collective 'stories'" (p. 558); the sixth stage is taking that story into the world; and the seventh stage is shifting realities.

Anzaldúa explains that one does not always or ever go through these stages in a linear way and instead suggests that these stages are fluid. The stages Anzaldúa lays out as part of a conocimiento process can be traced in some realist fiction texts within Chicanx children's and young adult literature—which is referred to as "conocimiento narratives."

In this way, conocimiento presents an opportunity to know differently and in this way participate in a healing process. Conocimiento narratives are explained as a way to read Chicanx characters and stories in Chicanx children's and young adult literature that lend themselves to the healing process that Anzaldúa explains. Conocimiento narratives provide a unique opportunity to examine a healing process within realist fiction about Chicanx children and young adults because these texts can then be used as tools from which actual Chicanx children and young adults can learn and begin their own healing process that challenges and transforms the oppressions they may experience. Herrera's *Downtown Boy* is an example of a conocimiento narrative because readers can trace Juanito's healing process.

By giving a name to what Juanito experiences young readers can find solace in knowing that their struggle is part of a larger process. In this way, understanding an arrebato like a father's absence, for example, can be contextualized and processed in safe and healthy manners.

DOWNTOWN BOY: "THE WATER WILL HEAL YOU"

Juan Felipe Herrera's *Downtown Boy* tells the story of ten-year-old Juanito Palomares and the distress he feels at not having his father near. For the majority of the young adult novel written in verse, his father's absence haunts Juanito like a ghost. The absence becomes more palpable for Juanito at moments when his masculinity is tested by those around him.

While he recalls his father's advice on how to be a man and what kind of man he wants Juanito to become, Juanito cannot reconcile his father's advice with his absence. Instead Juanito is left feeling conflicted and lost. Interestingly, much of Mr. Palomares' absence has to do with his own desire to find healing due to his struggle with diabetes.

Throughout the novel he insists that water has healing capabilities and tries to impart this knowledge on Juanito. However, Mr. Palomares falls short in explaining the significance of healing to Juanito because for the majority of the novel all Juanito understands is that his father is not present.

The father/son relationship in *Downtown Boy* suggest that father and son are in search of very similar things—a sense of belonging, a home, and healing. Though their searches do not seem to bring father and son together but instead separates them. In this section, Juanito's struggle with his father's absence as the thing that impacts his construction of his own masculinity and as the reason that he is caught in "nepantla." Furthermore, Mr. Palomares as what Sara Ahmed terms a "melancholic migrant" as a means to analyze the tension that exists between father and son's search for healing. Reading these characters in these ways further allows readers to explore their father/son relationship and consider how their individual healing processes contests Chicanx masculinity.

Furthermore, the chapter elaborates on the complicated ways that Juanito's conocimiento process is linked to Mr. Palomares' desire to find happiness. Juanito is well aware of the impact that his father's absence has had on their family; therefore, it is difficult for him to comprehend his father's search for healing as a necessity or urgency. Juanito expresses, "At Patrick Henry Elementary, my new school, sometimes it looks like he's standing under the black clock by the door, waiting for me, wearing his straw white hat and his favorite blue coat. If he was here Mami wouldn't have to work so hard" (p. 61).

Mr. Palomares' absence has meant that his family has had to move around often and that Juanito's mother has had to work more to sustain the family. Juanito sees his father's role, and by extension the role of men, as the provider. In this way, searching for healing is not recognized as a productive act because it is not providing for the family. Furthermore, his absence is felt as more of a form of abandonment rather than a necessary journey toward healing.

Juanito's view signals that men have limited access to healing because of certain gender expectations. That Mr. Palomares has abandoned his masculine duties—that of father, man of the house, and provider—in search for water that will heal him threatens his masculinity. Mr. Palomares' absence further threatens their family dynamics because the mother having to work more to make up for the lack of contribution from her husband also means that she cannot be the mother she's expected to be.

It is telling that while at his new school Juanito imagines his father picking him up from school but in reality since his father is not there and his mother is at work it is probable that no one is there to pick him up. Juanito, then, finds himself isolated and without a real sense of belonging.

In "now let us shift . . . the of conocimiento . . . inner work, public acts," Anzaldúa (2002) explains nepantla as the second stage of conocimiento that serves as a "liminal, transitional space, suspended between shifts, you're two people, split between before and after. Nepantla, where the outer boundaries of the mind's inner life meet the outer world of reality, is a zone of possibility" (p. 545). In this way, Nepantla is the stage where one can evaluate the multiple possibilities and knowledges available. Juanito is in a constant state of nepantla throughout the novel. His father's unexplained absence positions him in an in-between space where Juanito must contend with the various expectations placed on his gender in order to construct his own understanding of Chicanx masculinity.

Understanding Mr. Palomares as what Sara Ahmed (2010) calls a "melancholic migrant" figure allows me to demonstrate how his focus on healing is at odds with Juanito's own conocimiento process for various reasons including how his "melancholia" limits his ability to father. In other words, Mr. Palomares is so invested in his own search for healing and happiness that he neglects his son and his needs.

In *The Promise of Happiness* (2010) Sara Ahmed discusses the phenomenon of happiness and its complicated relationship to constructions of citizenship and subjectivity and argues that "we are directed by the promise of happiness, as the promise that happiness is what follows if we do this or that" (p. 14). In this way, happiness serves as the driving force that dictates one's actions. Mr. Palomares is convinced that the right water will cure his diabetes and therefore travels in search of it because a cure might mean he can live longer and be happier for a longer time.

In a discussion about British Asian migrant experiences, histories of empire, and the promise of happiness, Ahmed reads the film *Bend It Like Beckham* (2002) as a way to explore how migrants disrupt the idea of "happiness in imperial history." Ahmed explains that colonization and imperialism are understood as necessities for the improvement and civilization of natives which serve as reasons for happiness; in this way, unhappy migrants disrupt nation building projects because they are a reminder of the atrocities and violences of colonialism and imperialism.

She writes, "The figure of the melancholic provides 'us' with a wound; by providing a sore point, the melancholic might allow us to keep what is sore at that point. This is how the melancholic migrant *comes to figure*: if the migrant is a sore point, then soreness can be attributed to the migrant" (p. 141). Migrants that are unable to assimilate or prosper in ways imagined by the nation represent and become sore points in these larger histories of empires that make it difficult to progress. Ahmed reads *Bend It Like Beckham*'s Jess' father as a "melancholic migrant" figure because of the tension he creates for his daughter around her desire to play football (soccer) despite it being something that will make her happy. While considering one of the father's speech acts in the film Ahmed argues:

> The figure of the melancholic migrant appears as the one who refuses to participate in the national game. Suffering becomes a way of holding to a lost object. We can certainly see how the father's idea of himself, or his ideal self, is threatened by the experience of racism ("I was the best fast bowler in our school"). Racism becomes an explanation for the failure to live up to an ideal ("when I came to this country, nothing"). (p. 142)

The father suffers over a potential "ideal self" that becomes unattainable after migrating; furthermore, the father's suffering signals the ways in which the nation has failed its migrants. In this way, pointing out the racism that has made it difficult to achieve his "ideal self" signals the "sore point" that exists within nation building projects. Ahmed further argues:

> The melancholic migrant appears as a figure in this translation from experience to explanation. Racism as an explanation of migrant suffering functions to preserve an attachment to the very scene of suffering. Bad feeling thus originates with the migrant who won't let go of racism as a script that explains suffering." (p. 143)

This way, the father's lack of attainment is understood as an individual problem rather than a larger systemic issue. His suffering then becomes an obstacle for the nation's own happiness and progress. The "melancholic migrant" is a threat to the nation because this figure challenges notions of national progress by being a constant reminder that the system is fraught or even broken.

In *Downtown Boy,* Mr. Palomares' search is often described with longing and nostalgia. Juanito is not aware that his father searches for a cure to his diabetes and thus the longing and nostalgia are also for his father. Mr. Palomares refuses to look for medical treatment and instead puts his faith that the power of water will heal him; as a result, Juanito often associates his father with water.

Juanito recalls his father and his mother arguing, "'The water will heal you,' he says. 'Why don't you go to a doctor?' Mami says. 'All they know is knives and pills! Water, you drink it and it cools you, warms your heart.

Cleans your liver. Water is . . . Precious'" (Herrera, 2005, p. 171). Mr. Palomares' obsession with water throughout the novel is linked to a desire for a home and a sense of belonging. He wanders looking for water but even Juanito has an inkling that he searches for so much more, "Maybe that's why Papi looks for water. Water that will cure him. So he can feel at home" (p. 77). Mr. Palomares' suffering, physical and spiritual, indicates larger systemic oppressions in place that make it difficult for him and his family to move forward, begin healing, or find happiness.

Ahmed continues to argue that, "It is important to note that the melancholic migrant's fixation with injury is read as an obstacle not only to his own happiness but also to the happiness of the generation to come, and even to national happiness" (Ahmed, 2010, p. 144). Mr. Palomares' fixation on water and what water represents interferes with Juanito's own healing including Juanito's desire to have a united family and a stable home.

Because of this, Juanito finds himself in nepantla unsure of what he needs to do in order to pursue his own healing separate from his father's. Ahmed further explains that "the second generation children are the ones who desire their own happiness. The nation must intervene to protect the second generation from the first, those who have failed to let go of their past attachments and who hence can only suffer and transmit their suffering, which easily gets turned into terror and rage" (p. 148). Juanito and Mr. Palomares are part of a greater system of oppression that seeks to pit them against each other.

The tensions between father and son extend beyond generational differences wherein the first generation (Mr. Palomares) represents "past attachments" and the second generation (Juanito) stand in for progress and mobility. Ahmed argues that the nation has the second generation's interest in mind precisely because they symbolize the futurity of the nation and if the first generation's "terror and rage" get passed on to the second generation then that impedes the progress of the nation. The passing on of "past attachments" is clearly present in Mr. Palomares' relationship with Juanito. His teachings on the importance of water tell Juanito something about Chicanx masculinity, conocimiento, and citizenship.

Juanito remembers that when they lived on a farm in central valley California he spilled a pitcher of water and his father made him refill it in order to learn its value: "Water is life, son! It can heal you! Now you take this empty bucket and walk through the forest until you get to town. And when you get there, find a way, a faucet, fill the bucket with water. Bring it back full. Maybe, then you'll learn how precious water is" (p. 43)! Mr. Palomares expects to teach Juanito the value of water by correlating it with manual labor.

In this way, water is precious because the journey to acquire it is difficult. Later in the novel when Mr. Palomares briefly returns to the family he insists on taking Juanito to the ocean: "'Let's go to the ocean,' he says, 'tomorrow, very early. And I'll show you how to drink water from the ocean,'" (p. 192). Mr. Palomares' desire to show Juanito to drink from the ocean is an attempt to share part of him with his son.

It is an effort to bridge the gap that exists between them. By asking that Juanito trek to refill the bucket of water Mr. Palomares teaches his son about hard work and providing for a family—which are traditional values and expectations often placed on Chicanx masculinity. However, teaching Juanito about drinking from the ocean is a more personal lesson about sensitivity and connection with something greater than one's existence. Mr. Palomares further challenges traditional norms placed on their gender and ethnicity. Mr. Palomares' desire to teach Juanito about the water is also a need to teach his son about their culture.

Juanito does not seem to know much about his father's past nor does he really understand his father's obsession with water. He does understand, though, that his father is absent. However, the relationship between the water and their Mexican heritage is significant because it helps to clarify the "past attachments" that make Mr. Palomares a "melancholic migrant." Juanito assumes that his father travels a lot because he searches for water but does not really know where he goes. He says, "I think of Papi, somewhere in the desert in Chihuahua, swimming in an *ojo de agua*. Why doesn't he write?" (p. 37). For Juanito Chihuahua is a distant and vast place to which he does not feel a personal tie. The desert, Chihuahua, and *ojo de agua* are strange places that have taken his father and keep him from writing.

Again, Juanito does not understand that he too is somehow connected to these places and spaces but knows that his father is absent. Later in the novel Juanito shares similar sentiments at not having his father near: "Papi's somewhere in Mexico or New Mexico—I forget which Mexico—looking for water that will cure him. Why does he need water? What's wrong with him" (p. 62)? That Juanito does not know in which Mexico his father is located is a further indication that he does not have all the information.

This lack of knowing serves to distance him from his father and to keep him in a state of nepantla—an in-between space where he is mad at his father but still wants his affection. Mexico or New Mexico, in this case, continues to represent far off places to which only Mr. Palomares has attachments. Mr. Palomares' search for water is indeed a search for home as Juanito points out earlier in the novel. That home is somehow connected to Mexico and is a reminder that such home was not attainable in the United States.

Like in *Bend It Like Beckham*, the father suffers over a lost home or lost self; he is fixated on the life he had or on the life he did not get to live in the new country. Mr. Palomares' suffering is definitely for his health but it could also be for the better life for which his family (im)migrated in the first place.

Mr. Palomares suffers because he has been failed by the American Dream and the promise of happiness and as a result his family suffers as well.

The novel opens in 1958 a few years after the legal implementation of "Operation Wetback," a strategy intended to deport undocumented Mexicans after the influx of (im)migrants during the Bracero Program. Operation Wetback was a discriminatory and violent tactic that targeted and uprooted Mexicans in the United States; as a result, many U.S. citizens of Mexican descent were also deported. While the operation is not directly addressed in the novel it is not far-fetched to suggest that the Palomares' could represent a family impacted by it.

The anti-Mexican sentiment further marginalized Mexican populations which made it increasingly difficult to utilize resources and services available such as public schools and medical centers. Mr. Palomares' refusal to visit a doctor for diabetes treatment could be rooted in the long history of discrimination and violence against people of color by medical facilities which certainly were not improved by policies like Operation Wetback.

Mr. Palomares feels the full effect of this discrimination when his leg must be amputated because of the diabetes. I argue, in light of Ahmed's explanation, that his amputation can be understood as a way the nation contends with the "melancholic migrant" which in a painful twist results in Mr. Palomares staying home like Juanito wanted.

While at the hospital Mrs. Palomares explains to Juanito that Mr. Palomares' leg must be amputated:

> That means that they are going to have to cut off/ his leg. A terrible infection. Gangrene./ His diabetes is so bad that his blood/ reaches his feet very slowly. He can't heal well./ But he never listens. And he never visits the doctor./How's he going to walk?"/ But how's he going to go to the Plazita every morning?/ How's he going to find water? (pp. 225–6)

Mr. Palomares' loss of mobility does not end his suffering but it does impede his search. It is the process of searching, after all, that symbolizes his melancholia and unrest. The act of searching was the threat to the nation, the nation's happiness, and the second generation's happiness. The loss of his leg almost serves as a warning to stop searching and to accept the powers that be—the power of the hospitals, the doctors, and the state. Mr. Palomares "can't heal well" because of his diabetes and because of his "past attachments" to Mexico and now that his leg has been amputated his healing must take a different form.

Mr. Palomares can no longer define healing as something that can be reached via water and/or his past attachments; instead he must heal within the systemic structures that most likely wounded him in the first place. Although

Mrs. Palomares is concerned with her husband's ability to walk because, among many reasons, it threatens his ability to work and provide for the family, Juanito is concerned with his father's inability to search for water.

After his father comes to stay with the family Juanito has a difficult time understanding his father as stationary. Despite Juanito's insistence throughout the novel that he wants his father near he is also disappointed with the father he gets after the amputation.

His father is depressed and Juanito notices: "Papi says he's going to build himself a leg out of plywood. But he won't. He just says things now and stares out the window. He doesn't go anywhere anymore. No Plazita, no fountain. No water. Papi doesn't even shave anymore" (p. 228). Mr. Palomares' depression keeps Juanito in nepantla because although he wanted his father to stop searching for water now that he has stopped his father still does not seem to be fully present and Juanito remains unfulfilled.

As the novel progresses, Mr. Palomares reveals that he has more children and that they are also a reason why he has been away. His other children are also a part of his "past attachments" and are also representative of his shortcomings and serve as more reasons for his melancholia. Mr. Palomares' focus on his own healing and happiness, however, came at the cost of Juanito's own conocimiento.

Although Juanito spends the majority of the novel in a state of nepantla, he eventually confronts his father and moves out of nepantla and into the fourth stage of conocimiento, the call to action. Almost in tears Juanito yells "I don't want to be a chump/ like Chacho said!" . . ./ "But that's all I am!" (p. 267). Juanito recalls the beginning of the novel where his cousin Chacho encourages him to box despite Juanito's own reservations and hesitations about the sport because his father always warned him against fighting. His cousin taunts him and poses the question, "You wanna be a chump/or a champ?" (p. 7). Chacho asks Juanito to decide what kind of man he wants to be. His cousin's taunts and his father's advice set up a binary for what masculinity can look like—a fighter and not a fighter.

Juanito relates his father as not a fighter; however, that understanding of masculinity is also connected to his father's absence. Therefore, not fighting threatens his masculinity. Even though Juanito agrees to box, which is a result of his anger at his father's absence, Juanito still feels like a chump. He does not feel like a man and he associates that with not having his father there.

After hearing his son call himself a "chump," Mr. Palomares explains, "It wasn't you, *hijo*;/ it was me . . . I am/ so sorry, Juanito/ I love you, Son;/ you are my only one now./ And I promise/ never to leave you/ again" (p. 268). Mr. Palomares' apology challenges the champ/chump binary on masculinity by suggesting that masculinity, and being a father, is more complicated than that. By taking the blame Mr. Palomares recognizes the impact his absence has had on Juanito and further propels Juanito on his conocimiento journey.

Juanito could not move on with his conocimiento process until he reconciled with his father and his absence. By the end of the novel Mr. Palomares is in positive spirits and there is a sense of family unity. Mr. Palomares' focus on his family allows Juanito to better understand his father's fixation with water and what the water represents—that is, healing, happiness, and culture. As the novel closes Juanito is seen filling paper cups with water for "precious Papi,/ precious Mami,/ precious every moment—/ precious, like water" (p. 293). That Juanito is the one that gathers water for his parents is symbolic of what he has learned from his father and suggests that he is now the man he wants to be—a "champ" not unlike his father but more like himself.

CONCLUSION: "YOU WANNA BE A CHUMP/OR A CHAMP?"

Anzaldúa (2002) explains in her foundational essay that conocimiento presents the opportunity to transform realities. The different stages of conocimiento aim to take one from a place of unknowing or pain to a new space of empowerment—inner work leads to public acts of transformation. It is this potential for individual and communal change that makes conocimiento an important lens to introduce to Chicanx children and young adults. Chicanx young adult texts like Herrera's *Downtown Boy* are described as conocimiento narratives because it is important to understand (and to inform our students) that the personal struggles children and young adults of experience are rooted in larger systems of oppression and that despite the insidious, and often tragic, consequence of these systems there is the potential for transformation.

For example, Juanito demonstrates that while a new kind of masculinity where boys and men are encouraged to show emotion is desirable there are, nonetheless, several systemic and institutional oppressions that make this new masculinity very difficult to achieve—like the medical institutions his father is weary of and then amputate his leg. While by the end of the story, Juanito is able to move out of nepantla and as a result feel more comfortable with his masculinity this change takes place in the private sphere. Such shift is definitely still important and needed in the lives of Chicanx boys. Furthermore, the definitions of masculinity created by the characters gesture at the significance of being able to express themselves in a safe space.

In writing about the importance of having children's literature that represents an alternative masculinity Serrato argues that "A compelling means by which children's understanding of masculinity can be broadened beyond dominant definitions is through the dramatizations—and thus validation—of emotional vulnerability in boys" (p. 158).

As Serrato argues, more representation of masculinities "beyond dominant definitions" is necessary in order to encourage "emotional vulnerability" in young men of color. Still, these representations might also challenge dominant stereotypes of Chicanx boys and men where they are not always already thought of as "other," "deviant," "illegal" or "criminal." Being able to recognize the vulnerability, for example, in Andy Lopez might have saved his life.

After his death Andy was described in many ways by the media, his family, and his friends. The photos that were circulated depicted Andy as clearly a participant in youth culture from the beanie and loose clothes he wore to the diamond studs on his ears. Based on how Andy was read by the deputy that shot him and by society at large it is difficult to imagine that Andy could have been read any other way. But what if instead of the toy gun the Deputy would have seen Andy's smile? Andy smiles in the main picture that was circulated of him in the media. Photographs and youtube videos of the memorial and protest also show more pictures of Andy smiling.

On that tragic day the Deputy, and dominant society, could not see or even imagine a boy like Andy smiling. Larger histories of oppression, including the systems and institutions that continue to reproduce that violence today, have made it so that Chicanx boys are not recognizable as vulnerable, emotional, innocent, or even valuable.

It is for this reason that many Chicanx boys and men resort to surviving the best way they can. They exist in a society where being a chump or champ can be the difference between life and death. Stories like those written by Herrera create young Chicanx male characters that imagine them as vulnerable and valuable.

NOTES

1. The term "Latinx" is meant to serve as a gender-neutral identifier that challenges the gender specificity of the Spanish language attached to Latina/Latino. Latinx is more inclusive of trans, gender non conforming, and/or nonbinary people. I use the term Chicanx as a gender neutral identifier for people of Mexican/Mexican American descent I prefer Chicanx with an "x" as a way to suggest that my analysis of masculinity construction is not just applicable to straight and cis boys.

2. Cherrie Moraga "recounts the story of coyolxauhqui, the Aztec moon goddess who attempts to kill her mother, Coatlicue, when she learns of her mother's pregnancy. As we feministas have interpreted the myth, Coyolxauhqui hopes to halt, through the murder of her mother, the birth of the War God, Huitzilopochtli. She is convinced the Huitzilopochtli's birth will also mean the birth of slavery, human sacrifice, and imperialism (in short, patriarchy). She fails in her attempt and instead is

murdered and dismembered by her brother Huitzilopotchli and banished into darkness to become the moon" (*Loving in the War Years*, p. 147).

REFERENCES

Ahmed, Sara. (2010). *The promise of happiness*. Durham, NC: Duke University Press.

Anzaldúa, Gloria. (2002). now let us shift . . . the path of conocimiento . . . inner work, public acts. In Gloria E. Anzaldúa, & Analouise Keating (Eds.), *This bridge we call home: The radical visions for transformation* (pp. 540–78). New York: Routledge.

Anzaldúa, Gloria. (2007). La conciencia de la mestiza/ Towards a new consciousness. In *Borderlands/La Frontera: The new mestiza* (3rd ed., pp. 99–120). San Francisco: Aunt Lute Books.

Cacho, Lisa Marie. (2007). 'You Just Don't Know How Much He Meant': Deviancy, death, and devaluation. *Latino Studies, 5*(2), 182–208.

Cacho, Lisa Marie. (2012). *Social death: Racialized rightlessness and the criminalization of the unprotected*. New York: New York University Press.

Herrera, Juan Felipe. (2005). *Downtown boy*. New York: Scholastic Press.

Mungin, Lateef. (2013, October 25). Deputy kills 13-year-old carrying fake riffle. *CNN.com*.

Serrato, Phillip. (2012). Transforming boys, transforming masculinity, transforming culture: Masculinity anew in Chicanx and Latina children's literature. In Pedro Noguera, Aída Hurtado, & Edward Fergus (Eds.), *Invisible no more: Understanding the disenfranchisement of chicanx men and boys*. New York: Routledge.

Steinmetz, Kathy. (2013, October 25). "Toy guns, deadly consequences." *Time*.

Chapter 8

Representations of Sexual and Queer Identities in Chicana/o-Latina/o Children's Literature

Cecilia J. Aragón

During the past decades, there has been a strong record of publication in Chicana/o-Latina/o Children's Literature. To demonstrate growth in this area, Shirley A. Wagoner in her article, "Mexican-Americans in Children's Literature since 1970," presents an annotated bibliography of over twenty-seven children's books dealing with Mexican American experiences in the United States (1982). Educational scholar Gloria T. Blatt in her article, "Mexican-Americans in Children's Literature," examines thirty-two children's books dealing with Mexicans and Mexican Americans (1968). Blatt and Wagoner posit that there is an overwhelming amount of books that deal with the Mexican culture and not so much the Mexican American experience in the United States.

Ruth Quiroa, a former bilingual second grade teacher and currently an Associate Professor of Reading/Language Arts at National Louis University, agrees that "Latina/o themed literature for grades pre-K-12 has emerged since 1993" and notices that there are a variety of topics being explored (2013, p. 45).

These leading experts agree that the Chicana/o-Latina/o themed books demonstrate growth and deal with a variety of topics from folk tales, immigration/deportation, migrant farm workers, family and community, cultural myths, history, important people, to the most recent educational issue of bullying and special needs. However, the representation of sexual identities is the least common theme represented and studied in Chicana/o-Latina/o children's literature.

While there are many studies that explore various ways of writing sexual identities in adult Chicana/o-Latina/o literature, there is a paucity of writings on sexual identities in this genre of children's literature and cultural production. Few Chicana/o-Latina/o writers have recently chosen to accentuate sexual and queer identities, a growing body of literature and a distinctive perspective rarely highlighted in Chicana/o-Latina/o children's literary studies (Esquibel, 1998; Trujillo, 2003; Herrera, 2003; Tijerina-Revilla, 2005; Perez, 2009; Serrato, 2012; Millán, 2015).[1] This chapter attempts to provide an analysis and critique on the representations of sexuality in the following Chicana/o-Latina/o children's books: *La Llorona: The Crying Woman*[2] (2011) and *Juan and the Jackalope* (2009) by Rudolfo Anaya, *Antonio's Card* (2005) by Rigoberto González, and *Call Me Tree* (2014) by Maya Christine Gonzalez.

In what follows, I first contextualize a theoretical framework of fantasy and feminism that purports a Chicana/o-Latina/o literary and cultural production model. Fantasy and feminist concepts derive from Gloria Anzaldúa, Cherríe Moraga, and Isabel Millán. This framework presents new possibilities for mapping sexual identities and constructing queertopias[3] in the literary texts of *La Llorona: The Crying Woman*, *Juan and the Jackalope*, *Antonio's Card*, and *Call Me Tree*. The texts exemplify the various sexualized personalities and attitudes that have surfaced recently in contemporary children's literature.

I argue that the authors and their texts provide a counternarrative to Chicana/o-Latina/o children's literature that creates sexual and queer imaginaries, as they begin to set the stage for social discourse on a wide array of sexual identities and cartographies in children's literature and culture.

THEORY OF CHICANA/O-LATINA/O FANTASY AND QUEERNESS

The concepts of fantasy in Chicana/o-Latina/o literature have often been used by many Chicana/o-Latina/o writers and scholars as a literary technique. Scholar, Luis Davila (1975), for example in his essay "Chicano Fantasy Through a Glass Darkly" examines how Chicano writers use magical realism and fantasy as literary tools to combine both fact and fiction. Similarly, scholars like Catherine Bartlett in her article "Magical Realism: The Latin American Influence on Modern Chicano Writers" (1986) and Ramón Saldívar in his article "Narrative, Ideology, and the Reconstruction of American Literary History" (1991) argue that Chicana/o-Latina/o writers use literary forms of magical realism and fantasy-structures in their writings to weave in and out of their own lived experiences, identities, subjectivities, and consciousness to create the new Chicana/o literary poetics and aesthetics.

Thus, these examples of incorporating fantasy, magical realism, autobiography, fact, and fiction have been a literary device to blur the boundaries between reality and fantasy to create writings about childhood, identity, space, and place.

To further advance this literary technique within Chicana/o-Latina/o Studies, Isabel Millán coined the term *autofantasía* and has led the charge on reconceptualization of fantasy (*fantasia*) and autobiography (*auto*), as it applies to Chicana/o-Latina/o children's literature (Millán, 2015). Millán borrows ideas from Gloria Anzaldúa's *autohistorias*, where the storyteller positions themselves central to the action, rewriting and retelling their own story, so that cultural and historical production holds value and legitimacy (Keating, 2009).

Millán surmises that "the utility of *autofantasía* lies in emphasizing both autobiographies and fantasies as forms of fiction . . . where *fantasia* is a form of fiction that engulfs everything that can be imagined or fantasized" (pp. 203–4). She concludes her theory by stating that *autofantasía* ultimate goal is "steeped in personal experience, observations, political commentary, and utopian idealism meant to both educate and entertain children and the adults around them" (p. 206).

Within this theoretical framework, Chicana/o-Latina/o children's literature cannot be read solely as a stand-alone text, but rather as a text that inscribes the authors' personal lived experiences, imaginary space/place, and intended political messages for the audience.

Critic and literary fantasist Ruth Nadelman Lynn in her book *Fantasy Literature For Children and Young Adults: An Annotated Bibliography* reminds us that:

> Fantasy has been variously describes as imaginative, fanciful, visionary, strange, otherworldly, supernatural, mysterious, frightening, magical, inexplicable, wondrous, dreamlike, and paradoxically, realistic. It has been termed an awareness of the inexplicable existence of "magic: in everyday world, a yearning for a sudden glimpse of something strange and wonderful, and a different and perhaps truer version of reality." (p. xxi)

Lynn proposes that fantasy for children is a different approach to reality and an alternative technique for understanding journeys into the subconscious mind and discovering something real about the human spirit.

The other conceptual framework for this project is based on the pedagogies and theories of Chicana feminism and queer theory posited by Chicana feminists, the late Gloria Anzaldúa and the prolific Chicana writer Cherríe Moraga. Both Anzaldúa and Moraga recognize the centrality of gender and sexuality to their lives and the importance of incorporating these issues into their politics. They challenge the construction of female sexuality by the family, the state, the church, and criticize the traditional roles between Chicano men and women.

As literary scholar Yvonne Yarbro-Bejarano points out, many of the positions Moraga speaks to are the sexual specificity of the Chicana lesbian gender, body, and desires.[4] In Moraga's book, *Loving in the War Years*, she deconstructs conventional sexual norms that govern the female's desire and body. Anzaldua's writing is part of the process of dismantling and recomposing concepts of sexuality as ever-changing and what Anzaldúa calls "our shifting and multiple identity."[5]

Yarbro-Bejarano argues that Anzaldúa and Moraga's writing embodies a "sexual/textual project that disrupts the dualisms between mind and body, writing and desire"[6] that culminates in their cowritten book, *This Bridge Called My Back*.[7] To add to the discourse, I therefore take on the task of including Chicana/o-Latina/o children in the conversation, as it highlights and recognizes the natural progression and development of children as sexual beings through a literary Moragan and Anzaldúan "sexual/textual" analysis.

ANAYA'S FANTASY LAND AND MYTHS

Rudolfo Anaya's children's literature and young adult books within the past ten years has recently received national attention since his world renowned book *Bless Me, Ultima*—the seminal novel that set the momentum for Chicano literature in 1972. Anaya noted as the Godfather of Chicano literature, has made his mark in children's literature with acclaimed awards and publications with over ten books for pre-K-12, two juvenile literature books, and two plays with child protagonists. With children and young adult readers, Anaya has found a younger and larger readership. With his children's books, publishers have publicized him as the "*cuentista*"—the storyteller and mythmaker.

Two great examples of creating mythical characters are found in his books *La Llorona: The Crying Woman* (2011) and *Juan and the Jackalope* (2009). In *La Llorona,* Anaya recounts the mythical and a didactic story of *La Llorona*—the relationship between *La Malinche* and Cortez as symbolically represented in Maya and Señor Tiempo. Maya the main character is described as, "Maya is a child of the Sun. She will never die" (p. 2). Maya grows up and discovers that there are Gods at the top of the volcano such as Señor Tiempo. Señor Tiempo states, "I am the father of Time! . . . This girl will never perish! And if she has children, they will live forever. I cannot allow that!" (p. 4). Maya's parents fear for their daughter, so they take her up the volcano into the place of a mythical jungle—a "fantasy land," where she lives alone and away from angry Señor Tiempo.

Through time, Maya becomes lonely and her friend Señora Owl tells her "it is time for you to have *niños*" (p. 10). As instructed by Señora Owl, Maya makes a clay pot. "When the moon is full, take it to the lake and fill it with fertile earth. You will be given seeds to plant in the pot" (p. 10). As the story goes on, Maya does as she was told by Señora Owl. She meets up with a young man who she encountered by the lake. Thus, the story of a "fantasy sex" is described of how children are made. A story of love and sexuality is created by objects as manipulated by female, in this case, Maya and Anaya's nondescript indigenous male "the young man" (p. 12).

Although overt sexuality is usually avoided in books for children and young adults, Anaya is echoing Millán's purpose of fantasy, as he describes how Maya's children are fertilized, conceived, and born:

> Just then a young man came walking by. "That's a beautiful pot," he said. "What are you going to plant?" "Señora Owl told me this is the way to make a baby," Maya answered. "I, too, spoke to Señora Owl, . . . She told me to put the corn in the pot. This way you will grow a lovely child." He sat beside Maya and took kernels from his leather pouch. He planted the corn in the pot and added water from the lake. Maya thanked the young man and returned home. She placed the bowl on the window ledge. Each night the moon shone on the bowl, and the sun warmed it by day. Many months later, Maya heard a whimper. Curled up in the bowl lay a baby girl. "¡*Mi niña!*" Maya cried. She took the baby and wrapped her in feather blankets. "You are as beautiful as the tassels of a corn plant," Maya whispered. "I will name you Corn Maiden." (pp. 12–14)

Throughout the book, this process of social interaction with the young man, planting his seeds of chile, beans, squash, mangos, papayas, lemons, and oranges, and the incubation of months later (sun and moon blessing the pots), always brings forth a new child.

Maya not escaping Señor Tiempo's devious tactics, he seeks to steal Maya's children from her. Señor Tiempo tricks Maya into breaking the pots and throwing them in the lake and she does so. After seeing a terrible storm, the children are frightened and Señor Tiempo takes them to the lake and tosses them into the water. Returning to the lake, Maya finds that the shattered pieces of the pots were dissolved by the water, therefore, metaphorically, Señor Tiempo drowns her children: "Maya realized she would never see her children again. She ran along the edge of the lake, crying "¡*Mis niños! ¡mis niños!*" (p. 34). In Anaya's story Maya transforms into *La Llorona*, the crying woman and Señor Teimpo as symbolic of the deceitful Cortez threatening to take the children away and eventually drowning them."

Indeed, Anaya's book *La Llorona: The Crying Woman* asserts the norms of heterosexuality with the traditional and conventional masculine procreation acts of "planting the seeds." According to Millán's *autofantasía* theory, Anaya creates a literary world where he conceptualizes the role of women as he fantasizes about the biological process of pregnancy, sexual acts, and conventional relationships between mother and child. He asserts that "the children will make Maya happy, be her companions, she will teach them to grow vegetable and weave baskets, she tells them stories, and sings songs to them" (pp. 16–20). Anaya places gender roles in their traditional and provincial spaces creating the cultural norms for men and women, doing only what their roles necessitate and dictate. However, he does not shy away from symbolic representations of sexual engagements in his book.

Anaya further asserts both mythological creature, with what Millán posits as supernatural abilities, and heteronormativity sexual desires in his book *Juan and the Jackalope: A Children's Book in Verse* (2009). The book opens with grandfather rabbit telling the stories to his children about "The Great Grasshopper Race" and the prize Rosita awarded first place. The title character, Juan, a young buckaroo, wanted to win Rosita's love, but he is up against the competition of Pecos Bill, who rides "Hoppy a Grasshopper"—apparently, the fastest creature in town.

Similar to *La Llorona*, Anaya creates a "fantasy land—Unicorn Hill," where Juan encounters *La Llorona*, *Kookoóee*, trolls, dancing dragons, and of course the Jackalope that Juan will ride to win the competition and therefore, win the prize Rosita and Rosita's famous rhubarb pie. Millán states that in creating such a magical land the author inserts self with fantasy fiction. With his supernatural powers, the Jackalope takes Juan on a marvelous fantasy ride around the world into space to visit the planets, the milky way, and returns with stardust, sparkles, and glowing with sexual prowess. Anaya ends the book stating:

> Everyone cheered when Rosita kissed Juan and gave him the pie he had bravely won. Juan asked Rosita, "Will you be my bride, and ride on the Jackalope by my side? I'll marry you and ride by your side, rich or poor I'll be your bride. Fly to the moon and the star-filled sky. We'll dine on beans and rhubarb pie." (pp. 27–8)

While this perspective positions the child to be inculcated with heterosexual desires for the opposite sex, there is still room for the child to fantasize about other sexual possibilities. For example, it allows the child to create a mythical place where the child can begin to take power and control over their own sexual desires and pleasures. Along the journey, this narrative perspective attributes to playing with notions of heterosexual and nonheterosexual sexual identities.

Anaya introduces a range of psychological ideas about childhood and sexuality. These particular books are discussed in order to critique how Anaya engages the child reader to a mythical land or a "fantasy land" and romanticizes sexual desires and contacts between male and female. Anaya does not deviate from traditional standards, but he does allow the child to visualize sexual agency. While he conforms and perpetuates the traditional Mexican gender ideology through a gender conforming dichotomy in which the former is a biological given and the latter a cultural construction, he creates characters that possess supernatural sexual powers.

Anaya approaches sexual identity as a realm of social interactions where fantasy occurs and advocates for the traditional female ideal and assumes male attributes such as the independence and prowess of machismo with "the young man," "Señor Tiempo," and "Juan and his Jackalope." While Anaya asserts issues of sexuality and desires among heterosexual relations and conforms to the suggestions of Millán's queer notions of "fantasy land," there are also contradictions and barriers to Chicana feminist thought and beliefs.

In ascribing to Millán's *autofantasía*, Anaya presents us with alter egos of himself and human and animal characters that have supernatural powers and sexual agency. In this sense, the Jackalope represents more than a mythological creature; he represents a queer child that is a conduit to a fantasy world where sexual identities and polyamorous relations can be imagined. Here, the state of queerness functions as the animal supernatural characteristics as well as the sexual choices one has when Juan enters "Unicorn Hill" or Maya enters "the volcano into the place of a mythical jungle." Millán's theory would conclude that this is what is called *fantasia*, a place where sexual realities are imagined and this quickly reveals Anaya's place of sexual counter-heteronormativity.

RIGOBERTO GONZÁLEZ'S SAME-SEX ARTISTIC CREATIONS

While Anzaldúa and Moraga speak of acknowledging and transforming differences, sexual and queer notions are also seen in *Antonio's Card* (2005) written by award winning adult and children's writer, Rigoberto González. His previous children's book, *Soledad Sigh-Sighs* (2003) and *Antonio's Card* are children's literature targeted for the inclusion of Spanish language and geared toward beginning bilingual readers. In its bilingual format, the book depicts the protagonist, Antonio, as having two moms. It represents the diverse and complicated issues Antonio faces at school and at home.

The book begins with Antonio demonstrating his love for words, spelling, and drawing. Mami, Antonio's mom, helps to prepare Antonio for school. On their way out of the house, Leslie, Mami's partner, says "Adiós Antonio, see you later" (p. 4). This is the first time we are introduced to Leslie, Antonio's second mom. The next time we see Leslie is after school when she picks up Antonio. Leslie, a working artist, stands out in the crowd of parents, as she is very tall. She shows up with her splattered painted overalls and meets Antonio after school. Antonio overhears his classmates remarks about Leslie, giggling and with laughter, the kids remark, "That woman looks like a guy!";

"She looks like a box of crayons exploded all over her. . . . She looks like a rodeo clown" (p. 6). For Antonio these remarks are hurtful and for the first time he experiences a place of contradictions and uncomfortable feelings about his relations with his two moms.

It is at school—the public forum, where the consciousness of the sexual borderlands comes to the forefront as Anzaldúa herself expresses in her preface to *Borderlands*, "The Borderlands are physically present wherever two or more cultures edge each other, where people of different races occupy the same territory where under, lower, middle, and upper classes touch, where the space between two individuals shrinks with intimacy."[8] Anzaldúan and Moragan theory would reaffirm that this is a pivotal point in Antonio's life where he recognizes the fight against patriarchal and homophobic institutions, as the same-sex relationship between Leslie and his Mami represents the sexual contradictions to social norms.

Antonio's dilemma is further expanded with pressure when the teacher asks the classmates to make cards for Mother's Day, and "Antonio hunches over the piece of paper on his desk, protecting it from anybody else's sight. He presses the fat green crayon into the page. He draws his mother and Leslie sitting next to him as they read a book together. He writes in letters like pretty birds among the leaves: F-A-M-I-L-Y" (p. 15). Adding to Antonio's psychological pain, the teacher announces that the cards will be displayed up in the cafeteria and "Antonio's hand freezes on his card. The taunting of the kids echoes in his head: *Look, there's that rodeo clown!*" This passage captures Antonio's marginalization and vulnerability combined with the realization and his growing awareness of both of his mom's lesbian sexuality, given the urgency of his need to come to terms with their sexual identity and nonconforming gender identities.

Antonio's eventual coming to terms with his family's identity is facilitated by both his mom's. Leslie reinforces Antonio's self-confidence by painting a family picture with them sitting at the park under a tree with Antonio in the middle reading a book and Leslie on one side and Mami on the other side of him. Antonio's drawing and Leslie's painting emulate each other's emotions and reaffirm their own confidence and notions of family. It was this self-reflexive examination that allowed Antonio finally to make the connections between the sexual and the social aspects of his cultural identity.

In touch with Antonio's psychological fears and isolation, Mami reinforces the notions of accepting differences. She says to Antonio, "Leslie dresses and walks like Leslie, just like Antonio dresses and walks like Antonio. We're all a little different from each other. That's what makes each one of us an individual" (p. 18). Mami and Leslie both reinforce strength and support that is central to Antonio's understanding of his oppression incited by his classmates. Antonio makes a bold decision to display his Mother's Day card at the cafeteria card showcase. Presenting a straightforward visual representation, with Antonio Mother's Day card and Leslies painting of a lesbian family, creates explorations of nonheteronormative modes affirming their gender and sexual identities.

Antonio's Card illustrates Moraga's "theory in the flesh" and calls for women of color and lesbians to examine their own lives and to understand the oppressive systems and structures within which they live as part of their larger project to "change the world."[9] Moraga is referring to the experientially acquired knowledge that manifests itself in survival mode, which is also described by Anzaldúa as *la facultad*, a skill developed by marginalized people as a survival skill that allows to adjust quickly and gracefully to threatening changing circumstances. According to Anzaldúa, *La facultad* involves a loss of innocence and an initiation into an awareness of fear, but gaining knowledge and self-confidence to confront complex situation, as in the case with Antonio.

Millán's theory suggests that in his writing, Rigoberto González enacts his *autofantasías* by giving voice and visibility to that which has been silenced in our society. González uses the metaphor of words, letters, drawing, and a tree to explore the potentially conflictive and fatal perils of lesbian existence. As an *autofantasías* the tree symbolizes a significant space where family is rooted, and for Leslie and Mami, it is a public space where lesbian sexuality and desire come together to define family. González engages the reader to participate in this radical promotion of eco-spirituality, acceptance of same sex relations, and embracing nonconforming gender and sexual identities.

GENDER FREE AND NONCONFORMING IDENTITIES

The admiration of trees as symbolizing beauty, family, and the magnitude of nature is a familiar theme in many children's books. Anthropomorphizing a tree in *Call me Tree* by Maya Christina Gonzalez helps children to identify with desires, gender, and identity differences. It is known as a children's book that challenges gender stereotypes and reinforces a self-designed gender identity. Much like *Antonio's Card*, *Call me Tree* is a bilingual picture book that inspires children to reach, dream, and be as free as trees.

Maya Christina Gonzalez author and illustrator is a widely exhibited artist known for her brightly vivid imagery of strong women and girls. With nearly over twenty children's books, the most recognized include *Laughing Tomatoes: And Other Spring Poems* (2005), *From the Bellybotton of the Moon: And Other Summer Poems* (2005), *Angels Ride Bikes: And Other Fall Poems* (2005), and *My Colors, My World* (2013). To avoid the she/he pronouns, Gonzalez in *Call Me Tree* begins with a nondescript, nonconforming, nongendered character in a fetal position surrounded by cocentric layers—the brightly yellow inner circle where the character lies denoting a dream or fantasy-like state, the second outer layer is depicted by earth tone circular rock-like structures floating about signifying earth and rocks, and the blue outer circle enmeshed with stars within circles is clearly symbolically mimicking the sky, stars, moon, and other celestial features.

The child character reaches and stretches one hand outside the symbolic earth circle, awakening and rising above earth to greet and engage with nature. When the character comes to an eco consciousness, there is a realization of other different child bodies seen at the center of other trees, as stated, "Trees! More and more trees. Trees and trees just like me!" (p. 13). The character states, "A tree I am A tree I stand on a sidewalk on a mountain by a river or a road" (pp. 15–16). These passages can be understood as the importance of seeing one's self reflected in one's world.

In *autofantasías* theory, the author and character use the power of dream and fantasy to take ownership of creating and visualizing multiple identities. Moraga describes this process as an example of how "our bodies and our experiences are that complex site of conflict through which our political work is mediated" (p. 59). Gonzalez deftly combines the visual, realism, and fantasy with the text. Another issue that Gonzalez cleverly illustrates is the underlying assumption of equity issues that are evident in this picture book. Equity issues in terms of gender, eco-consciousness, race, and culture are covertly expressed.

Gonzalez does not stereotype gender, but rather creates visual representations and a text that are suitable for both genders. In doing so, Gonzalez illustrates gender as a nonfixed identity and malleable according to the natural order of nature and environment.

In the final page of the book, the reader has to rotate the book clockwise to view the breadth of the tree, standing at the root is the child character with reaching hands to the sky. In the final passage the character proclaims, "Call me tree because I am tall I am strong and like a tree I am free" (p. 22). This forces the reader to view the textual and the visual aspects in a different perspective.

Moreover, the peculiar details of physically changing viewpoints enables the reader to generate questions, thus engaging them to read actively. As an adult reader, I found this particular technique intriguing as I kept on thinking about the reasons as to why the author/illustrator drew visuals that allowed for sexual/textual manipulations and transformations.

The child character reminds me of how Anzaldúa and Moraga describe a growing awareness of "transformation of experience" has happened in light of a new perspective or reinterpretation on the social, or in this case, the environmental world within which that experience has meaning. As a result, the child character's newfound identity is more epistemically and socially salient than the former identity insofar as it more accurately refers to the complex and multiple ways that self-concept and identities change within the ecosystems of the indoor space and the outdoor space, as indicated in the beginning pages.

In *Call Me Tree*, the *autofantasías* is when the author connects children with nature to diversify their outdoor experience. Nature is used to connect with children's social and cognitive developments. Author Gail F. Melson, in her book, *Why the Wild Things Are: Animals in the Lives of Children*, suggests that children, nature, and animals share significant ties for reassurance, support, and contact comfort of touch that appeal to the child sensibilities; as Melson states, "animals as symbols . . . appeal to the children's imagination" (p. 6).

Children are like animals at this point, learning from what they see, hear, smell, taste, as they take it all in and, thus, form themselves into what they are to become. Melson asserts that children use "creatures great and small to explore, clarify, and reflect different facets of the child's sense of self" (6). Children can relate to the "character" nature or animal in a fantasy way without feeling compromised.

CONCLUSIONS: SEXUAL IDENTITY AND CHILDHOOD

The queer aesthetics and eccentricities of these books create what Millán calls a *autofantasías*—a "fantasy land" much like that found in Anaya's mythical work of *La Llorona* and *Juan and the Jackalope*. The paintings/drawings of *Antonio's Card*, and the inner world/outer world of *Call Me Tree*, are a biographical and a fantasy space where identities can be played out and constructed by the child having agency over their decisions, dreams, and sexual identities. The characters have a "fantasy escape" that is a safe zone space that helps them move away from innocence to knowledge.

In *Antonio's Card* and *Call Me Tree*, there is a queer nostalgia—a longing not just for a different place to play out their fantasy but for a place where same-sex relations and queerness is accepted and embraced. *Autofantasías* applies similarly to both authors' claim to a newfound queer society that yearns for inventing new queer mythology through the use of the natural world—trees to appeal to a child reader. Anzaldúan theory places both the authors, the lived experiences, and the political message at the heart of queer engagement. As she states in her essay "La Prieta" that:

> We are the queer groups, the people that don't belong anywhere, not in the dominant world nor completely within our own respective cultures. Combined

we cover so many oppressions, but the overwhelming oppression is the collective fact that we do not fit, and because we do not fit *we are a threat*. (p. 50)

As the overarching political commentary and the utopian ideals, Millán and Anzaldúa theory suggests that this is where the author's voice—*auto* merges with the utopian idealism that is meant to education, entertain, and empower children.

I argue that the queer tendencies of *Antonio's Card* and *Call Me Tree* contextualize their narratives in indoor/outdoor—private versus public spaces, play with notions of queer fantasies, and find places where they are free to exercise the queer identities. For Antonio and the nongendered child character, it is in same-sex relations and nonconforming ideals that they find comfort and solace. These books are juxtaposed with Rudolfo Anaya's children's literature and how he promotes a heteronormative discursive practice but allows for sexual agency within the child.

I argue that while the literature in all of these children's books are characterized by the use of bilingualism, *Antonio's Card* and *Call Me Tree* challenge the hegemonic and traditional views of childhood sexuality and engage the child reader to fantasize about queerness. All of the books create a "fantasy land" or dream-like world, be it the drawings/paintings, outer space/inner space, where queerness, same-sex, and heterosexual desires can be expressed, understood, normalized, and socially accepted for children. I argue for the inclusion of these texts as valued resources in elementary educational settings.

What prompts my political stance are personal experiences, as I am witnessing my own daughter, nine years old, being consumed by what Millán calls in her essay title, "Que(e)ries into . . . *Autofantasías*" (2015). My daughter continually explores places and spaces to play out her sexual identities and queerness wherever and whenever she can. Texts such as *La Llorona, Juan and the Jackalope, Antonio's Card*, and *Call Me Tree* serve as a guide for my daughter's own sexual and queer journeys. I look around my daughter's classroom, and see other children hungry for texts such as these that explore issues of sexuality and queerness. I can only imagine how many more students would benefit from having these texts readily available to them located on the bookshelves of their classrooms or libraries. To have these books in the classroom reminds me of what feminist author and scholar bell hooks says about educational spaces:

> to be changed by ideas was a pure pleasure. But to learn ideas that ran counter to values and beliefs learned at home was to place oneself at risk, to enter the danger zone. Home was the place where I was forced to conform to someone else's image of who and what I should be. School was the place where I could forget that self and through ideas reinvent myself. (p. 3)

This quote highlights how valuable resources in the classroom can celebrate the power of ideas to experience human compassion and change peoples' perceptions and also addresses the imaginative *autofantasías* posited by Millán.

The texts of Rudolfo Anaya's *La Llorona: The Crying Woman*, and *Juan and the Jackalope*; Roberto González's *Antonio's Card*; and Maya Christina Gonzalez's *Call Me Tree* present new possibilities for mapping out sexual imaginaries and sexual identities with children and also construct new queertopias in Chicana/o-Latina/o children's literature. These books begin to take a greater account of the way social contexts and social processes shape children's development and sexual identities. They draw attention not only to the cultural origins of childhood, but also to gender and sexual constructs. Above all, these books examined in this chapter explore the children's ability to understand and make decisions on their own behalf, giving children agency over their activities and making decisions concerning their welfare by themselves and for themselves.

ACKNOWLEDGMENTS

I am indebted to Daniel Enrique Perez and David Miller for their comments on earlier versions of this chapter. I am very thankful for coeditors Dr.'s Laura Alamillo, Cristina Herrera, and Larissa Mercado-López for their inspirational direction they provided for this chapter and also for their unyielding patience and their valuable feedback . . . *mil gracias, mujeres!*

NOTES

1. These authors have similar themes of writing about queer childhood experiences.

2. Preceding *La Llorona: The Crying Woman*, Rudolfo Anaya published in 1997 a children's book, *Maya's Children: The Story of La Llorona*. Both of Anaya's children's books focus on the retelling La Llorona's story as a character who does not harm her children, rather a story that focuses on the creation of the *mestizo* race, a mythical indigenous land, and the sexual desires of *La Llorona* to engage in procreation.

3. I agree with the claims of Benjamin Bateman who states that "Queer culture . . . must imagine a political order in which the needs of children are not inimical to the interests of queers, and it must celebrate . . . that which is most queer, and queer-able in children" in *The Future of Queer Theory*. The Minnesota Review. Ns 65–66, 2006. Available at: http://www.theminnesotareview.org/journal/ns6566/bateman_r_benjamin_ns6566_stfl.shtml. Also see Kenneth Kidd, "Queer Theory's Child and Children's Literature Studies," PMLA, 2011. 182–8; Karín Lisnik-

Oberstein, "Childhood, queer theory, feminism." *Feminist Theory*. December 7, 2010, 11: 309–21; and Lisnik-Oberstein, and Stephen Thomson, "What is Queer Theory Doing With the Child?" in *Parallax*. Routledge: Taylor & Francis Ltd.: United Kingdom, 2002. Vol. 8, No. 1, 35–46.

4. Yvonne Yarbro-Bejarano, "Deconstructing the Lesbian Body: Cherrí Moraga's *Loving in the War Years*" in *The Lesbian and Gay Studies Reader* eds. By Henry Abelove, Michéle Aina Barle and David M. Halperin (New York: Routledge Press, 1993), 595–615.

5. Preface, *Borderlands/La Frontera: The New Mestiza* (San Francisco: Spinsters/Aunt Lute, 1987), "N.pag."

6. Yvonne Yarbro-Bejarano, "Deconstructing the Lesbian Body: Cherrí Moraga's *Loving in the War Years*" in *The Lesbian and Gay Studies Reader* eds. By Henry Abelove, Michéle Aina Barle and David M. Halperin (New York: Routledge Press, 1993), 596.

7. Cherríe Moraga, and Gloria Anzaldúa, eds., *This Bridge Called My Back: Writings by Radical Women of Color* (Watertown, MA: Persephone Press, 1981; 2nd ed. New York: Kitchen Table Press, 1983).

8. Gloria Anzaldúa, *Borderlands* Preface (1987), "N. pag."

9. Moraga, Cherríe, and Gloria Anzaldúa. "Entering the lives of others: Theory in the flesh." *This bridge called my back: Writings by radical women of color* (1981): 21–2.

REFERENCES

Anaya, Rudolfo. (2009). *Juan and the jackalope: A children's book in verse*. Albuquerque: University of New Mexico Press.

Anaya, Rudolfo. (2011). *La Llorona: The crying woman*. Albuquerque: University of New Mexico Press.

Anzaldúa, Gloria. (2009). "La Prieta." In AnaLouise Keating (Ed.), *The Gloria Anzaldúa reader* (pp. 38–50). Durham, NC: Duke University Press.

Bartlett, Catherine. (1986). Magical realism: The Latin American influence on modern Chicano writers. *Confluencia, 1*(2), 27–37.

Blatt, Gloria T. (1968). Mexican-Americans in children's literature. *Elementary English, 45*, 446–51.

Davila, Luis. (1975). Chicano fantasy through a glass darkly. In *Otros mundos, otros fuegos; Fantasía y Realismo Mágico en Iberoamérica,* [Papers of the] XVI Congreso de Instituto.

Esquibel, Catrióna Rueda. (1998). Memories of girlhood: Chicana lesbian fictions. *Signs: Journal of Women in Culture and Society, 23*(3), 644–81.

Gonzalez, Maya Christina. (2014). *Call me tree/Llámame árbol*. New York: Children's Book Press.

González, Rigoberto. (2005). *Antonio's card/La Tarjeta de Antonio*. San Francisco: Children's Book Press.

Herrera, Juan Felipe. (2003). *Super cilantro girl/La Superniña del Cilantro*. San Francisco: Children's Book Press.

hooks, bell. (1994). *Teaching to transgress: Education as the practice to freedom.* New York: Routledge.
Internacional de Literatura Iberoamericana (pp. 245–48). East Lansing: Latin American Studies Center of Michigan State University.
Keating, AnaLouise. (2009). *The Gloria Anzaldúa reader.* Durham, NC: Duke University Press.
Latina-themed literature. In Jamie Campbell Naidoo & Sarah Park Dahlen (Eds.), *Diversity in youth literature: Opening doors through reading* (p. 48). Chicago: ALA Editions, American Library Association.
Lynn, Ruth Nadelman. (1996). Fantasy literature for children and young adults: An annotated bibliography. *Utopian Studies, 7*(1), 129–31.
Melson, Gail F. (2001). *Why the wild things are: Animals in the lives of children.* Cambridge: Harvard University Press.
Millán, Isabel. (2015). Contested children's literature: Que(e)ries into Chicana and central American *Autofantasías*. *Signs: Journal of Women in Culture and Society, 41*(1), 199–224.
Perez, Daniel Enrique. (2009). *Rethinking Chicana/o and Latina/o popular culture.* New York: Palgrave Macmillan.
Quiroa, Ruth. (2013). Promising portals and safe passages: A review of pre-K-12 Latino- and Saldívar, Ramón. (1991). Narrative, ideology, and the reconstruction of American literary history. In Héctor Calderón & José David Saldívar (Eds.), *Criticism in the borderlands: Studies in Chicano literature, culture, and ideology* (pp. 11–20). Durham, NC: Duke University Press.
Serrato, Phillip. (2012). Transforming boys, transforming masculinity, transforming culture: Masculinity anew in Latino and Latina children's literature. In Pedro Noguera, Aída Hurtado, & Edward Fergus (Eds.), *Invisible no more: Understanding the disenfranchisement of Latino men and boys*. New York: Routledge.
Tijerina-Revilla, Anita. (2005). Raza Womyn Mujerstoria. *Villanova Law Review, 50*(4), 799.
Trujillo, Carla. (2003). *What night brings.* Evanston, IL: Northwestern University Press.
Wagoner, Shirley A. (1982). Mexican-Americans in children's literature since 1970. *The Reading Teaching, 36*(3), 274–9.

Section III

TRANSFORMATIVE PEDAGOGIES: REFLECTIONS FROM INSIDE AND OUTSIDE THE CLASSROOM

"If reading were not a bitter obligation, if on the contrary, studying and reading were sources of pleasure and happiness as well as sources of knowledge we need to move about the world, we would have indexes that were more indicative of the quality of our education" (Freire, 1998). Freire in *Teachers as Cultural Workers* critiques the manner in which reading is approached in education. His lens can also be used to critique the manner in which children are subjected to school literacy programs that place children into reading levels limiting access to certain literature. This context poses challenges for Chican@ children who because of their English Learner label or status are often labeled as struggling readers, requiring reading intervention. In a review of children's literature used in reading intervention programs, Chican@ children's literature are often left out of these programs.

Section 3 includes chapters for educators who are interested in reexamining and resisting teaching practices that young, Chican@ children are subjected to in the context of school-based literacy reforms. These reforms limit access to the literature presented in these chapters. The preselected literature does not always reflect the lived experiences of Chican@ children. The authors present Chican@ children's literature that validate and affirm the linguistic diversity in the classroom. For example, Laura Alamillo poses an additive way in viewing the fluidity of language practices in schools and how Chican@ children's literature affirms these practices. Cibils and coauthors raise awareness as to how educators can build linguistically sustaining classrooms using Chican@ literature.

Elena Avilés presents how Chicana feminist-illustrator, Maya Cristina Gonzalez, uses color and images to show the connection between language and pedagogy. Avilés' proposed use of chillante pedagogy affirms the multiple identities experiences of Chican@ children through the use of text images. Katherine Bundy discusses two books that can raise the consciousness of young readers to serve as springboards for activism and social change in their community. Each chapter presents Chican@ children's literature that can spark a deeper interest into reading quality children's literature and affirm cultural and linguistic identities. The authors explore themes within Chican@ children's literature that can be used to raise the consciousness of young children in the classroom by presenting themes in the literature that reflect their lived experiences. These themes can be further explored in the classroom transforming pedagogy to be more inclusive of Chican@ children.

Chapter 9

Chillante Pedagogy, "She Worlds," and Testimonio as Text/Image: Toward a Chicana Feminist Pedagogy in the Works of Maya Christina Gonzalez

Elena Avilés

There are often understudied interactions between how illustrations create stories that interact with verbal texts. The rise of the graphic novel and visual narratives is opening new lines of critical inquiry to literary boundaries and contesting the disciplinary terrain of what is literature. However, even within these trending fields, where the visual and literary worlds are represented, critics have noted the stark under representation of the multiculturalism and diversity of experience by people of color (Aldama, 2009, 2010). The same holds true in the publication of children's literature by and for diverse populations.

The presence of Chicanas in authorship roles and as navigators of children's imaginative kingdoms remains largely invisible among children's literature and scholarship. This chapter examines how text and image interact in children's literature written and illustrated by Maya Christina Gonzalez to demonstrate how she uses the visual and literary arts as an embodied practice to rewrite the cultural histories of historically underrepresented communities. Her approach to bilingual storytelling is one reflective of the idea that learning about Chican@ history and culture is itself international learning. By offering works in bilingual formats, she reaches various audiences: monolingual English speakers, monolingual Spanish speakers, children growing up in bilingual language environments, and children who are heritage speakers of Spanish. As a feminist, her investment in multilingual storytelling brings to young audiences the philosophies of language being twin skin to identity as Gloria Anzaldúa and Cherríe Moraga address in their early writings on the need to cultivate a voice of one's own. In terms of gender and sexuality, her works create a revolution.

Many Chican@ children are Spanish language heritage learners. They weave languages and code-switch, reminding us that language is an expressive and inventive work of art with myriad combinations and shifts. Chican@s often grow up learning various forms of shame and guilt about the languages they speak, do not speak, and have internalized these views due to sociocultural forces that define who is native or not. Gonzalez understands the complexities of language in Chican@ culture. She uses bilingualism to raise cultural sensitivity and consciousness on the importance of placing a positive value on all languages, inclusive of the survival of indigenous registers.

Her dedication to publish in English and Spanish challenges language hierarchies and English-only perspectives. She uses children's literature to respond to anti-Chican@ rhetoric by showing how the Chican@ experience is universal. In her work, she presents universal themes, concepts, offering counternarratives to the stereotypical representations of Chican@s in society. Adopting the pedagogical teachings of Gloria Anzaldúa's seminal chapter "How to Tame a Wild Tongue," in *Borderlands/La frontera: La nueva mestiza* (1987), Gonzalez shows the value of multiple tongues, bilingual storytelling, and the power of wild tongues.

Furthermore, as a result of her lens, she promotes the celebration of the Chican@ experience that defines U.S. multicultural society. As a border crosser she codes books with multilingual, experiential, and visually intermixed narratives. For example, she offers narratives of trans-American history and culture that speak of the cultural histories of historically underrepresented communities to minority groups like Chican@s, who often do not see themselves represented in books. In this regard, she uses literature and art as two ways to interpret storytelling. She writes words to tell a story in the same way that she uses visual imagery to decipher the meaning of texts. For children, color offers a medium through which meaning manifests. She understands this fundamental principle, and is able to use color to whisper stories into the little eyes and ears of her readers. For this reason, a section of this chapter elaborates on the use of text and image as the practice of testimony.

Publications where she has served as the illustrator such as—*My Very Own Room* (2000), *My Diary from Here to There* (2002), and *Nana's Big Surprise!* (2007) written by Amada Irma Pérez—allow children to see the practices of their communities and homes in print. Discussing everyday practices of public and private life in culturally specific terms enables Gonzalez to bridge Chicana feminist praxis of breaking stereotypes through storytelling and testimony. For children of color in the United States, the validation of home values, which at times may be different than the values of dominant society, is transformative.

Her stories speak to the need to continue to break stereotypes and show women telling stories, or application of testimony as a methodology, is transnational by nature for feminists of the Americas. The materiality of her books also teaches children a sense of belonging that is valued in the public sphere, and which is significant for Chicanos as a historically stigmatized group. Gonzalez generates visibility of Pre-Columbian text and images largely through visual representation. Her Chicana feminist methodology positions itself within a borderlands framework and as such conveys to readers Chicana ways of knowing based on *la conciencia de la mestiza*, that borders are imaginary.

In addition, she also encourages Chicano children to see themselves as part of a global community. Her wide range of visualizing topics and themes as seen in the following publications—*Just Like Me: Stories and Self-portraits by 14 Artists* (1997) by Harriet Rohmer, *Fiesta Femenina* (2001) by Mary-Joan Gerson, and *Animal Poems of the Iguazú* (2008) by Francisco Alarcón—illustrates such goal. In this sense, she also rewrites cultural traditions of underrepresented communities by using images as a gateway for teaching cultural competency, nonviolence, and love for difference.

Many of the contributions Gonzalez has made to Chicano children's literature are yet to be written, but the most salient one is how she channels Chicana feminist pedagogy in children's narratives. Keeping aware the interaction between text and image, this chapter outlines the advancement of Chicana literary and visual perspectives in children's book genre. This chapter presents how Gonzalez infuses children's narratives and her own perspectives within a Chicana feminist identity. Her use of color references the long historical relationship mestizos have with aesthetic practices that reflect their unique experiences and ways of seeing the world.

Building on the critical inroads made by Tomás Ybarra Faustro on rasquachismo and Amalia Mesa-Bains' extension of rasquache aesthetics into Chicana feminist art practices through her elaboration of domestic, this chapter illustrates how Gonzalez learns from these masters and partakes in a Chicana feminist practice of chillante pedagogy within the genre of children's books.

Gonzalez paints a Chicanita literary space, or "she" worlds. "She" worlds, read through the lens of Chicana feminism, is a form of what Gloria Anzaldúa and Cherríe Moraga refer to as "theory in the flesh," bringing subjectivity to what has traditionally been cast as an object. The tales Gonzalez offers about "she" worlds, where women are heroes and the main protagonist, set the historical script of the role and position of women of color. Likewise, for other tales, a feminist lens remains operational. In the "she" worlds, creativity and imagination in textual and visual expression function independently and together to decolonized history.

Gonzalez inserts Chicana subjectivity in children's books to show women and men of all ages to honor the power of diverse forms of knowledge transmission through Chicana power. Her books are artifacts that show us how to understand Chicana power, using it as an antidote to safeguard oneself from violence against women of color and the importance of Chicana power to combat cultural erasure and amnesia.

GONZALEZ AS A PIONEER OF CHILDREN'S BOOKS ARTIVISM

Gonzalez approaches art as a powerful tool that can nurture forms of expression often undervalued and underutilized. She considers the practice of art a form of empowerment and self-affirmation. For her, creativity is a powerful site for the preservation of certain languages and forms of expressions that are disappearing, becoming lost, or silenced in modern Western thought and life. Across time, the artist has created a discourse that frames art production as a community practice and as a positive social justice space. Art became the space in which Gonzalez depicted a "critical discourse from within," as art historian Holly Barnet-Sanchez has observed about the distinctive art practices of Chicana artists ("Tomás Ybarra-Frausto," 2005).

Gonzalez invokes a critical discourse reflective of her subject position as a Chicana feminist. She first cultivated her distinct artistic sensibility by making and selling jewelry in Oregon. This craft granted her the time and space to develop her own artistic philosophy. She developed a critical sense of art as a nonverbal language by examining how colors spoke to her as they had when she was a child. In the quest to clarify the mysteries of her own phenomenological experience with an entity she describes as a radiating light that awakened her one night as a child, Gonzalez turned to art to channel her visions of the world and to finally give voice to the enchanting and spiritual aspects of nature defining the memories of her childhood.

Because she is a Chicana of mixed ancestry, Gonzalez experienced the effects of language shifts and loss. Though her Mexican American father grew up as a fluent Spanish speaker, she also experienced firsthand the effects of racial and ethnic discrimination during the early part of the twentieth century when children were reprimanded and punished for speaking Spanish at school. As a result of the language trauma he endured, he did not actively teach his daughter Spanish.

Her mother's own assimilationist perspectives added to the sense of internalized colonialism the Chicana felt throughout her childhood. Likewise, she faced discrimination and oppression as the only Chicana when her parents decided to move from California to a rural town in Southern Oregon. Her adolescent years were marked by constant reminders that she was culturally, historically, and linguistically different.

Thus, as a woman of color, she faced many forms of violence because of her identity. Although the intent of Gonzalez's parents was to spare their daughter from the effects of what Anzaldúa termed "linguistic terrorism," her home life experiences simultaneously narrated the hidden cultural practices developed among Chicano communities that resisted and subverted the same "linguistic terrorism" (Anzaldúa, *Borderlands*, 1987). These include establishing Spanish as the language of home, passing on cultural values in domestic settings, and forging strong familial and community ties.

Despite her mother's own personal views and her father's own language trauma, Spanish might not have been the language of her public life, but it also was not a dead language at home. The artist recalls that Spanish was a language spoken at home, the language that defined her cultural interactions with family and community members (Interview, 2014).

Her community taught her alternative modes of discourse rooted in hybridity that circumvented and nullified the messages transmitted in dominant and public discourses that sought to oppress minority populations. She recalls Spanish being the language of family functions and which defined the communicative transactions of personal affairs.

In other words, developmental moments in her own personal identity formation were not divorced from the transmission of oral traditions in Spanish that characterizes the cultural practices of Mexican American and Chicano communities in the United States. But because during her early childhood Spanish was publicly considered a subordinate language, the Chicana channeled her sense of love and pride for her culture through art.

For this reason, her art reflects the development of a critical discourse rooted in the practice of oral traditions and in feminist practices rooted in domesticity that celebrates a Chicana/o heritage speaker's sense of *mestizaje* with the same openness and sense of love she felt among her family and friends.

In works she has written and illustrated such as *Call Me Tree* (2014), *My Colors, My World* (2011), and *I Know the River Loves Me* (2009), you will note the celebration of visual imagery that is layered and mixed, like her own historical experience. For example, her artwork is reflective of the traditions of Latin American textiles and use of color and storylines that value nature and one's connection to the world.

Afraid of losing the wealth of knowledge about history, culture, and nature embedded in the languages of her lived experience, Gonzalez was determined to preserve her cultural heritage. She realized that positive cultural memories could be kept alive by creating visual narratives of a community celebrating itself. In the case of missing or lacking narratives, the artist's role could be one of activist; the artist also had the ability to invoke the imagination to create new stories that would bring justice to fragmented or missing life tales. In memory of her father, she decided to use art as a tool for social justice.

In 1994, after working several years as a jewelry maker, she moved to San Francisco to dedicate herself to painting. That same year she had a show for *Día de los Muertos* at La Galería de la Raza. She sold most of her work. Impressed, Harriet Rohmer, an editor for Children's Book Press, invited the artist to work for the press. Rohmer was in need of someone to illustrate Gloria Anzaldúa's *La Prieta and the Ghost Woman/Prietita y La Llorona* (1995). Gonzalez realized she had the ability to illustrate the rich oral traditions of her culture—stories, songs, and histories—passed on to younger generations by translating the words of Chican@ tales into visual narratives.

During her early years with the children's publishing house, she learned that the transmission of culture could exist outside of written forms. To really influence children to think positively about themselves she knew it was important to speak to them in languages comprehensible to them; after all, she knew firsthand the power of visual images in the formation of children's identities. Then she decided to become a pioneer Chicana artivist of children's books.

ARTIVISM: A SPIRITUAL CALL TO ACTION FROM WOMEN GLOWING IN THE DARK

Gonzalez's lively and colorful visual narratives allowed her to view the creative process as a spiritual tool to heal one's mind and soul from traumas, such as the feeling of not belonging, not being good enough, having your language and culture oppressed and silenced. Art allowed her to represent herself in image and text, to etch her identity into existence by becoming visible. "I believe that belonging is one of the subtexts that can be found in all of my books in some way," the artist notes ("Maya Christina Gonzalez," 2).

For example, in the following passage, Gonzalez expresses a Chicana vision as she expresses her approach to the practice of art:

> It's in the way that I paint, the way I develop the characters, the environments I create, even the intention with which I paint. At each step in the process, I hold my own heart as a child in my awareness, as I hold the collective heart of the children I paint for. I focus on a sense of belonging, of being reflected, on the reality of being a child in this world. I imagine my father at five years old as he entered a school where only English was spoken. He spoke only Spanish. Although half of my family spoke primarily Spanish at family events, I was not taught Spanish growing up. The lesson of my father and much of our culture at that time was of assimilation. On one level, I am painting these books for the little boy my father used to be and hoping that our world is changing, expanding its perceptions. ("Maya Christina Gonzalez," 2014)

With the three principles that guide her work—everyone is an artist; there is never a right or wrong way to make art; and art is always an act of courage—Gonzalez's art reflects a high level of social consciousness that defies conventional art dogmas ("Maya Christina Gonzalez," 2). Her own art philosophy reflects a critical discourse reflecting the influences of Chicana feminist politics.

But her world vision also affords the creative process as a means to empower the voice that lives as a heritage language. Through such action, she reframes heteroglot elements in all multiethnic, minoritized, subaltern, and colonized peoples. *Laughing Tomatoes and Other Spring Poems/Jitomates Risueños y otros poemas de primavera* (1997), *Iguanas in the Snow and Other Winter Poems/Iguanas en la nieve y otros poemas de invierno* (2001), *Animal Poems of the Iguazú/Animalario del Iguazí (2008)*, and *Angels Ride Bikes and Other Fall Poems/Los Ángeles Andan en Bicicleta y otros poemas de otoño* (2014) are stellar representations of her art, and in action, her activism.

Written by Francisco X. Alarcón, the books listed above show her interest of publishing culturally specific children's books. As a dynamic duo, always at play, these publications show how artist and writer can work to rewrite cultural histories of underrepresented communities. The development of a visual language emerging from hybridity reflects the flourishing of her Chicana approach to use language and to work within the system of visual language to assert new possibilities for self-love among children.

Gonzalez states, "When I paint a book, I'm constantly thinking of a child in the classroom or library grazing the book spines with her fingers, her eyes searching for something that catches them like sunsets caught mine" ("Maya Christina Gonzalez," 2014). Notice the subject in her imagination is a female in search of a book, reflecting the gaze of curious eyes in search of information and knowledge. While Gonzalez's close creative bond with Alarcón allowed them to produce books by and for Chicanos, additional collaborations reflect her particular interest to advance Chicana ways of seeing.

I offer *Prietita and the Ghost Woman/Prietita y La Llorona* (1995) as one of the first examples where Gonzalez puts into visual practice Chicana literary perspectives. Gonzalez began her career as a children's book illustrator when contracted to illustrate Gloria Anzaldúa's children's book. Tey Diana Rebolledo explains the significance of the parallel between the rise of children's literature showing Chican@s in a positive light with the evolution and progress of Chican@ literary expression. In *Prietita y el Otro Lado: Gloria Anzaldúa's Literature for Children*, the critic writes:

> Chicana writers began to be noticed in the 1980s, although they had been writing since the beginning of the Chicano movement of the 1970s. It soon became

clear that there was a need for books that provided cultural knowledge and role models for children. In elementary and middle schools, most books represented mainstream children and children's lives. Children of color would never see themselves reflected in these narratives. Some small presses, such as Children's Book Press, Bilingual Review Press, and Arte Público, began to publish books by authors of color, most with beautiful illustrations by artists of color. Writers such as Pat Mora, Rudolfo Anaya, Carmen Lomas Garza, Sandra Cisneros, Lucha Corpi, Gary Soto, and Gloria Anzaldúa understood the importance of cultural transmission to children through books written for them. (2006)

As Rebolledo points out, artists of color became the visual copilots of a new revolution taking place within literacy initiatives for younger audiences. As literal superheroes, writers often partnered with artists of color who understood the kinetic power of words and images.

In *Prietita*, Gonzalez captures that fulcrum of change that defined Chicana feminist efforts of the early 1990s, which used the creative process to ignite a method of lucid dreaming propelling Chicanas to exploit the plentiful resource of their collective memories to advance a new Chicana identity. The epistemologies of Anzaldúa's "border thinking" concentrated on narrating a more favorable depiction of women in history through concepts such as *conocimiento* and *facultad* because they embrace cultural memory and subaltern wisdom (Saldívar, *Trans-Americanity*, 2012).

Anzaldúa inverts La Llorona's role as a child-stealing she-monster witch into a guiding force that fosters the young protagonist's understanding of *curanderismo* and also protects her from the evils of the Texas Rangers. Gonzalez compliments the literary empowerment of Chicana politics and action by deciphering a new way to communicate to children through art.

Aware of the pre-Hispanic connection that theorizes La Llorona and La Malinche to be the same person, the characterization of La Llorona-La Malinche as a guide or interpreter by the author is reinforced visually by the illustrator who reenvisions the narrative of folkloric, historical, and forgotten women. Images of women and of Chicana sensibilities infuse each page. In both text and image of *La Prietita*, the negative stereotype of La Llorona-La Malinche is replaced with a feminist reading and method of representing women in accordance with Chicana discourses. In visual representation, La Llorona is depicted as a woman glowing in the dark.[1] She is a light form that serves as a spiritual guide for the young protagonist who ventures to the external world in search of a medicinal plant to give to her grandmother to help her mother heal from a sickness.

As an apprentice to Anzaldúa's philosophy, the artist contributed to a developing Chicana visual culture where images operated to convey new symbolic thought about the life of La Llorona structured through Chicana feminist languages of domestic life that mirror the politics of *la mujer chicana*. Parallel to Anzaldúa's own empowerment through writing, engaging in Chicana notions of artistic process allowed Gonzalez to use art as a dream catcher to present new visions to end the negative stereotyping of female cultural archetypes of La Llorona. At the same time, she offers visual representations of women of color in a positive light and at center stage.

CHICANITA LITERARY SPACES AND THE MAKING OF VISUAL "SHE" WORLDS

Born during the early years of the Chicano Movement (January 24, 1964), this California native channels the core principle of being tied to land and the significance of the sense of place that roots Chicano politics. Her first self-written and illustrated book, "My Colors, My World/Mis colores, mi mundo" (2007) taps into the collective power of memory. She describes the memories of her childhood as follows:

> I grew up in the Mojave Desert of Southern California in the 1960s and 1970s in a town called Lancaster. I felt like I was out in the middle of nowhere. The world was all sky and desert. My father was a lineman and my mother was a homemaker. My father is Mexican American and my mother is white. I have a younger brother close to my age named David. ("Maya Christina Gonzalez," 2014)

In this seemingly "unassuming" narrative of her own childhood memories, the author lays the groundwork for inspiring young readers to consider their social location and social space as important to the shaping of their identity. The interaction between space and place to notions of identity reference the power of memory. Gonzalez's multicultural identity made her unique and publishing on her life itself proves how she writes new cultural histories in Chican@ children's narratives.

During her adolescent years, she turned to writing to express this difference and the notion of difference that led to a feeling of shame when her family moved from California to Oregon. This motivated her to pursue a degree in creative writing at the University of Oregon. In college, Gonzalez saw literature as a way to connect to the world. She read emerging Chicana writers and identified most with the experiences of subaltern and multiethnic literatures of the world. It was not until near the completion of a writing program at the University of Oregon that she discovered art.

Gonzalez enrolled in an art history course after a friend pleaded for company, but, once in class, she realized art was the language of her spirit. She best explained the relationship between the desert and her own identity formation as a Chicana and artist when she stated in an interview:

> My favorite thing about the desert was the sunset. In general, there wasn't a lot of vibrant color. Things were very beige and muted. But nearly every evening, the sky at the end of our street looked like smeared fuchsias—all reds, pinks, purples and oranges. I became fixated on what I used to call Hot Pink. It was my personal color. The sky presented it to me every night in a passionate way that I took very personally. ("Maya Christina Gonzalez," 2014)

The art history class reignited the stored memory of her childhood about herself as an artist. In fact, the study of art reawakened the spiritual ties to landscapes her mind and soul had enjoyed as a child. Gonzalez recognized that she had developed an artistic sensibility from her connection to mother earth.

The creation of a space for herself—the self-portrait of a little Christina—too channels a momentous act where theory and practice merge. She not only "theorizes a new flesh" for herself in self-characterization and self-representation, she also closes the gap within the dominant literary world and the lack of Chican@ children's book by offering her story and vision of a "she" world (Andaldúa and Moraga, 1983). And in this world she had voice and subjectivity at a young age. For this reason, I read her first self-authored/self-illustrated work as a reflection of the importance of building identity by locating meaning through places and landscape of the mind and its memory.

At the same time, *My Colors, My World/Mis colores, mi mundo* pays homage to the tradition of self-portraiture within Chican@ art practices. Advocacy for the idea that it's all about perspective, we see in this publication Chicana acts of crossing black and white lines that dominate children's narratives. For example, she uses a different color to express a mood.

This also allows children to begin associating colors with texts and with experiences. In *My Colors* the protagonist sees beauty in her life, in who she is and in nature. Like the beauty of nature, she describes the beauty she experiences via color. The use of color reads as one way Gonzalez embodies a Chicana positionality to rewrite the cultural histories of historically underrepresented communities which speaks about her expression of chillante pedagogy but also of a women's way of interpreting the world.

Her Chicanita world theorizes a new flesh for her younger audiences; "she" worlds place colored bodies back into visual and literary spaces. Through the use of color, she too recolors the world, not from Western eyes, but from the eyes of our ancestors, our collective memory, our family history, or own eyewitness account. For example, when the protagonist frames the world with her fingers and eye, she becomes the author of her world, and her perspective reflects the process of making "she" worlds because the body becomes the mechanism through which she controls worldviews.

As she assimilates what she sees, she captures through her eyes, like a camera lens, images of what she considers beautiful. The overarching positive view of the world from this subjective lens becomes a definitive trait in Gonzalez's "she" world. Why not be positive, perhaps stands as the most powerful tool for creating another way to be women in "she" worlds. It is creating a positive world of possibility, a world where women think of color, words, and images to form positive identities.

Her multiethnic stories come to life in vibrant and colorful illustrations that celebrate Chicano/a visual practices of chillante aesthetics. Chillante aesthetics is a practice and politics of expressive culture that is uniquely Chicano. Tomás Ybarra Frausto and Amalia Mesa-Bains' scholarship on Chicano rasquachismo position us to understand the power of color and the operational use of color as a form of renegotiation and creativity in Chican@ expression. While their critical writings have paved inroads to understanding the roots and evolution of Chican@ aesthetic practices, a few studies have traced the influence and impact of this tradition on the development of children's literature.

The literal definition of chillante, a word in the Spanish language, offers an adjectival dimension to the use of color. Chillante means a color that is lively/bright, what in Spanish is described as *muy vivo*. The use of chillantes as a practice, a style, and a methodology honors the use of expressive color that marks the art traditions of Chican@ visual practices and its connection to Latin American art. The illustrator's practice of chillante aesthetics within US multiethnic children's literature credits the legacy of the Chicano Movement and the development of Chican@ identity in the United States. At the same time, chillante aesthetics advances the development of Chican@ visual and literary sensibilities and its appreciation to a new generation of readers.

Gonzalez's work examines essential questions about the power of visual narratives in bilingual storytelling where chillantes function both as a form of affirmation and of resistance that color a new vision of storytelling in literature that is uniquely Chican@. Her stimulating take on contemporary Chican@ culture and society uses color to allure new audiences not to fear color. She works with the visual, figurative, and literal language of color to speak to young readers who respond with open eyes to the symbolic form and structure of her technicolored drawings.

For insiders to Chican@ culture, Gonzalez offers culturally coded images that promote bilingual storytelling and pride of chillante forms meant to awaken to imagination and the symbolic language that lead one toward a path of *mestiza* consciousness. She uses colors as a form of storytelling and as a Chicana remedy to racism in educational institutions that are already linguistically and visually diverse but often made invisible. For adults, she offers a way to go back to the memories of their childhood and reclaim that collective memory of themselves in order to recolor memories in positive and vibrant contexts.

CHICANA *TESTIMONIOS* AS TEXT AND IMAGE

Finding a calling in the need to foment the visual and literary sensibilities of the Chicano imagination, Gonzalez became a pioneer in the illustration world and debuted as children's book author with *My Colors, My World/ Mis colores, mi mundo*. Because she paved a new visual social space for the promotion of Chicano children's literature, Gonzalez is a Chicana groundbreaker that has brought social justice to the world of children's books. With this publication, we see Gonzalez implementing the techniques and styles of textual and visual *testimonio* Chicana feminists use to tell their stories and the centrality of imagery to the act of storytelling across oral, written, and visual frames.

Parallel to the developments in Chicana literature of Chicana *testimonio* and *(auto)historia* booming in the 1990s, Gonzalez begins to etch a place and space for *testimonios* within children's literature. She uses Chicana/Latina feminist approaches to re-envision storytelling methodology to bring undocumented voices to the fore, what she calls "first voice." In "Polka Dots, Self-Portraits, and First Voice Multicultural Children's Books," her *auto-historia* comes to life. Reading like a Chicana version of Jorge Luis Borges' infamous short story about the metaphysics of existence in "El Aleph,"[2] she states:

> I noticed over the years that even if someone is only making a polka dot, it is visibly theirs and no one else's. How we hold a pencil is uniquely our own. No one can make a polka dot the same way. Somehow, some way our body, our stories, our thoughts, our selves make a basic mark that is uniquely our own, however subtle, however small, this mark shows something about us. To me, this is the beginning of art. This is the beginning of expressing something that is ours and ours alone.

For this reason, I read her first self-authored/self-illustrated work as a reflection of the empowerment in reclaiming history and the voices of the underrepresented. By representing herself, she is able to reclaim her past, celebrate her memory and her present love of her collective experiences. She further elaborates:

> The power of the polka dot is amplified when we go beyond that initial mark and express ourselves more fully, through self-portraiture or words. I like beginning with acknowledging the polka dot, because it hints at the vast and multidimensional levels available to us when we engage in creation/expression. This

includes not only our own exceedingly unique and individual experience, but also all of our cultural, social and historical influences as well. (n.p.)

She also closes the gap within the dominant literary world's lack of Chican@ subjects. But perhaps, what is most important to consider is how across text and image she offers the reader a "she" world with an ever-present voice as subjectivity. Imagine what the world would look life if women of color were taught to have voice since childhood, instead of being taught traditions of silence and invisibility?

Maya Christina Gonzalez offsets linguicism, racism, and other forms of discrimination in Chican@ social and cultural experiences by rewriting cultural traditions of underrepresented communities as a Chicana feminist. Similar to Chicana authors of children's literature like Gloria Anzaldúa, Pat Mora, and Sandra Cisneros, she offers a radical perspective for the hybridity of language use among Chicanos. Her books channel a Chicana feminist spirit that advises that language equals power; and that power equals presence.

This chapter concludes with the suggestion that Gonzalez's children's books are also decolonial gifts to the next generation of Chican@s. She makes the history and modern day experiences of Chican@ culture visible and present for audiences both young and old through the interaction between word and image. She offers a radical perspective for understanding the hybridity of language use among Chicanos reminiscent of Chela Sandoval's notion of decolonial acts of love. Her illustrations create stories that dialogue and advance Chicana visual and literary practices and pedagogies. What a beautiful way to teach a new generation the power imbedded in the love to read, ¿qué no?

NOTES

1. A popular curandera book published in 1997 by Elena Avila with Joy Parker also holds the same title: *A Woman Who Glows in the Dark: A Curandera Reveals Traditional Aztec Secrets of Physical and Spiritual Health.*

2. Written in 1949 by Jorge Luis Borges in *El Aleph and Other Stories,* "El Aleph" is a Spanish-language short story that characterizes a point as a mark that contains all space.

REFERENCES

Aldama, F. L. (2009). *Your brain on Latino comics: From Gus Arriola to Los Bros Hernandez*. Austin: University of Texas Press.

Aldama, F. L. (2010). *Multicultural comics: From zap to blue beetle*. Austin: University of Texas Press.

Anzaldúa, G. (1987). *Borderlands/La frontera: The new mestiza*. San Francisco, CA: Aunt Lute.

Anzaldúa, G., & Moraga, C. (Eds.). (1981). *This bridge called my back: Radical writings by women of color*. Watertown, NY: Persephone Press.

Anzaldúa, G., & Gonzalez, M. (1995). *Prietita and the Ghost Woman/Prietita y La Llorona*. San Francisco, CA: Children's Book Press.

Barnet-Sanchez, H. (2001). Where are the Chicana printmakers? In C. Noriega & H. Barnet-Sanchez (Eds.), *Just another poster?* (pp. 118–49). Santa Barbara: University of California.

Barnet-Sanchez, H. (2005). Tomás Ybarra-Frausto and Amalia Mesa-Bains: A critical discourse from within. *Art Journal, 64*(4), 91–3.

Barnet-Sanchez, H. (2007). Chicano/a critical practices: Reflections on Tomás Ybarra-Frausto's concept of *Rasquachismo*. In K. Mercer (Ed.), *Pop art and vernacular cultures* (pp. 56–87).

Freire, P. (1998). *Teachers as Cultural Workers. Letters to Those Who Dare Teach. The Edge: Critical Studies in Educational Theory*. Boulder, CO: Westview Press.

Gonzalez, Christina. (n.d.). Polka dots, self-portraits, and first voice multicultural children's books. *Children's Book Academy*, n.p., Web. April 15, 2016. Retrieved from http://www.childrensbookacademy.com/blogettes/polka-dots-self-portraits-and-first-voice-multicultural-childrens-books#sthash.wkFPQBGg.dpuf

Gonzalez, M. C. (2014, January 03). Telephone interview. "Maya Christina Gonzalez." (2014, June 6). Retrieved from http://eds.b.ebscohost.com.libproxy.unm.edu/ehost/detail?sid=ac910d13-35bc-438c-bea45d2004c3904b%40sessionmgr113&vid=4&bk=1&hid=102&bdata=JnNpdGU9ZWhvc3QtbGl2ZSZzY29wZT1zaXRl#db=brb&AN=203106656

Mesa Bains, A. (1999). "'Domesticana': The sensibility of Chicana Rasquache. *Aztlán: A Journal of Chicano Studies, 157*. General OneFile. Web.

Rebolledo, T. D. (2006, January 01). Prietita y el Otro Lado: Gloria Anzaldúa's Literature for Children. *PMLA, 121*(1), 279–84.

Saldívar, J. D. (2012). *Trans-Americanity: Subaltern modernities, global coloniality, and the cultures of greater Mexico*. Durham, NC: Duke University Press.

Saldívar-Hull, S. (2000). *Feminism on the border: Chicana gender politics and literature*. Berkeley: University of California Press.

Sandoval, C. (2000). *Methodology of the oppressed*. Minneapolis: University of Minnesota Press.

Ybarra-Frausto, T. (1991). Rasquachismo: A Chicano sensibility. In R. Griswold del Castillo, et al. (Eds.), *Chicano Art* (pp. 155–62). University of Arizona Press, AZ.

Chapter 10

Was It All a Dream? Chicana/o Children and Mestiza Consciousness in *Super Cilantro Girl* (2003) and "Tata's Gift" (2014)

Katherine Elizabeth Bundy

This chapter explores problem solving through identity negotiation within a dream state in two contemporary works that are considered part of Chican@ literature and cultural works for children: *Super Cilantro Girl/La Superniña del cilantro* (2003) by Juan Felipe Herrera with illustrations by Honorio Robledo Tapia, and "Tata's Gift" (2014), a short film written and animated by Dionisio Ceballos along with artisan Marie-Astrid Do-Rodriguez. Through a blending of the technological with the folkloric, the visual and textual portrayal of the young Chicana/o protagonists in both of these works opens up a series of questions regarding the ability to resolve and navigate complex problems through hybrid identities and youth activism during the dream state. In both works, the blurring of borders and enhanced perceptions between the dreaming and waking states trace back to a specific *facultad* in Gloria Anzaldúa's *mestiza consciousness* which she describes in her classic text, *Borderlands/La Frontera* (1987). Through an analysis of key moments performed within the dream states in both works, this chapter recognizes the developing identities of Chican@ youth as abled cultural activists equipped with eclectic technologies and heritages for hybrid problem solving. Additionally, two different middle grades educational activities are proposed to encourage critical literacy of these cultural works within a Language Arts and Ethnic Studies/Cultural Studies classroom.

In an article written by Stephanie L. Schatz (2015) concerning Lewis Carroll's approach to children's fiction and the dream state as medical debate during the Victorian era, she identifies Carroll's use of the term "dream-child" that characterizes the depiction of Alice in his famous novels, *Alice and Wonderland* (1865), and its sequel *Through the Looking-Glass* (1871). Schatz asserts that: "because Wonderland involves a merger of dream-states with waking consciousness, Carroll's 'dream-child' represents a state of consciousness or modality that is more akin to a way of seeing than simply an object to be perceived" (96). Like Carroll's "dream-child," the state of dreaming in the two Chicano works for children discussed in this chapter can be considered as active modes of consciousness-building rather than passive explanations of impractical fantasies.

The shift from the perception of dreaming as a passive stream of the subconscious toward an active stance of incubation, consciousness building, or pre-performance of future activism is a step toward bolstering otherwise marginalized voices such as those of children of color into cultural works for and about children. Rather than the dismissive and clichéd, "It was all just a dream," the seemingly impossible performance of heroism or magic in the dream state can leak into a material reality and assert agency for children living in a world dictated by adults.

A long way from the Victorian children's novel, the dream state is still being featured in the genre of Multicultural and Chicano children's literature, which has only begun to have a prominent presence in U.S. Children's Literature in the last few decades. Specifically in Chican@ juvenile literature, the function of dreams can provide a space for expressing desires for the future, listening to the advice of ancestors that have passed on, and/or rehearsals of activism in a nonmaterial state of consciousness that can help resolve problems in the child's waking life. For example, Carla Trujillo's *What Night Brings* (2003) features the dreams of an adolescent Chicana girl, Marci, who prays and dreams of changing into a biological male in order to date other girls. This clear affirmation of her queer objectives is certainly possible in the dream state, even to the point where she feels and fantasizes with her male genitals during the sleep state, only to realize upon waking that her sex had not, in fact, changed at all. This rehearsal of queer desire and transformation in the dream state during the novel serves as a private space of experimentation with bodies, sexualities, and transgressions of the boundaries that were otherwise binding and polarizing for Marci to question as a young adolescent girl.

Another well-known Chicano young adult's novel, Rudolfo Anaya's *Bless Me, Última* (1972) engages with the dream state when the protagonist, Antonio perceives his own birth, the future conflicts and deaths in his families, as well as a mix of religious and shamanistic symbols with the help of Última, Antonio's grandmother as well as the community's *curandera*. In this story, the dream state functions as a medium of spiritual insight and incubation of future decisions in a different state of consciousness that permits the blurring of physical, chronological, and conceptual boundaries in the mind of a young person.

Within Chicano children's literature, the dream state carries its own significance that is tied to Chicano culture with syncretic influences that move beyond a fantastic flight into passivity and rather engage with the dream state as a source of knowledge, predictions, and spiritual communication that can have an effect in the waking state. From a cultural standpoint, the Chicana/o protagonists in *La Súperniña del Cilantro* and "Tata's Gift" are examples of Chicano dream-children who activate their *mestiza consciousness* to navigate a borderless realm between waking and dreaming states.

Throughout the chapter, I will analyze two Chicano cultural works for children that incorporate a dream state in order to resolve the problems that affect the young protagonists. The first work examined is *La Súperniña del Cilantro* or *Super Cilantro Girl* (2003), a bilingual children's picture book by author Juan Felipe Herrera, who is currently the first Chicano Poet Laureate of the United States as of 2014. "Tata's Gift" is a short film made collectively by the Los Cenzontles Mexican Art Center in collaboration with animator Dionisio Ceballos and artisan Marie-Astrid Do-Rodriguez in 2014.

In dialogue with the plot and character analyses, I will reference Gloria Anzaldúa's term, *mestiza consciousness*, which equips the protagonists for manifesting activism by using traditional and contemporary cultural tools available to these young Chicano subjects. The *mestiza consciousness*, or, the consciousness of the mixed-race woman, is a call-to-action for a breakdown of subject-object duality and therefore the transcendence of binary limitations that the hybrid subject such as the mestiza or the chican@ embodies and performs as border identities. In her famous text that blends creative verse with the theoretical and the anecdotal, *Borderlands/La Frontera: The New Mestiza*, Anzaldúa dialogues borders that are geographic, material, sexual, gendered, racial, and psychological with the hybrid *facultad* that equips border identities.

By specifically thinking of Chican@ children in this article, Anzaldúa's *mestiza consciousness* is a useful concept to apply to consciousness building in young people who are developing their worldviews as marginalized border identities, and hopefully future activists who understand several cultural registers that are needed to resolve complex problems such as the borders themselves. Anzaldúa's focus on children throughout her career as an educator as well as her authoring of children's books including *Friends from the Other Side/Amigos del otro lado* (1993) and *Prietita and the Ghost Woman/ Prietita y la Llorona* (1995) is a testimony to her commitment to help shape awareness of cultures, power dynamics, and cartographies of problem solving for future generations.

Be it magical shape-shifting into a super heroine or confronting a bully in a videogame world, I propose that both of the Chican@ dream-children in these cultural works perform empowerment with *mestiza consciousness* as preactivism in their prospective spaces within dreams rather than in the defined and bordered realities of the material state. By interpreting this dream state as an empowering rehearsal of play and pretend for a Chicano child inside a world colonized by adults, I hope to emphasize the ability of Latino and Chicano children's literature to shape future activism and self-image of diverse young readers in the United States. I also hope to emphasize the importance of viewing and analyzing children's literature as sites of critical theory in K-12 classrooms as well as in institutions of higher education.

JUAN FELIPE HERRERA'S SUPER CILANTRO GIRL (2003)

Named the first-ever Chicano U.S. Poet Laureate in 2014, Juan Felipe Herrera is the author of numerous literary works for children, young adults, and adults that highlight the cultural heritage and political activism in the daily life of Mexicans and Chicanos living in the United States. His most recent publication, *187 Reasons Mexicanos Can't Cross the Border: Undocuments 1971–2007*, is an exploration of the undefined identities of the undocumented, yet he explains in a 2015 interview, "We do have documents, and we do have texts, and we do have a history, and we do have a culture (DemocracyNow!)." For a young audience, his children's and young adults' books of prose and poetry focus on the blend of cultural identities that Chicano children face when navigating daily life in the United States.

Super Cilantro Girl (2003) is no exception to his exploration of the highly politicized U.S. and Mexican border from the perspective of a child who dreams of a world without borders. The young protagonist's fluidity as a subject not only navigates the dreaming and waking worlds as a self-fashioned super heroine, but she also resolves the complex problems that result from borders of all kinds.

Super Cilantro Girl is a picture book that tells the story of Esmeralda Sinfronteras, a young Chicana girl living in the United States who worries about the safe return of her mother on the other side of the Mexican and U.S. border. Anxiously waiting with her grandmother at home, Esmeralda picks a bouquet of cilantro from the garden and recites a nighttime incantation before falling asleep with the cilantro in her hands. The next morning, Esmeralda notices that she is slowly taking on characteristics of the cilantro as her hands, eyes, and teeth turn green; her hair turns into thick green vines; and she grows too tall to even fit in her house as she physically transforms into *Super Cilantro Girl*.

With a newfound agency as a super heroine, she flies across the border, finds her mother in a border detainment facility, and rescues her in order to bring her back home safely across the border. Before leaving the borderland, she reforests the border between the United States and Mexico with luscious plants, plentiful animals, and Spanish-speaking white men who were formerly border patrol officers. When she wakes up in the morning, her Super Cilantro body has morphed back into Esmeralda, and she realizes that her flight was only a dream, but not without both visual and textual clues that would suggest otherwise.

"TATA'S GIFT" (2014): A COLLECTIVE SHORT FILM ABOUT CHICANO IDENTITY

Although produced more than ten years later than *La Súperniña del cilantro*, the creators of the short film, "Tata's Gift" similarly portray the complexities of cultural identity as a young Chicano child, and the blend of contemporary and indigenous technologies that can empower children who struggle with the pressures and effects of marginalizing discourses about Chicanos living in the United States. The animation, sound effects, music, and editing of the "Tata's Gift" bring the story to life without dialogue or many textual clues that assign meaning throughout the short film. Despite the lack of dialogue, the plot clearly illustrates the hybrid realities of a child who dreams of overcoming discrimination by embracing his cultural heritage while presenting relatable elements to young Chican@ children such as food, music, colorful cars, gaming devices, challenging video game levels and prizes, zombies, and typical altars for loved ones that have died in the home setting.

The protagonist in the silent short film, "Tata's Gift," is a school age Chicano boy who experiences troubles with bullying during his walk home from school in Los Angeles. At home, the boy appears uninterested and frustrated at the Mexican traditions and customs around him, and even daydreams of driving a fast convertible and listening to rock music at the kitchen table. When he drifts off to sleep in his bed with his gaming device in hand, the scenery shifts toward what appears to be a videogame world blending digital aesthetics and traditional Mexican textiles and iconography.

The protagonist advances through a series of videogame levels until sees his deceased Tata (grandfather) as a live character that presents a bag full of tools (a guitarrón, a nopali, a sombrero, a piñata, and a tortilla) for him to combat the forthcoming adversaries in the game world. With his grandfather's blessing, he advances several levels thanks to his customary maneuvers such as the "nopilazo" and the "tortillazo" which he throws at his obstacles who resemble cactus zombies.

Finally, in a beam of light, he rises up to the final level where he is confronted with the bully as the ultimate videogame "boss." Face to face, the main character closes his eyes and activates all of the tools in his bag. Increasing in size as the bully shrinks, the boy raises up his fist in an empowering gesture as his Tata smiles with approval. Having awakened from the dream state, the boy stares confidently into the camera, his feet planting on the ground. He leaves his room, hugs his abuela, waves to his father, and runs triumphantly through his neighborhood, with the landscape of downtown Los Angeles further ahead.

MESTIZA CONSCIOUSNESS IN *SUPER CILANTRO GIRL* AND "TATA'S GIFT"

Both *Super Cilantro Girl* and "Tata's Gift" feature the dream state in the stories and suggest leaks between the waking and dreaming dimensions. In the case of *Super Cilantro Girl*, Esmeralda wakes up from her dream near the end of the book and realizes that her mother has arrived in the middle of the night, apparently without Esmeralda's interference.

Although a more superficial reading of this scene could suggest that the heroic activism of a Chicano child is only possible in a dream world, a closer look at the text reads: "green feathers drift from the cups of lilies light and slow. And outside the window, a bird with a crooked beak pecks at the glass, then flies high over the green-green cilantro patch, free and *sin fronteras*" (p. 31). Perhaps Esmeralda's heroic journey erased the U.S. and Mexican border after all, and/or her dream allowed her to envision and resolve the hybrid cultural tools of her *mestiza consciousness*.

The presence of the bird with the crooked beak (who accompanies Esmeralda in the illustrations throughout her dream journey) suggests another nomadic subject that could function as both her guardian in the spirit world and a witness on the material plane. The illustrations also depict a blurring of reality and possibility when the cilantro-colored feathers seem to be floating into the bouquet of calla lilies. The birds painted on the vase of lilies appear to be flying off the surface, another sign of the transgression of borders between the dimensions of the dream world and the waking state.

Clues from the text and the illustrations near the conclusion of the story suggest that Esmeralda's dream world has blurred over into the waking state, which recognizes Esmeralda's visions of herself as a super heroine equipped with an activated set of tools and abilities from her heritage as well as her existence as a Chicana child in a contemporary context.

Similar to the conclusion of *Super Cilantro Girl*, the aftermath of the boy's victory within the videogame dream trickles into his waking life. The viewer takes note of this when a photograph of his Tata smiles wider as the child's abuela turns and looks knowingly at the picture, having just received a hug from her grandson.

This scene, along with the animated style and textures of the film both inside and outside of the dream sequence, suggests a harmony of playfulness and materiality that children can perceive more than adults, especially if they are navigating the complex world of cultural identity in spaces such as Los Angeles, California. Like Esmeralda Sinfronteras, the boy's love for contemporary videogames in his waking life blends with his heritage through his Tata to provide a hybrid space for problem solving through play and consciousness-building.

GLORIA ANZALDÚA, MESTIZA CONSCIOUSNESS, AND CHILDREN'S LITERATURE ACTIVISM

Super Cilantro Girl and "Tata's Gift" are both stories of optimism and encouragement for young audiences as well as adults who sympathize with the complex plight of children as cultural minorities in the United States. In the case of the young Chicano protagonists featured in these works, both of their problems and creative solutions bear likeness to the vision of *mestiza consciousness* that Gloria Anzaldúa describes in her chapter, "La conciencia de la mestiza/Towards a New Consciousness" in her book, *Borderlands/La Frontera* (1987). The *mestiza consciousness* is a state of being but also a project of activism in which the ambivalence of cultural, racial, political, and spiritual influences within one body create an inner restlessness that achieve a transcendence of dualities that have historically dominated and divided the oppressors and the oppressed. Anzaldúa upholds *mestiza consciousness* as an example of a multifaceted approach in which all minorities can find a way to participate as a collective consciousness to eventually erase *la frontera*.

The *frontera* (border) that is geographic, racial, gendered, and identifying can be evaded, blurred, erased, and even decorated with a revolutionary stance of ambiguity, just as Esmeralda Sinfronteras did when she reforested and therefore eliminated the geographic border between Mexico and the United States. In fact, Esmeralda's last name, Sinfronteras, dialogues appropriately with Anzaldúa's advice: "To survive the Borderlands you must live sin fronteras (and) be a crossroads" (p. 217). This embodiment of *mestiza consciousness* in young people and in adults prepares consciousness to be flexible and permissive to the contradictions and multiplicity of voices that inform the hybrid subject. Eventually, Anzaldúa visualizes "a massive uprooting of dualistic thinking in the individual and collective consciousness is the beginning of a long struggle, but one that could, in our best hopes, bring us to the end of rape, of violence, of war" (102).

The protagonist of "Tata's Gift" also activates this borderland as he embraces the cultural gifts from his Tata as a means of standing up to an oppressor in a videogame setting. These rehearsals of dream-activism serve as pre-performances of *mestiza consciousness* in a space without borders that can potentially activate agency in the waking state riddled with border problems.

Anzaldúa's vision of the border is more than a line, but that of a third culture which is a border culture that is seeking a *retorno* and a hybrid subject who embodies *mestiza consciousness* to revolutionize these spaces. Both Esmeralda Sinfronteras and the protagonist of "Tata's Gift" are examples of dream-children with *mestiza consciousness* who navigate multiple dimensions by piecing together elements of their specific worlds and performing hybrid resolutions.

CHILDREN'S LITERATURE AS A SITE OF CRITICAL ENGAGEMENT

While cultural works for children are often overlooked when considering cultural representation and activism, the impact of children's literature on young readers should be recognized as a source of potential influence and empowerment. In her article about resistance strategies in bilingual children's literature, Taran Johnston emphasizes: "Not only is children's literature politically charged and historically generated, but it actively shapes consciousness, which in turn shapes action" (p. 45). This is to say that when adults read to children, or when children read for themselves, consciousness is being constructed and embedded that could lead toward future activism or behaviors.

Among other theorists and academics who write for young readers such as Chela Sandoval and Cherríe Moraga, Gloria Anzaldúa specifically reached out to Latina/o and bilingual children in her picture books *Friends from the Other Side/Amigos del otro lado* (1993) and *Prietita and the Ghost Woman/ Prietita y la Llorona* (1995). In an interview with Karin Ikas, Anzaldúa discusses her focus on writing for children:

> I also want Chicano kids to hear stuff about *la Llorona*, about the border, et cetera, as early as possible. . . . With my children's books I want to provide them with more knowledge about their roots and, by doing so, give them the chance to choose. To choose whether they want to be completely assimilated, whether they want to be border people, or whether they want to be isolationists. (p. 234)

Anzaldúa recognized children as dwellers in a state that she called "conocimiento" or "la facultad" (Rebolledo, 2006, p. 281). *La facultad* that Anzaldúa refers to is an extra sensitivity that marginalized populations have as a matter of survival under oppressive circumstances. Seeking to reach out to *la facultad* in her young readers, Anzaldúa wrote her children's books to resurrect Chicano and Mexican mythologies, and to recount her childhood adventures in order to, in her words: "encourage children to look beneath the surface of what things seem to be in order to discover the truths that may be hidden" (*Interviews*, 39).

Thus, the dream state of the Chicano child in *Super Cilantro Girl* and "Tata's Gift" is not so much a Freudian revelation of the oppressed subconscious desire as it could be a state of pretend in which the dreamer is rehearsing their *facultad*, or an early stage of *mestiza consciousness*.

This practice of visualization and manifestation evokes Anzaldúa's words (1987): "Awareness of our situation must come before inner changes, which in turn come before changes in society. Nothing happens in the 'real' world unless it first happens in the images in our heads" (p. 109). This progression from dreaming to activism is a part of *mestiza consciousness* that can be empowering for young Chicana/o readers who struggle with similar problems to those of Esmeralda Sinfronteras and the boy in "Tata's Gift."

Both stories discussed in this chapter include an activation of *mestiza consciousness* that occur within the dream state of the Chicano child regardless of gender or age. The successful resolutions of the protagonists' problems in the dreams are not only limited to those realities, but are empowering messages to encourage Chicano children to embrace their cultural identities, regardless of how hegemonic discourses in the United States might not value a Chicana superhero with cilantro-colored hair or a Chicano boy who throws magical tortillas at cactus zombies in a videogame. These playful and imaginative stories that represent Chicano children can affect young readers who read them, and they can further complicate and inform the discourses that affect children and their developing agency as future adults in a diverse world.

CLASSROOM APPLICATIONS OF DREAM-TO-ACTIVISM LITERATURE AND *MESTIZA CONSCIOUSNESS*

Within the K-12 classroom, critical literacy is a pedagogical tool that acknowledges the power dynamics of texts as well as the agency of readers. When students look at literature or cultural products with a critical lens, Jones (2006) explains that "it is an understanding that language practices and texts are always informed by ideological beliefs and perspectives whether conscious or otherwise" (p. 65). Critical literacy practices dive deeper than reading comprehension activities since "critically literate students have mastered the ability to read and critique the messages in texts in order to better understand whose knowledge is being privileged" (Norris et al., 2012, p. 61).

Both of the Chicano cultural works discussed in this article can serve as sites for critical literacy and analysis with children and young adults in a Language Arts setting as well as part of a Cultural or Ethnic Studies program.

I propose two different activities for middle grades students (ranging from grades 5–8) that require a varying amount of preparation and materials depending on the resources available to teachers.

As a supplement to viewing both *Super Cilantro Girl* and "Tata's Gift" in the classroom, the following questions can be a guide for students to preview and/or review the book and film as a discussion or a journaling activity:

- What is the difference between dreaming and thinking while you're awake? What are some common things that are said about dreams in movies or songs that we know? Why do you think dreaming is important?
- Why do you think we dream at night? Why is dreaming different or the same as real life? Have you ever dreamt about something that came true? Is that possible? Why or why not?
- Did you ever have a problem, and then you dreamt about how to solve it? Why could it be better to dream about it first when you're sleeping?
- Did you ever have a problem, and wished you were a super hero to solve it? What super power do you want to make the world better? What do you think super heroes dream about?

ACTIVITY PROPOSAL FOR MIDDLE-GRADE LANGUAGE ARTS CLASSROOM

Over the span of a few days (or a weekend), students will keep a dream-journal about their dreams and/or write down the dreams of their family members. Teachers may want to find examples of dream journaling or short videos that discuss dream journaling beforehand. Dream journaling could be useful for writing practices since the process of writing down dreams can serve as a template for arranging events in a narrative order since dreams do not always follow a chronological sequence, or even playing with rearranging sequences for the story to "make sense" or for it "not to make sense."

Once the dreams have been written down and brought into class, students can even interpret dreams by reading about common dream scenarios as a research component to the activity. To connect the activity to *Super Cilantro Girl* and "Tata's Gift," students can write letters to the protagonists in the works to describe their dreams and make connections with the characters' dreams in the stories. In response to the letters written to the protagonists, other students can research the significance of dreams in Mexican and Chicano traditions to answer the letters. For a creative written product, students can use the collection of dream journals or dream interpretations as inspiration for creative writing by using dream-like elements as central components for a poem, short story, or visual art activity that relates back to the students' lives and cultures.

ACTIVITY PROPOSAL FOR MIDDLE-GRADE ETHNIC STUDIES/CULTURAL STUDIES CLASSROOM

After viewing both works in Spanish and/or English, students can imagine themselves as super hero(ine)s and write and illustrate themselves into a blank storyboard or comic strip with cloze passages from *Super Cilantro Girl*. To complete the cloze passages, students can fill in their own key words in Spanish or English that point to their influences that help them solve problems that are concerning to them. The cloze passages are helpful since they incorporate Juan Felipe Herrera's literary structures and patterns in *Super Cilantro Girl* and provide a structure that will be more manageable for creative writing and structuring for middle grades students outside of a Language Arts classroom, while still incorporating cultural description and imaging.

Like *Super Cilantro Girl* and "Tata's Gift," the students should decorate their super hero(ine) selves with items that are important to them and their family's cultural heritage. As an extension of the activity, students can even dress up or bring in props to embody their own version of a super hero(ine) and give presentations in Spanish and/or English about their missions in an in-class or out-of-class setting.

In both of the activities proposed, critical reading is taking place in the form of self-reflection in the prereading and postreading discussion questions, as well as in the creation of a product that personally connects with the dream state and *mestiza consciousness* demonstrated by the protagonists in *Super Cilantro Girl* and "Tata's Gift." By creating a product with a specific voice informed by a young person's personal influences and dreams, this is one such example of a practice through critical reading and creativity of Anzaldúa's *mestiza consciousness*. In describing an activist approach of mestiza consciousness, she advises the following:

> At some point, on our way to a new consciousness, we will have to leave the opposite bank, the split between the two mortal combatants somehow healed so that we are on both shores at once and, at once, see through serpent and eagle eyes. Or perhaps we will decide to disengage from the dominant culture, write it off altogether as a lost cause, and cross the border into a wholly new and separate territory. Or we might go another route. The possibilities are numerous once we decide to act and not react. (*La conciencia de la mestiza*/Towards a New Consciousness, 101)

This permissible and multifaceted approach to problem solving and critical engagement of *mestiza consciousness* is not limited to adults but also extended to the developing consciousness and activism of children as dwellers in the geographic borderlands, but also between borders of symbolic language and ordering. The inclusion of multicultural children's narratives as sites of critical engagement for adults and young people alike is increasingly important in K-12 classrooms (and beyond) in order to provide examples and pathways to fluid and tolerant postures of activism rather than reactions to rigid discourses of hegemony.

CONCLUSION

When bell hooks was asked in a *New York Times* interview this year how she believes theory can function as a place of healing, she responded, "I always start with children. Most children are amazing critical thinkers before we silence them" (2015). This statement about the colonization of the child's mind by adults insists that research and activism revisit the assumptions that children's literature only belongs in a classroom setting, or that a simplistic message lacks depth in the world of children and adults alike. Terry Eagleton also comments on the role of children in *The Significance of Theory*: "Children make the best theorists, since they have not yet been educated into accepting our routine social practices as 'natural'" (1990). More scholarly research in fields beyond Pedagogy and Literacy Education is acknowledging the legitimacy of cultural products for children and young adults as an important site of understanding key topics such as human and language development, child psychology, power dynamics, political and social ideologies, as well as race, class, and gender subjectivities for young persons.

As a scholar who hopes to research and contribute to the genre of Latina/o children's and young adult's literature in relation to cultural identity in the United States, the recognition and critique of multicultural works meant for children must acknowledge the power of the messages sent to young readers navigating worlds mapped out by adults.

REFERENCES

Anzaldúa, G. (1999). *Borderlands/La Frontera: The new mestiza* (3rd ed.). San Francisco: Aunt Lute Books.

Ceballos, D., & Do-Rodriguez, M. (Producers). (2015, October 20). *Tata's Gift* [Video file]. Retrieved from https://www.youtube.com/watch?v=hlGEjj394FM

Felipe Herrera, J. (2015, October 9). First Latino US poet Laureate Juan Felipe Herrera on migrant farmworkers, the border and Ayotzinapa [Interview]. Retrieved April 26, 2016, from http://www.democracynow.org/2015/10/9/first_latino_us_poet_laureate_juan

Herrera, J. F., & Tapia, H. R. (2003). *La Súperniña del Cilantro/Super cilantro girl*. San Francisco: Tapia.

Jones, S. (2006). *Girls, social class, and literacy: What teachers can do to make a difference*. Portsmouth, NH: Heinemann.

Keating, A. (2008). *Entre mundos/among worlds: New perspectives on Gloria E. Anzaldúa*. New York: Palgrave Macmillan.

Norris, K., Lucas, L., & Prudhoe, C. (2012). Examining critical literacy: Preparing preservice teachers to use critical literacy in the early childhood classroom. *Multicultural Education, 19*(2), 59–62.

Rebolledo, T. (2006). Prietita y el Otro Lado: Gloria Anzaldúa's Literature for Children. *PMLA, 121*(1), 279–84.

Schatz, S. L. (2015). Lewis Carroll's dream-child and Victorian child psychopathology. *Journal of the History of Ideas, 76*(1), 93–114.

Yancy, G. (2015, December 10). Bell Hooks: Buddhism, the beats and loving blackness. *The New York Times*. Retrieved December 11, 2015, from http://opinionator.blogs.nytimes.com/2015/12/10/bell-hooks-buddhism-the-beats-and-loving-blackness/?_r=0

Chapter 11

Translanguaging *con mi abuela*: Chican@ Children's Literature as a Means to Elevate Language Practices in Our Homes

Laura Alamillo

> The rest of the winter, while Mami and Papi are at work, Abuela waits for me to get home from school. Then we bundle up thick socks and handmade sweaters to walk to the park and toss bread to the sparrows. My *espanol* is not good enough to tell her the things an abuela should know. Like how I am the very best in art and how I can run as fast as the boys. And her English is too *poquito* to tell me the stories I want to know about Abuelo and the rivers that ran outside their door.—Mango, Abuela and Me by Meg Medina and Angela Dominguez

In this story by Meg Medina and Angela Dominguez (2015), Mia's abuela visits the family every winter leaving behind her home "between two snaking rivers." Language loss and language revitalization is a central theme in this story transforming into language lessons between Abuela and Mia.

As we look deeper into this story, monoglossic views on bilingualism, language loss and societal normatives on language underpin the playful story in Mango, Abuela, and Me. This chapter expands on previous work (Alamillo & Arenas, 2012) on accuracy and authenticity in which I codeveloped considerations when evaluating Latino children's literature.

This chapter examines the way in which Chican@ literature appropriates language as heteroglossic, drawing on children's ways of knowing, sharing, and being closer to the complex and diverse multilayered forms of communication found in Chican@ homes. I argue that the medium of text highlights the tensions that happen when monoglossic approaches are privileged.

It also examines Chican@ children's literature investigating the ways that this appropriates translanguaging practices, interconnectedness, and leverages community funds of knowledge in particular from grandmothers and children. Chican@ children's literature provides for the cultural and linguistic transborder crossing with historical roots that comprise a mixing, *el mestizaje*, of English, Spanish, Calo, Chicano Spanish, and Chicano English, and the cultural, historical, sociocritical voices, and lived experiences of Chican@ families in the United States (Anzaldua, 1987).

The literature surfaces themes that are central to Chican@ families such as interdependence between generations, family, and community. It also privileges the heritage ways of knowing and being of Chican@ children, a *conocimiento* that draws on community and the interconnected funds of knowledge of families (Moll, 2006).

Chican@ children's literature counters deficit contextual elements that make up the ecology of schools, surfacing the tensions and offering the possibility for counternarratives (Yosso, 2006) and the emergence of a third space. Language loss (Wong-Fillmore, 1991), hybridity (Gutiérrez, Baquedano-López, & Tejeda, 1999), language maintenance, and translanguaging (Garcia, 2014) are prevalent issues discussed in the literature.

An analysis of three examples *Nana's Big Surprise* by Amada Irma Perez, *Grandma and Me at the Flea* by Juan Felipe Herrera, and *Mango, Abuela and Me* by Meg Medina presents diverse language practices between grandmothers and grandchildren in the context of monoglossic language beliefs and practices in our schools. The authors beautifully tell stories of relationships between grandchildren and grandparents, demonstrating the acceptance of children's language practices and how children navigate their everyday language practices.

The abuelas are agents of change in the lives of their grandchildren by using and accepting translanguaging in the exchanges with their grandchildren. As agents of speech/social change, the relationships and their language practices used counter the raciolinguistic ideologies (Flores & Rosa, 2015) existing in our society.

Anzaldua (1987) describes *el mestizaje* as being neither accepted in the United States or Mexico in terms of language use and cultural identification. "Because I, a mestiza, continually walk out of one culture and into another, because I am in all cultures at the same time, alma entre dos mundos, tres, cuatro, me zumba la cabeza, con lo contradictorio. Estoy norteada por todas las voces que me hablan simultaneamente" (p. 77). Chican@ children's literature provides a space where children can see the various language practices they engage in with family and community.

It promotes and validates the *conocimiento* they acquire in their homes interacting with family, abuelos, and community. The final area the literature draws on are funds of knowledge connections. Family are experts in the lives of their children. In these examples, the abuelas are the sources of knowledge and agents of speech as they interact with their grandchildren in the language(s) situated in the task.

CURRENT CONTEXT OF RESTRICTIVE LANGUAGE SPACES

Policies such as English for the Children (Proposition 227) (Gandara & Contreras, 2009), deficit views of linguistically and culturally diverse children (Flores, Cousin, & Diaz, 1991), and anti-immigrant rhetoric frame the context for understanding the importance of providing a space to use Chican@ children's literature.

Flores describes the historical context embedded in policies that attempt to eradicate nondominant languages by imposing policy goals centered on monolingual English criteria ignoring the multilingual, multicultural funds of knowledge children and families bring to classrooms.

A UCLA professor asked preservice teachers to consider, when a student presents themselves with their *maletas* (suitcases) filled with family, culture, language, and community at the entrance to the classroom door, will the teacher allow each *maleta* into the classroom. How does the teacher decide which *maleta* comes in or not and what informs these decisions?

Classrooms that allow for all the richness of students' cultural and linguistic heritage and everyday knowledge facilitate expansive ways of knowing and leveraging students' repertoires of practice (Gutierrez, 2008). Garcia and Wei (2013) describe the contradictions between describing bilingualism based on monoglossic views of bilingualism, "from the perspective of bilingual people themselves, nothing is dual, nothing is simply two, or just three, or even more" (p. 100).

Despite Garcia's approach to viewing bilingualism, schools continue to describe emergent bilingual children as English Learners (EL or ELLs), Limited English Proficient (LEP), and Standard English Learners (SEL). These labels deny the linguistic complexity of Chican@ children and perpetuate monoglossic understandings of bilingualism. Garcia argues for schools to transform their perceptions surrounding how they approach bilingualism to "translanguaging as a bilingual pedagogy."

Official policy such as Proposition 227 in California placed many parameters on how emergent bilingual children learn and maintain Spanish and English. When it passed in 1987, schools began the difficult process in deciding what to do with Spanish curriculum including Spanish language textbooks and bilingual children's books. There was little direction on what to do after the initiative was passed. Many schools threw out literature in fear they would be penalized for having Spanish textbooks. The initiative institutionalized restrictive language policies and set in place dominant contextual normative structures that continue to play a role in how language is used in the classroom.

The current views on bilingualism and language development are driven by policies such as 227, outdated pedagogical theories to teach language, and by societal expectations of assimilation and acclimation for emergent bilingual children. These views also stem from deficit views of families who speak two languages. As a result, as an act of social justice, Chican@ children's literature authors are playing out these themes in their literature for young children.

Flores and Rosa (2015) describe raciolinguistic biases that determine how fluency is defined within our society. These biases shape how bilingualism is viewed in our society and further stigmatize the use of Spanish in our society. Schools also impact these strict views regarding multilingualism by perpetuating these biases in their curriculum and assessments. For example, in Spanish, dual language immersion (DLI) programs, children are taught Spanish and English in strict, structured 90/10 or 50/50 models.

Teachers also enforce this strict separation by not allowing children to speak Spanish during English time and vice versa. Contrary to research on second language development, dual language instruction continues to follow this model.

The restrictive language spaces in the classroom and predominance of English in United States, English-only policies transpired into bilingual education advocates in appropriating monoglossic structures to privilege minority languages in DLI programs. Bilingual teachers in DLI classrooms teach language by keeping them separate throughout the day.

A common practice is for bilingual teachers to privilege the target language structuring of their programs so as to appear to students as monolingual speakers mindful of their use of language in the presence of students so as to not allow young dual language learners the knowledge that they are English speakers. Many DLI teachers keep this strict separation of language in order to "ensure" fluency in two languages.

Informal restrictive language policies perpetuate this notion that children aren't fluent or proficient if they speak Chicano English, Chicano Spanish, or any other variety. Garcia's (2014) theory of translanguaging presents a more realistic notion of how emergent bilinguals speak two languages. Garcia's lens provides a space to view bilingual children as learning two languages in dynamic and fluid spaces. It also elevates various forms of bilingualism in our society.

This chapter highlights the purposeful inclusion of these linguistic practices in Emergent Bilingual families and how Chican@ children's literature authors present thoughtful and accurate representations on how Chican@ families talk in their communities. The authors use translanguaging as a means to elevate the use of two languages by speakers of Spanish and English. The use of Chican@ books such as these in classrooms with young children is an act of social justice. The literature offers a means for countering raciolinguistic ideologies and disrupts the deficit monolingual language discourse in schools.

Chican@ children's literature serves as a tool to reinforce student's voices and rich varied linguistic practices presenting an alternative to conceptions of language development idealized as optimally occurring in rigid and separate spaces. Instead, we see literature representing a more realistic picture of how Chican@ children talk in everyday conversations with friends, family, and their community. Children's talk is socially constructed (Gee, 2015) and not developed hierarchically by strict models in first and second language development, but instead according to the social context (speakers, community, etc.).

"El Mestizaje, Toward a New Consciousness"

Garcia, Johnson, and Seltzer (2016) leverage translanguaging in the classroom by developing a practical way to apply it in the classroom. Translanguaging can be seen as theory not applicable to the classroom. "An approach to bilingualism that is centered not on languages as has been the case, but on the practices of bilinguals that are readily observable. These worldwide translanguaging practices are seen here not as marked or unusual, but rather taken for what they are, namely the normal mode of communication that, with some exceptions in some monolingual enclaves characterizes communities around the word" (44).

Translanguaging pedagogy as Garcia describes moves teachers in to viewing language practices as "translanguaging corriente, dynamic translanguaging progressions and finally translanguaging pedagogy" (p. xi). Translanguaging is a "*corriente*" means it flows in classrooms. Garcia describes it as not always seen but always flowing constantly and consistently.

Teachers can observe this corriente by "stepping back" and watching and listening to children in the playground, in their communities, with their parents and siblings. These conversations untap this corriente that is not fixed but moving steadily throughout the day. Instead of correcting this *corriente*, a translanguaging teacher allows it and brings in tools to nurture and leverage the flow of language in everyday practices. "A translanguaging stance sees the emergent bilingual child's complex language repertoire as a resource not as a deficit" (p. xiii).

Chican@ children's literature are tools that leverage these practices and counter the status quo. Translanguaging constructs a social space for bilingual individuals within families and communities that enables them to bring together all their language and cultural practices. Translanguaging in the context of raciolinguistic ideologies and archaic descriptions of language development is essential in order to understand the importance of the use of translanguaging in Chican@ children's literature.

Placing the literature in the context of current ideologies in schooling of emergent bilingual children and in addition to restrictive language policies in schools, current ideologies restrict the acceptance of children code-switching, translating, and hybrid language practices. Emergent bilinguals are defined as deficient or not fluent in either language. Chican@ children who are often emerging bilinguals are restricted in how they communicate in classrooms that restrict translanguaging practices. These norms counter current research in second language development and restrict identity development of Chican@ children.

Palmer and Martinez (2016) reexamine "what teachers need to know about language" by having teachers look at language as practice, "language as a form of action, that emerges in particular social and cultural context" (p. 381). They argue that emergent bilinguals "do bilingualism" and that children engage in hybridity as a normal function of bilingualism.

Bilingual children switch naturally from one language to another as a normal way of communicating. Dual language teachers should be aware of language variations, language development as dynamic and not compartmentalized into separate language systems. Understanding that language is dynamic, not static, and socially constructed is essential in classrooms where bilingual children can feel at ease in showing their understanding of classroom content.

Moving away from strict rules in language separation allow Chican@ children to thrive in school and also in identity development. Flores and Rosa (2015) also critique "appropriateness-based approaches to language diversity in education." Flores and Rosa question the additive approaches to education by critiquing the underlying "appropriateness" of language use that lies at the core of additive approaches.

Flores and Rosa propose undoing appropriateness in language education and not using standard forms at the comparison. Instead, classrooms must "engage, confront and ultimately dismantle" the racialized hierarchy in U.S. society by engaging in critical language discussions.

Chican@ children's literature disrupts raciolinguistic ideologies. The text opens a space for Chican@ children to become critical language detectives and develop a critical language awareness in order to investigate the many forms of language use in their communities. Chican@ authors and illustrators such as Juan Felipe Herrera, Amada Irma Perez, and Gloria Anzaldua challenge these norms in the illustrations and text. Authors challenge the raciolinguistic ideologies by presenting heteroglossic examples of bilingualism.

Nana's Big Surprise

Nana's Big Surprise (Irma Pérez, 2007), depicts an elderly, Spanish-speaking grandmother who visits her grandchildren. "Nana had been lonely and sad every since our grandfather, Tata, died. But in just a week, Nana would arrive by bus all the way from Mexicali. The coop was a special surprise for her—she knew everything about raising chickens. I just knew our coop would make her smile." The family decided to build her a chicken coop to welcome nana to their home.

Nana is at the forefront of the story countering stereotypical, Mexican grandmothers as docile and weak. The children are concerned she may not like it in the United States, and feel out of place. The chicken coop may help her adjust. The story depicts everyday experiences of Chican@ children having family from Mexico visiting in their homes. They are excited, hopeful, and view the visit in a positive manner. "Finally the day arrived when we all piled into our old blue station wagon and drove to meet Nana at the bus station. There she is! I cried. Through the window, I could see Nana's flowered *rebozo*. It was strange not seeing Tata next to her."

The author demonstrates the excitement in these visits and describes nana as the "expert" in the family. Translanguaging is used as a means to elevate and leverage the use of two languages in this dynamic and fluid manner. "Translanguaging is the discursive norm in bilingual families and communities. For example, the only way to communicate in bilingual/multilingual family events is to translanguage.... A bilingual family conversation about school might take place with speakers selecting features associated with the language dominant in society; whereas the same speakers, when conversing about intimate relationships might select very different features" (23).

The characters in the text use two languages to communicate in the story. The characters translanguage in this unique third space and present a more realistic example as to how Chican@ children and families interact.

> I remember Tata selling fruits and vegetables at the *mercado*, weighing them on his scale that looked like a cradle.
> There she is! I cried. Through the bus window, I could see Nana's familiar flowered *rebozo*. It was strange not seeing Tata next to her.
> Back at home again, we brought Nana to the backyard. Her sad eyes grew huge when she saw the chicken coop. *Mis nietecitos*, what a beautiful surprise.
> Nana smiled and said, *Familia mia,* I want you all to know that I will remember this time forever-even after I die. And we all hugged our Nana for a long, long time.

There are numerous examples of translanguaging throughout the text. Perez chose to use Spanish in the text in order to effectively communicate the character's thoughts and feelings. The story is bilingual yet Perez chose to use Spanish in the English portion of the story. Words like *rebozo*, *mercado*, *nietecitos*, and *familia* are not translated.

These words are not translated into English because they are closely tied to their connection with their grandmother. This space allows for translanguaging to take place in *Nana's Big Surprise.*

GRANDMA AND ME AT THE FLEA, *LOS MEROS MEROS REMATEROS*

"I love *remates*—flea markets—earthy makeshifts stores under big skies. When I was a child in California's San Joaquin Valley, remates were my favorite playgrounds. Our routine was always the same. My *mamá Lucha* and my *papi Felipe* would stop and and buy me a net-bag of juicy oranges. . . . At the remate I was one big family. When I saw children running around the booth, I joined them, and my heart felt happy and free."—Herrera writes from personal experience in many of his children's books.

This book takes him back to his childhood in Fresno, visiting the *remate* with his family. The remate reminds him of his family, his childhood, and his experiences with culture and language. These feelings are portrayed when he tells the story of a young boy visiting the *remate* with his grandmother. Herrera, Rohmer, and Cumpiano (2002) describe the grandma as a *mera mera rematera*.

The grandchild joins his grandmother in the flea market to learn how to sell and bargain with the vendors. Grandma starts the engine. "A real *rematero* makes times for songs!" she says in her husky voice, and winks at me. Herrera tells the story of the remateros in poetic words. The author uses Spanish throughout the story, sometimes translating the word immediately following the Spanish word. Herrera's play with words gives the reader access to both languages.

> *Danny makes funny faces and his pants always fall down, just like Cantinflas, the goofy comedian from Mexico. Floribey loves to read telenovelas, like photo comic books.*
>
> > *They laugh at my buzzed-off hair.*
> > *Pelon! They call me—baldy.*
> > *Follow me! I yell out around the Flea booths.*
> > *I wave a churro like a baton.*

Herrera's use of translanguaging leverages the language practices used between the grandmother and the grandson. The boy waves his *churro* like a baton reminding readers of buying *churros* at their local *remate* and it also allows readers to connect with the boy's experiences of visiting the *remate* with family.

Mango, Abuela, and Me

Medina and Dominguez portray an alternative depiction of a relationship between a child and her abuela. Unlike *Nana's Big Surprise* and *Grandma and Me at the Flea*, *Mango, Abuela and Me* touches on critical issues of language loss and the disconnect grandchildren encounter with Spanish-speaking grandparents. Wong-Fillmore (1991) describes the implications of learning a second language at the expense of losing their first language.

Children of immigrant parents may disconnect with grandparents due to losing the first language. Wong Fillmore describes language as the means to bridge connections between various generations within the family structure. Language loss contributes to a loss of family structure resulting in stress, anxiety, and emotional distress between family members.

Medina and Dominguez provide a space for the child and the grandparent to communicate despite this "obstacle." Instead, the two come together by teaching and sharing the language(s) that bring them together.

IMPLICATIONS FOR THE CLASSROOM

Martinez (1981) in his approach to Raza and Community Mental Health describes a bilingual child, Juanito, who first entered school with excitement and eagerness.

> Class, this is *Johnny*. Johnny come take a seat. (1981, p. 10).
> The family noticed a change in Juanito, he complained about going to school.
> Juanito jumped in alarm at the words he did not understand. Desperately searching for something familiar to help stop the pounding in his chest and the laughing in his ears, he turned his thoughts to the rainbow of the serape, the warmth in the virgencitas face, the strength in his abuelas eyes. He recalled the magic in the letters, JUANITO, as she wrote them on this brown bag.
> Now, every morning he complained of a head, tooth, or stomachache so he could stay home. He repeatedly asked why his abuela or *ama* couldn't be his teacher. The school teacher, through a translator, described him as culturally deprived or referring to him as having a language handicap. Speak English! Speak English! Some children like himself were quiet; others seemed to get angrier.
> How strange he thought that some no longer spoke Spanish and didn't recognize their names (p. 10).

Martinez tells the story of Juanito as an example of many school-aged *raza* children. Martinez describes *El No* as the internalization of children hearing in schools that they can't, or no *vales*, resulting in children not having the confidence to move forward.

These experiences shape their positive or negative outcomes in schooling. As we consider the socioemotional aspects of schooling, language acceptance influences children at all levels. Issues of language loss and monoglossic views on bilingualism ignore that language is tied to family, culture, and community.

Bilingual teachers who use Chican@ children's books that represent linguistic variation are taking into account the everyday talk of their emergent, Chican@, bilingual children. Children who speak two languages translanguage in their homes, with their parents, in their communities, and in the playground. Children are very much aware of these linguistic variations and are aware of who can and cannot participate in this fluid manner of speaking (Zentella, 1997).

Children like Juanito yearn to have educators who identify with them linguistically and culturally. Children flow between variations of English and Spanish with ease and no hesitation, very much aware of their speakers, listeners, and where the conversations were taking place.

Translanguaging in Chican@ children's literature validates and affirms the way children communicate within their own lives. The literature represents the heteroglossic ideologies in doing bilingualism. Instead of utilizing these skills in children, educators continue to keep languages separate. Baker (2001) describes translanguaging as an advantage in the classroom using it to challenge students cognitively. "It may promote a deeper and fuller understanding of the subject matter" (p. 64).

It not only promotes a deeper understanding, but it also provides a space for children to "digest" the material. Chican@ children's literature are tools that can be used to challenge students to think beyond the separation of languages. The text affirms and leverages language practices in their homes and communities.

In the literature presented, the authors presented *abuelas* and grandchildren as experts and language models. They challenge deficit views of emergent bilingual children by allowing a space for nontraditional representations of bilingual children. The text represents more accurate and authentic, heteroglossic representations of bilingualism.

INSTRUCTIONAL AND CLASSROOM RECOMMENDATIONS FOR TEACHERS OF CHICAN@, EMERGENT BILINGUALS

This section offers some instructional recommendations afforded when using Chican@ children's literature to transform classroom spaces both culturally and linguistically in ways that affirm and allow for the varied repertoires of practice (Gutierrez & Rogoff, 2003) that students bring to classrooms and the funds of knowledge (Moll, 2006) of the families that make up the ecology of classrooms.

1. Shift views on language development from monoglossic to heteroglossic views on bilingualism (Garcia, 2016).
2. Rethink, reexamine, and challenge labels and terms used to identify bilingual children. Terms such as EL, LEP, and SEL promote monoglossic ideologies and don't recognize the various language practices in children. It also implies children are letting go and leaving behind their first language.
3. Use all language practices as resources in the classrooms and not focus solely on moving or transitioning into Standard English. Instead, build critical language awareness in children to have them become critical language detectives in order to understand raciolinguistic ideologies in our society (Flores & Rosa, 2015).
4. Incorporate and use Chican@ children's literature as tools to build critical language awareness in children. Literature contributes to self-awareness and validates, leverages language use in their lives. It is a window to their world.
5. Incorporate a funds of knowledge lens into your teaching. *Abuelas, abuelos, tios, tias,* parents, and community are sources of knowledge and can be used as tools in promoting content in the classroom.

These instructional recommendations shift teaching practices to those that include a more transformative pedagogy, raise consciousness, and raise language awareness in linguistically and culturally diverse children. Chican@ children's literature with themes of abuelas and abuelos as funds of knowledge and agents of speech elevate a positive awareness of Chican@ families and the resources they bring into the classroom.

REFERENCES

Alamillo, L. A., & Arenas, R. (2012). Chicano children's literature: Using bilingual children's books to promote equity in the classroom. *Multicultural Education, 19*(4), 53.

Anzaldua, G. (1987). *Borderlands/La frontera*. San Francisco: Aunt Lute.

Baker, C. (2001). *Foundations of bilingual education and bilingualism*. Clevedon: Multilingual Matters Limited.

Barrera, R. B., Quiroa, R. E., & Valdivia, R. (2003). Spanish in Latino picture storybooks in English: Its use and textural effects. *Multicultural Issues in Literacy Research and Practice*, 145–65.

Barrera, R. B., Quiroa, R. E., & West-Williams, C. (1999). Poco a poco: The continuing development of Mexican American children's literature in the 1990s. *New Advocate, 12*, 315–30.

Flores, B., Cousin, P. T., & Diaz, E. (1991). Transforming deficit myths about learning, language, and culture. *Language Arts, 68*(5), 369–79.

Flores, N., & Rosa, J. (2015). Undoing appropriateness: Raciolinguistic ideologies and language diversity in education. *Harvard Educational Review, 85*(2), 149–71.

Fox, D. L., & Short, K. G. (2003). *Stories matter: The complexity of cultural authenticity in children's literature.* Urbana, IL: National Council of Teachers of English, 1111 W. Kenyon Road.

Gandara, P. C., & Contreras, F. (2009). *The Latino education crisis: The consequences of failed social policies.* Cambridge, MA: Harvard University Press.

García, O., & Wei, L. (2013). *Translanguaging: Language, bilingualism and education.* New York: Springer.

García, O., & Wei, L. (2014). Translanguaging and Education. In *Translanguaging: Language, Bilingualism and Education* (pp. 63–77). UK: Palgrave Macmillan.

Gee, J. (2015). *Social linguistics and literacies: Ideology in discourses.* New York: Routledge.

González, N., Moll, L. C., & Amanti, C. (Eds.). (2006). *Funds of knowledge: Theorizing practices in households, communities, and classrooms.* New York: Routledge.

Gutiérrez, K. D., Baquedano-López, P., & Tejeda, C. (1999). Rethinking diversity: Hybridity and hybrid language practices in the third space. *Mind, Culture, and Activity, 6*(4), 286–303.

Gutiérrez, K. D., & Rogoff, B. (2003). Cultural ways of learning: Individual traits or repertoires of practice. *Educational Researcher, 32*(5), 19–25.

Herrera, J. F., Rohmer, H., & Cumpiano, I. (2002). *Grandma and me at the flea.* San Francisco, CA: Children's Book Press.

Lewis, G., Jones, B., & Baker, C. (2012). Translanguaging: Origins and development from school to street and beyond. *Educational Research and Evaluation, 18*(7), 641–54.

Martinez, S. C. (1981). *Hijos Del Sol: An approach to Raza community mental health* (Vol. 1). Familia Counseling Service.

Medina, M., & Dominguez, A. (2015). *Mango, Abuela and Me.* Somerville, MA: Candlewick Press.

Palmer, D., & Martínez, R. A. (2013). Teacher agency in bilingual spaces a fresh look at preparing teachers to educate Latina/o bilingual children. *Review of Research in Education, 37*(1), 269–97.

Palmer, D. K., & Martínez, R. A. (2016). Developing Biliteracy: What do Teachers Really Need to Know about Language?. *Language Arts, 93*(5), 379.

Pérez, A. I. (2007). *Nana's big surprise.* San Francisco, CA: Children's Book Press.

Riojas Clark, E., Bustos Flores, B., Smith, H., & Gonzalez, D. (2016). *Multicultural literature for Latino bilingual children: Their words, their worlds.* New York: Rowman and Littlefield.

Wong-Fillmore, L. (1991). When learning a second language means losing the first. *Early Childhood Research Quarterly, 6*(3), 323–46.

Yosso, T. J. (2006). *Critical race counterstories along the Chicana/Chicano educational pipeline.* New York: Routledge.

Zentella, A. C. (1997). *Growing up bilingual: Puerto Rican children in New York.* New York: Wiley-Blackwell.

Chapter 12

Identity Texts in Linguistically and Culturally Sustaining Classrooms: Chican@ Children's Literature, Student Voice, and Identity

Lilian Cibils, Enrique Avalos, Virginia Gallegos, and Fabián Martínez

As educators focused on cultural responsiveness, high among our priorities are creating classrooms where the students' sense of belonging is strengthened in the teaching-learning process. The authors of this chapter embrace identity texts as a central component of a rich environment to foster student voice. Further, we propose that the close relationship between reading and writing warrants the expansion of the term *identity texts* (Cummins & Early, 2011)—which in the literature refers strictly to those created by students—to also include those works which serve as springboards for student reflection and the creation of their own texts.

We call identity texts, whether read/experienced or written/created by students—which are central to the development of voice, agency, and community in linguistically and culturally sustaining classrooms. It is within this framework and the context of our dynamic multilingual community in the Southwest Borderlands of the United States—where translanguaging (García, 2009; Baker, 2011; Lewis, Jones, & Baker, 2012) and codeswitching are everyday practices—that the incorporation of Chican@ children's and young adult literature to our curriculum becomes an organic part of the continuum of our lives inside and outside the classroom.

The present chapter emerged from our critical work in a graduate course in our TESOL/Bilingual Education program in which we problematized traditional theories of Second Language Acquisition (SLA) by reading them vis-à-vis Norton's work on identity. The coauthors of this piece participated in the class, Lilian as instructor, and Enrique, Virginia, and Fabián as students who also presented a panel on identity texts at a regional literacy conference. In our combined experience of teaching and learning in community, grade school, and university settings in the Southwest of the United States, the authors recognize the need to challenge static perspectives on culture and identity as a central factor in cultural responsiveness. Specifically, for us this implies promoting a shift away from monolithic and essentialist understandings of what being Latin@ means (Segura, 2007; Zavella, 1991).

As dynamic social constructs, culture and identity are in constant flux and subject to negotiation and redefinition through time and across contexts (Gutiérrez & Rogoff, 2003; Nieto, 2010). With our identity texts created in response to a selection of Chican@ children's literature—which are also included in our definition of identity texts—we hope to contribute nuance and texture to the larger tapestry of what constitutes being Latin@[1] teachers and students in the United States.

CONTEXTS:
THEORIES IN OUR GRADUATE CLASSROOM

Central to our reading of theory against the grain is a focus on the power dynamics at play and the negotiation of identities involved in the process of acquiring an additional language, especially after immigration. Norton (2013) shines a bright light on this gap in SLA theory, which has tended to keep understandings of the language acquisition process and considerations of its context separate. In her critical study, Norton insists on a focus on language learning as "socially, historically and politically constructed, and the classroom as a site of identity negotiation" (Norton, 2013, p. 15). Thus, Norton points to the significance of the strategic choices to be made, since "Particular pedagogical practices in language classrooms can either constrain or enable students in their reimagining possibilities for both the present and the future" (p. 17).

This collaborative piece was further inspired by the recent call for a culturally sustaining pedagogy to deepen the educational impact of the constructs of cultural responsiveness and relevance by continuing to build on their foundation (Paris, 2012; Paris & Alim, 2014; Ladson-Billings, 2014). Critical educators and scholars have long propelled a move away from subtractive and assimilative approaches and the resulting erasure of students' linguistic practices from US classrooms. Yet, there is a long way to go in our pedagogical orientations so as to make lasting inroads into the destructiveness of deficit discourses, since "the dominant society tries to maintain control by addressing minoritized students' underachievement itself, rather than turning to and learning directly from minoritized communities" (Sleeter, 2013, p. 254). In our college, K-12, and community teaching/learning settings, it is up to us educators to create spaces where students who may otherwise experience marginalization and isolation may instead be part of the process of building a sense of belonging in a community which embraces them.

Countering the assimilationist perspective often underlying the pedagogical models associated with Teaching English to Speakers of Other Languages (TESOL) requires an antideficit approach centered on human agency as one of its guiding premises (Valencia, 1997, p. 251). The development of such agency in the classroom calls for openness to students' expression of their thoughts and feelings within safe spaces where they are valued (Gay, 2010, p. 51). Thus, an authentic linguistically and culturally responsive pedagogy involves shifting the teacher-student relationship paradigm to create a genuinely student-centered environment by encouraging the emergence of student voice (Sleeter, 2013). Although the notion of student-centered classrooms is not new, it is imperative that we insist on its tight link to cultural responsiveness and student voice. In Knaus' (2013) words:

> Centering students in the classroom ultimately entails centering the cultural contexts students bring; developing voice allows other students (and teachers) to learn how culture operates on a daily basis in students' lives. The more focused a curriculum and teaching approaches are on developing student voice, the easier centering the cultures of the students will be. (p. 79)

Ladson-Billings (1998) defined culturally relevant pedagogy as a "theoretical model that not only addresses student achievement but also helps students to accept and affirm their cultural identity while developing critical perspectives that challenge inequities that schools (and other institutions) perpetuate" (p. 204). A culturally sustaining pedagogy further proposes creating spaces in teacher education in which our students can find ways "of both naming and conceptualizing the need to meaningfully value and maintain the practices of their students in the process of extending their students' repertoires of practice to include dominant language, literacies, and other cultural practices" (Paris, 2012, p. 95).

In working with emergent bilinguals in the United States, this demands of educators an approach akin to the balance described by Delpit (2006). In an equitable and empowering pedagogy, educators accept "the responsibility to teach, to provide for students who do not already possess them, the additional codes of power" while embracing the linguistic and cultural diversity of the community (Delpit, 2006, p. 40).

CONTEXTS: BILINGUAL EDUCATION AND TESOL IN NEW MEXICO

Our work in the US Borderlands with preservice and in-service teachers to encourage a culturally sustaining pedagogy may not differ from that carried out in other regions, in that it involves understanding students' backgrounds to strengthen the family-school connection by developing an antideficit perspective based on family and community funds of knowledge (González, Moll, & Amanti, 2005).

However, there is some singularity to our context. According to the US Census Bureau, in 2014, in the State of New Mexico, 36.2 percent of persons ages five and above spoke "a language other than English," and 28.8 percent of the population over five spoke Spanish at home (American FactFinder). Some of our teachers in training who have not experienced migration or immigration—even if earlier generations of their families have—may find themselves teaching students from migrant agricultural communities or recent immigrants in varied circumstances. Our program then provides opportunities for future teachers to enhance their insight and sensitivity and better support the learning processes of students in our context.

EXPANDING THE CONCEPT OF IDENTITY TEXTS AND CREATING COMMUNITY

In the search for creative means of encouraging the development of student voice and expanding the concept of literacy, several educators have proposed the notion of *identity texts* (Bernhard et al., 2006; Giampapa, 2010; Taylor & Cummins, 2011), defined in these terms:

> Identity texts described the products of students' creative work or performances carried out within the pedagogical space orchestrated by the classroom teacher. Students invest their identities in the creation of these texts—which can be written, spoken, signed, visual, musical, dramatic, or combinations in multimodal form. The identity text then holds a mirror up to students in which their identities are reflected back in a positive light. (Cummins & Early, 2011, p. 3)

At the center of this approach is the fostering of a sense of belonging and acceptance in classrooms where students experience being valued and thus become empowered in the process. Trust is a crucial component of such an environment as students may need to become vulnerable to speak their minds and embrace their own creativity. As the community of learners and the larger community celebrate their work, students are validated in the expression of their culture(s) and identities: "When students share identity texts with multiple audiences (peers, teachers, parents, grandparents, sister classes, the media, etc.) they are likely to receive positive feedback and affirmation of self in interaction with these audiences" (Cummins & Early, 2011, p. 3).

That reading and writing are tightly intertwined processes cannot be stressed enough. As Cixous (1993) expressed it over two decades ago: "Writing and reading are not separate, reading is a part of writing. A real reader is a writer. A real reader is already on the way to writing" (p. 21). Based on this interdependence, we propose expanding the concept of identity texts to include those texts that help students and teachers explore their lived stories, reflecting on who they are, where they come from, and where they are going.

The reading and creation of identity texts become community-building experiences where we learn about and from our students, and students from each other, where relationships are strengthened, and curriculum becomes relevant. In such communities, "Individual identity takes form in the contexts of relationships and dialogue; our concern must be to create the kinds of contexts that nurture—for all children—the sense of worthiness and agency" (Greene, 1995, p. 41). Thus, teachers allow themselves the opportunity to consider the work of children (as well as of youth and adults) who would otherwise be given deficit labels and to see instead their talent:

> to break the hold of some specific fixities and constructed categories, to let (as it were) specific children go. Attending concretely to these children in their difference and their connectedness, feeling called on truly to attend—to read the child's word, to look at the child's sketch—teachers may find themselves responding imaginatively and, at length, ethically to these children. To respond to those once called at risk, once carelessly marginalized, as living beings capable of choosing for themselves is, I believe, to be principled. (Greene, 1995, pp. 41–2)

A strong sense of community is created when students develop voice and agency through story-telling and writing stimulated by the power of carefully selected readings (Christensen, 2000).

IDENTITY TEXTS, CHICAN@ CHILDREN'S LITERATURE, AND DIVERSE VOICES IN THE CLASSROOM

In the rest of this chapter we illustrate the notion of identity texts, as we extend it beyond its original meaning of those authored by students, to encompass also works which serve as springboards and inspiration for writing and thus contribute to the creation of spaces of agency, voice, and empowerment. Our autobiographical pieces, crafted in response to texts from Chican@ children's and young adult literature, cut across space and time, crisscrossing different points in our lives, from scenes in our childhood to echoes from classrooms where we were sometimes students and sometimes teachers. Our texts are interlocked here with those of authors we have read in a counterpoint of voices of readers, writers, teachers, and students. Just as in music counterpoint results from individual melodic lines contributing to the texture of a piece, here each unique voice contributes to the art/work of being Latin@ teachers and students in the Southwest of the United States.

GARY SOTO'S ODES

One of the most cherished texts read with preservice bilingual teachers in one of Lilian's courses was "Ode to la Tortilla" from Gary Soto's *Neighborhood Odes* (1992). This poem abounds in evocative sensorial images such as "The tortillas are still warm/ In a dish towel,/ Warm as gloves just/ Taken off, finger by finger./ Mamá is rolling/Them out. The radio" (p. 4). This identity text created a space for reflection and sharing which would not have existed but for this reading.

Childhood reminiscences about growing up in the Southwest gave way to deeper conversations about intersecting identities of race, ethnicity, class, and gender. One student raised poignant questions of gender roles and different expectations which determined who among her siblings was in charge of preparing the tortillas when their mother was away. Another student discussed the significance of extended family in growing up, and the value of preparing a meal together for a special celebration. A basis for autobiographical writing, this text also fostered reflection on student voice and exploration of cultural identity in their own future classrooms.

Enrique, one of the coauthors and a Social Studies preservice teacher specializing in TESOL, was teaching within a practicum experience in two different ESL (English as a Second Language) adult education settings at the time he wrote his identity text. In it, Enrique relates to the scenes depicted in Soto's work through childhood memories as well as through his connection with his adult students who are learning English as he embraces the process of learning Spanish.

ENRIQUE'S REFLECTION ON "ODE TO THE SPRINKLER"

The poem I chose, "Ode to the Sprinkler" by Gary Soto (1992), describes in detail an episode in the life of a young person. The children do not have access to a swimming pool but make do with a sprinkler for recreation. After the child (the poetic persona) gets stung by a bee, the mother brings out Kool-Aid and the swollen toe eventually heals. My initial reaction to the piece was to remember similar scenes from my own childhood. Although I lived in several parts of the United States, on my vacations I would return to New Mexico where my cousins and I would find various ways to play, which often included water. One was using water to slide on a plastic surface, another one was running around the sprinkler.

The memories are fond, but they are also of competing identities. Returning to New Mexico and hearing my family speak Spanish, a language I do not speak, meant there was always a disconnect between me and my cousins.

They told jokes I did not understand and used phrases I had never heard. The poem, in its use of Spanish slang, elicited these memories and the feelings associated with them. In this context, it was difficult to assert myself in the dynamics of the group and have a voice.

For example, when a game was decided the roles we were to play were out of my control. I might have suggested something different, but because I could not speak Spanish I had no voice. Though I did have fun, ultimately it was not of my own choosing. In the end, there was solace in leaving to languages I knew and environments in which I could participate more fully.

Some years later, I came to realize why until then I had had no interest in learning Spanish. In fact, I had made efforts to avoid it despite knowing how useful it might be. In my experience, it was just a language that left me on the outside. Now, my relationship with Spanish has changed in that I am actively trying to acquire it through my interaction with English learners. Not only am I inspired by their efforts, but I also feel the need to learn Spanish to better relate to my students. I am in their shoes, connected, not on the outside, but as a fellow learner.

LILIAN'S REFLECTION ON SANDRA CISNEROS' "MY NAME"

The House on Mango Street by Sandra Cisneros (1984) is another text often read in my courses, as it offers inspiration for autobiographical writing through reflection centered on identity. The vignette titled "My Name" becomes a remarkable springboard for sharing and writing. We begin the discussion with an in-depth analysis of the linguistic resources used by the author to create the nuances of meaning associated with the character's name, Esperanza.

In the first two sentences of this first-person text, Esperanza introduces her bilingualism indirectly, as she refers to the meaning of her name, hope, and plays with the idea of the Spanish sounds in an English-speaking context by mentioning how, "In Spanish it means too many letters" (p. 10). In the poetic balance that characterizes the whole piece, this foreshadows the later comparison of the seemingly painful process of the pronunciation of her name at school—in humorous reference to English speakers attempting to mouth Spanish words—with the smooth-sounding Spanish.

The meaning of her name is then associated with sadness and waiting, in a direct reference to how the word for hope is derived from the verb *esperar*, which means to wait. Among the sensorial images with which Cisneros explores the richness of the narrator's name, her comparison with "the Mexican records my father plays on Sunday mornings when he is shaving, songs like sobbing" vividly evokes the sadness mentioned earlier (Cisneros, 1984, p. 10).

The figure of Esperanza's great-grandmother, her namesake, dominates the center of the vignette. Internal tension builds in the contrast between her description as "a wild horse of a woman, so wild he wouldn't marry" and how "she looked out the window her whole life, the way so many women sit their sadness on an elbow" (p. 11). The resistance to scripted gender roles by a cultural insider is captured thus by Esperanza—and Cisneros, as a Chican@ feminist: "I wonder if she made the best with what she got or was she sorry because she couldn't be all the things she wanted to be. Esperanza. I have inherited her name, but I don't want to inherit her place by the window" (p. 11)

In this brief vignette, Cisneros creates a tapestry of varied textures, built with colors, sounds, and characters, moving across time and space into the history of her family and the generational difference between Esperanza and the women who preceded her while, at the same time, establishing the strong ties to them. This tension illustrates the fluidity of culture and a dynamic and nuanced view of identity in which members of a community both embrace aspects of their heritage while they also adopt behaviors and cultural practices that are distinct from it and reflect the complexity of the intersections of their diverse social locations.

A student's freewrite about their own name follows this analysis. These texts then become the basis of a rich dialogue in which students share personal stories, which are later developed into more elaborate autobiographical pieces. In this context, students in small groups discuss the origin and meaning of their name or names, the family stories associated with how they got their name, who chose it or who they are named after.

This conversation creates a sense of community in which the moments of joy experienced by each family at the time of the student's birth or naming seem to reverberate in the classroom. Through these stories—some voluntarily shared with the whole class—a sense of intimacy is created in the group with opportunities for laughter and moments of respectful silence, depending on the lightness or seriousness of the family and community traditions. In opening up about the stories behind their names, about their family customs, and about the people who are important in their lives, students find a space to share detailed accounts reflecting their linguistic and cultural background.

For instance, after reading Esperanza's description of the different ways her name is pronounced in each context—"At school they say my name funny as if the syllables were made out of tin and hurt the roof of your mouth. But in Spanish my name is made out of a softer something, like silver" (p. 11)—students often reflect on how their own names are treated differently in various linguistic environments.

MI NOMBRE: FABIÁN'S POEM

Mi nombre es Fabián. Webster defines it as
A bean or bean farmer. Me dicen frijolero
But I would never be a farmer.
I say this with sass
For I have worked on too many [farms] and now I want to be proper
—When I was young, trabajé como un perro.
Fabián is also the name of a singer
Y me gusta andar con pelo suelto.
To this day, I ask my mom why she chose Fabián.
"Fabián Omar Martínez, ah qué bien,
Un nombre poderoso para mi único hijo,"
Eso es lo que dice y escribe in a black ink pen.
I have spent my entire life sin padre
Y la única influential person in my life era mi madre.
Eran tiempos celosos pa' mí, porque I saw my fellow peers
With a classic American family. Oh how I use to shed tears.
No más, I grew up and became a man,
One madre could be proud of, who does not seek
Solace at the bottom of beer cans.
I would rather move forward to find my peak,
So that I may move on to bigger and better plans.

THE CIRCUIT: STORIES FROM THE LIFE OF A MIGRANT CHILD—FRANCISCO JIMÉNEZ'S IDENTITY TEXT

Among the texts which Lilian often reads with her students at the beginning of the semester in her graduate and undergraduate Second Language Acquisition courses is an excerpt of the autobiographical novel by Francisco Jiménez, *The Circuit: Stories from the Life of a Migrant Child*. In the scenes we generally focus on, as readers we are privy to the first-person narration by the child protagonist who has just arrived in Fresno, and needs to go back to school after having spent the previous months working in the field with his family, while his older brother stays on. We accompany him on his way from their new place where they have just unpacked, on his bus ride to school on his first day, to the day when he gets back from school and sees all of their belongings packed in boxes—a sign that he and his family are moving once again.

We experience firsthand what it feels like to negotiate all of these unfamiliar spaces, as the young protagonist shows up at a new school once the school year has already begun. We can almost feel his heart pounding in our chest and in our ears as the narrator sits alone in the back of the bus and describes how, "When the bus stopped in front of the school, I felt very nervous" (p. 67). As he walks into the principal's office, we sense the vulnerability of suddenly being immersed in the English-speaking world of a US school:

> When I entered I heard a woman's voice say, "May I help you?" I was startled. I had not heard English for months. For a few seconds I remained speechless. I looked at the lady, who waited for an answer. My first instinct was to answer her in Spanish, but I held back. Finally after struggling for English words, I manage to tell her that I wanted to enroll in the sixth grade. After answering many questions, I was led to the classroom. (p. 68)

Again, we accompany the protagonist into the classroom—yet another unfamiliar space he needs to negotiate—where they are reading in English and he is asked to read aloud. We feel the dryness in his mouth, as if it were ours; as his eyes well up, we empathize, feeling overwhelmed and unprepared to read. Finally, we share the relief of our protagonist when his teacher Mr. Lema agrees to help him with reading and devotes lunchtime to him.

After some weeks, as the teacher invites him to the music room and plays the trumpet, we feel the child's excitement, "The sound gave me goose bumps. I knew that sound. I had hear it in many *corridos*" (p. 69). We are moved by the teacher's kind gesture of offering to teach him how to play the trumpet, as our narrator expresses his wonder at his teacher guessing his thoughts, "He must have read my face" (p. 69). We embrace the budding comfort of his newly found place in the school environment, thanks to an understanding teacher who reaches out and makes a difference.

The class discussion and group reflection which follow the reading of the vivid description of the intense experience in this first-person narrative allows in-service and future teachers to be immersed in this fictional student's world and empathize with him, as he negotiates his linguistic and cultural identities in the abrupt first encounters with the reality of a school and a classroom which feel distant from his everyday life. Our classroom dialogue allows us to explore this situation creatively and work with different scenarios of how each character in this setting could have responded to the circumstances at hand, and what we would each borrow or do differently if these were scenes in our real life.

In the identity text, Virginia, one of the coauthors who is both a bilingual teacher and an MA student in the Bilingual Education program, offers a personal reflection on how she relates to the experience of the protagonist in Jimenez's work. Virginia establishes further connections between the narrator and the lives of her own students, in the dual language middle school classroom where she teaches 8th grade in Las Cruces, New Mexico.

VIRGINIA'S REFLECTION ON *THE CIRCUIT*

Cajas de Cartón[2] is a novel that depicts the life of many migrant workers, their travels from field to field looking for work to make sure their families have the money to live day to day, although in this story we are looking at the migrant life from the viewpoint of a young child. He tells of his journey from the field to the classroom and how each stage feels. He starts sharing his feeling of leaving one field and moving to another to continue earning money. When he describes the feeling of talking to a coworker and that being the last time he saw him reminded me of classmates that would attend my school for a certain amount of time and then would not come back because their families had moved to another location or had been deported.

Living in an area where agricultural work is very common meant that many of my classmates were children of migrant workers and although they did not work in the fields themselves, like Panchito in this story, the majority of the students left after a year and did not return. I lost many good friends that way over many years and I couldn't understand how their parents did not do what my father did. My father was a field worker for many years but he bought a home for us and eventually gave us a legal immigrant status so that we didn't have to move or fear the threat of deportation.

Panchito tells of his experience of having to hide from the school bus in order to not get into trouble when they were not attending school in order to work. I personally never had to do this but I always had to be careful of what I said regarding my immigration status. I was brought to the United States at a very young age but until I was eleven I was not considered a legal resident. My older brother and I always had the fear of someone knowing about it and calling immigration, and of having to go back to Mexico. I can see how hiding to not get in trouble is something that everyone has had to do as a young child, for small things, like for breaking something. But to fear being taken away from your parents or sent somewhere you are not used to living is a fear no child should face. But the most touching part of this story is the sense of losing something you didn't know you wanted.

Panchito felt as an outsider at every school he went because not only was he entering the school later than the other kids but his English proficiency was not very high. As he sat at the desk and the teacher asked him to read you could almost feel what he was feeling, that sense of not belonging and not knowing how to answer a simple question. The teacher was very understanding and later became his best friend who not only helped him with English and reading but also found a topic they could learn more about, music.

Unfortunately, when he felt most happy with school and looked forward to going back and learning, his hopes are shattered with the news that once again they are moving. I can only imagine his feelings when he walked into the shed and saw all their belongings packed up. What could he do? Nothing, that feeling of helplessness derived from the fact that no matter how much he might want something, he still couldn't have it.

Telling his parents about his desire to stay or of the opportunity to learn how to play the trumpet would not change the fact that they were moving to their next work destination. He couldn't even say goodbye to his teacher, the person who helped him so much. There was no time. Anyway, how could he say his goodbyes, if he really didn't want to leave?

All these emotions for a boy so young would be hard to understand. Would he hold it against his parents, or would his future education benefit from this experience? These are questions that I ask myself when I see students move after doing so well in our school. I have had students who grew immensely academically and socially at our school because of the size of the school and the electives it offers, and then, due to circumstances out of their control, they had to go somewhere were this was no longer the situation, and they regressed in their development. This is a story which reflects my own childhood but also provides insight into the lives of many of the students I serve now.

CONCLUSION

In reading Chican@ children and young adult literature in culturally and linguistically diverse classrooms, in responding to it in enlivened personal discussions, and in creating their own identity texts inspired by the authors' work, students and teachers embrace a dynamic rather than a static concept of culture and identity (Nieto, 2010; Norton, 2013).

In identifying with some aspects of the cultural practices reflected in the readings while at the same time expressing their differences and distinctiveness, students experience the fluidity of culture as they contribute to define it. In this way in our classrooms we negotiate the tensions between linguistic and cultural historical repertoires of practice and those current practices in which individuals and communities choose to engage in and identify with, which may sometimes differ from intergenerational heritage practices (Gutiérrez & Rogoff, 2003).

As illustrated above, *The Circuit* by Jiménez, *The House on Mango Street* by Cisneros, and *Neighborhood Odes* by Soto are examples of Chican@ children's literature and Chican@ literature for young adults, which constitute identity texts in our extended meaning. When introduced into K-12, university, and community classrooms, they foster dialogue and may provide in turn the inspiration for rich identity texts in which students (and teachers) pour their own histories into poems or narrative pieces, and community is created. As Knaus (2013) points out:

> Centering students does not always have to be teaching about presumed monolithic identity groups (such as African American or Latino). Indeed, centering culture may mean letting students clarify what growing up as a multiracial African American and Latino person feels like. This is the purpose of voice: to clarify exactly what life is like from the perspective of the speaker, author, poet, playwright, actor, musician, artist, and student. (p. 79)

Students gain agency in a community of learners where they can find spaces to develop their own voice, as well as to explore and name their identities in their own terms. In Maxine Greene's (1995) words:

> Our classrooms ought to be nurturing and thoughtful and just all at once; they ought to pulsate with multiple conceptions of what it is to be human and alive. They ought to resound with the voices of articulate young people in dialogues always incomplete. We must want our students to achieve friendship as each one stirs to wide-awakeness, to imaginative action, and to renewed consciousness of possibility. (p. 43)

Community is built in classrooms based on trust in students' possibilities, where student voice is fostered in emancipatory spaces centered on respect for the unique identities of students. Our extended meaning of identity texts contributes to a more nuanced approach to identity and culture. Students may both identify with and embrace some aspects of their cultural heritage reflected in these texts while at the same time finding spaces to distinguish themselves from them by creating their own texts in a realization of identity as a forward-looking social construct.

NOTES

1. The authors use different identifiers, such as (in no special order) Latin@, Mexican, Mexican American, and Mexican@. The use of Latin@ is the choice of the first author and does not reflect the coauthors' preferences.

2. Title of *The Circuit* in its Spanish translation, often used in bilingual classrooms.

REFERENCES

American FactFinder. *Language spoken at home: 2010–2014 American community survey 5-year estimates*. Washington, DC: US Census Bureau. Retrieved from http://factfinder.census.gov/faces/tableservices/jsf/pages/productview.xhtml?src=CF

Baker, C. (2011). *Foundations of bilingual education and bilingualism* (5th ed.). Tonawanda, NY: Multilingual Matters.

Bernhard, J., Cummins, J., Campoy, F., Ada, A., Winsler, A., & Bleiker, C. (2006). Identity texts and literacy development among preschool English Language Learners: Enhancing learning opportunities for children at risk of learning disabilities. *Teachers College Record, 108*(11), 2380–405.

Christensen, L. (2000). *Reading, writing and rising up: Teaching about social justice and the power of the written word*. Milwaukee, WI: Rethinking Schools.

Cisneros, S. (1984). *The house on Mango Street*. New York: Vintage Contemporaries.

Cixous, H. (1993). *Three steps on the ladder of writing*. New York: Columbia UP.

Cummins, J., & Early, M. (Eds.). (2011). *Identity texts: The collaborative creation of power in multilingual schools*. London: Institute of Education Press.

Delpit, L. (2006). *Other people's children: Cultural conflict in the classroom*. New York and London: The New Press.

García, O. (2009). *Bilingual education in the 21st Century: A global perspective*. Malden, MA: Wiley-Blackwell.

Gay, G. (2010). *Culturally responsive teaching: Theory, research, and practice*. New York: Teachers College Press.

Giampapa, F. (2010). Multiliteracies, pedagogy and identities: Teacher and student voices from Toronto elementary school. *Canadian Journal of Education, 33*(2), 407–31.

Gonzáles, N., Moll, L., & Amanti, C. (Eds.). (2005). *Funds of knowledge: Theorizing practices in households, communities, and classrooms*. Mahwah, NJ: Lawrence Erlbaum Associates.

Greene, M. (1995). *Releasing the imagination: Essays on education, the arts, and social change*. San Francisco: Jossey-Bass, Wiley.

Jiménez, F. (1997). *The circuit: Stories from the life of a migrant child*. New York: Houghton Mifflin.

Knaus, C. (2013). You are the ones who need to hear: The role of urban youth voice in a democracy. In R. Brock & G. Goodman (Eds.), *School sucks: Arguments for alternative education* (pp. 64–98). New York: Peter Lang.

Ladson-Billings, G. (1998). Toward a theory of culturally relevant pedagogy. In L. Beyer & M. Apple (Eds.), *The curriculum: Problems, politics and possibilities* (2nd ed., pp. 201–29). New York: SUNY Press.

Ladson-Billings, G. (2014). Culturally relevant pedagogy 2.0: A.k.a. the remix. *Harvard Educational Review, 84*(1), 74–84.

Lewis, G., Jones, B., & Baker, C. (2012). Translanguaging: Origins and development from school to street and beyond. *Educational Research and Evaluation: An International Journal on Theory and Practice, 18*(7), 641–54. doi: 10.1080/13803611.2012.718488

Nieto, S. (2010). *Language, culture, and teaching: Critical perspectives* (2nd ed.). New York: Routledge.

Norton, B. (2013). *Identity and language learning: Extending the conversation* (2nd ed.). Tonawanda, NY: Multilingual Matters.

Paris, D. (2012). Culturally sustaining pedagogy: A needed change in stance, terminology, and practice. *Educational Researcher, 41*(3), 93–7. doi: 10.3102/0013189X12441244

Paris, D., & Alim, H.S. (2014). What are we seeking to sustain through culturally sustaining pedagogy? A loving critique forward. *Harvard Educational Review, 84*(1), 85–100.

Segura, D. (2007). Working at motherhood: Chicana and Mexican immigrant mothers and employment. In D. Segura & P. Zavella (Eds.), *Women and migration in the U.S.-Mexico borderlands: A reader* (pp. 368–87). Durham, NC: Duke University Press.

Sleeter, C. (2013). The quest for social justice in the education of minoritized students. In R. Brock & G. Goodman (Eds.), *School sucks: Arguments for alternative education* (pp. 245–66). New York: Peter Lang.

Soto, G. (1992). *Neighborhood odes: A poetry collection*. New York: Harcourt.

Taylor, S., & Cummins, J. (2011). Second language practices, identity, and the academic achievement of children from marginalized social groups: A comprehensive review. *Writing and Pedagogy, 3*(2), 181–8. doi:10.1558/wap.v3i2.181

Valencia, R. (Ed.). (1997). *The evolution of deficit thinking: Educational thought and practice*. Washington: Falmer Press.

Zavella, P. (1991). Reflections on diversity among Chicanas. *Frontiers, 12*(2), 73–85.

Index

absent fathers, 91–104
Acosta, Belinda, 77–89, 78
Acosta-Alzuru, M. C., 25
activity proposal: for middle-grade cultural studies classroom, 147–48; for middle-grade ethnic studies classroom, 147–48; for middle-grade language arts classroom, 146
Ada, Alma Flor, 53, 56
Ahmed, Sara, 95–98
Alarcón, Francisco X., 125, 129
Alice and Wonderland (Carroll), 137
"The Altar of the Family" (Wilding), 64
Alvarez, Julia, 77, 80–81
American Girl doll collection, 18
American Girl Place, Chicago, IL, 17, 19, 30
Anaya, Rudolfo, 49, 106, 108–11; fantasy land and myths, 108–11; gender roles and, 110; as the Godfather of Chicano literature, 106; heteronormativity sexual desires and the works of, 110; overt sexuality and, 109; role of women, conceptualizing, 109; sexual identity and, 111
Angels Ride Bikes and Other Fall Poems/Los Ángeles Andan en Bicicleta y otros poemas de otoño (Gonzalez), 113, 129
Animal Poems of the Iguazú/Animalario del Iguazí (Alarcón), 125, 129
anticolonial Chicana feminist movement, 14
Antonio's Card (González), 106, 111, 113, 115–17
Anzaldúa, Gloria, 4–5, 7–8, 10–13, 92–96, 93, 102, 106–8, 111–16, 123–31, 135, 139, 143–44, 152, 156; children's literature activism and, 143–44; mestiza consciousness and, 143–44
artists: Mexican, Chicanx picture books, 52–54; portrait as muchachito, 61–75
autofantasía, 107, 109, 111, 113–17
autohistorias, 107

Baker, C., 160
Bang, Molly, 38
Barnet-Sanchez, Holly, 126
Barrera, Rosalinda, 19–20
Bartlett, Catherine, 106
BeForever dolls, 18
Belpé, Pura, 49
Bend It Like Beckham (film), 96–97, 99
Berkshire, Geoff, 34

Bernal, Dolores Delgado, 51
bilingual children: as English Learners (EL or ELLs), 153; as Limited English Proficient (LEP), 153; as Standard English Learners (SEL), 153
bilingual education: in New Mexico, 165–66. *See also* emergent bilinguals
Bilingual Education program, 163, 172
bilingualism, 153; English for the Children (Proposition 227) and, 153–54; monoglossic views of, 151, 153, 160
Bishop, Rudine Sims, 34, 47, 48
Blatt, Gloria T., 105
Bless Me, Ultima (Anaya), 49, 108, 138
Blume, Judy, 49
The Book of Life (film), 33–34
Borderlands/La Frontera: The New Mestiza (Anzaldúa), 7, 112, 124, 139, 143
Borges, Jorge Luis, 134
Bracero Program, 100
Brady, Mary Pat, 36
Butler, Judith, 68–69

Caballero: A Historical Romance (González and Raleigh), 4
Cacho, Lisa Marie, 91
Cain, Will, 77–78, 81
Cajas de Cartón (Jiménez), 173
Calaca imagery, 38
Call Me Tree (Gonzalez), 106, 113–17, 127
Camino Real, 25, 27
Cantú, Norma E., 78, 79, 81, 88–89
Carroll, Lewis, 137
Castillo, Ana, 6, 8
Changes for Josefina: A Winter Story (Tripp), 21
Chato and the Party Animals, 51–52
Chicana: alienation, in ongoing colonial project, 11–13; defined, 8; feminism, 82, 107, 123–25; rites of passage, 79–82; sexuality, in ongoing colonial project, 11–13

Chicana feminist pedagogy: in works of Maya Christina Gonzalez, 123–35
Chicana/o children, 137–48
Chicana/o-Latina/o children's literature: Anaya's fantasy land and myths, 108–11; fantasy in, 106–8; gender free and nonconforming identities, 113–15; representations of sexual and queer identities in, 105–17; Rigoberto González's same-sex artistic creations, 111–13; sexual identity and childhood, 115–17
Chicana *testimonios* as text and image, 134–35
Chicana ya literature: for a liberatory future, 13–14
Chicana Young Adult (YA) literature: as an intervention strategy, 5–7
Chican@ children's literature, 163–75; classroom, 167; current context of restrictive language spaces, 153–58; "Grandma and Me at the Flea, *Los Meros Meros Remateros*", 158–59; implications for classroom, 159–60; instructional and classroom recommendations for teachers, 160–61; as a means to elevate language practices in homes, 151–61
Chican@ identity and consciousness, 1–2
Chicanita literary spaces, 131–34
"Chicano Fantasy Through a Glass Darkly" (Davila), 106
Chicano identity: "Tata's Gift," 141–42
Chicano Movement, 52, 131, 133
Chicanx picture books, 1–2; familia, 50–51; Mexican artists, 52–54; neighborhood, 51–52; personal reflections on reading, 47–56; sensibilities, 54–55; young reader and educator librarian, 48–50
childhood: sexual identity and, 115–17
children's books artivism: Gonzalez as a pioneer of, 126–28
children's literature: Día de los Muertos in, 33–44; as a site of critical

engagement, 144–45. *See also* Chican@ children's literature
chillante pedagogy, 123–35
Christensen, Linda, 50
The Circuit: Stories from the Life of a Migrant Child (Jiménez), 171–74
Cisneros, Sandra, 6, 135, 169–70
Civil Rights Movement, 9
Civil War, 23, 24
Cixous, H., 166
classroom(s): Chican@ children's literature, 167; Chican@ children's literature, implications for, 159–60; culturally sustaining, 163–75; diverse voices in, 167; identity texts, 167; linguistically sustaining, 163–75; middle-grade cultural studies, 147–48; middle-grade ethnic studies, 147–48; middle-grade language arts, 146; theories in graduate, 164–65
classroom applications: of dream-to-activism literature, 145–46; of mestiza consciousness, 145–46
colonialism, 5, 11, 14, 18, 21, 96, 126
community, 166–67
con mi abuela, 151–61
conocimiento, 91–104, 93–94; desconocimiento and, 93; seven stages of, 94–102
conocimiento narratives, 93–94, 102
Creación de las Aves *(Creation of the Birds)* (painting), 53
critical literacy, 6, 50, 52, 145
critical masculinity studies, 61–75
critical reading, 147
CTA California Read, 43
culturally relevant pedagogy: defined, 165; Ladson-Billings on, 165
culturally sustaining classrooms: identity texts in, 163–75
Cumpiano, I., 158

Damas, Dramas, and Ana Ruiz (Acosta), 77–89; Chicana rites of passage, 79–82; Mama Drama and, 82–87; maternal strife in, 82–87; mother-daughter strife in, 77–89; Niña A Mujer, 79–82; quinceañera celebration as "tradition," 79–82; teenage angst in, 77–89
Dávalos, Karen Mary, 78–81, 85, 88
Davila, Denise, 35, 44
Davila, Luis, 106
Day of the Dead skulls and skeletons, 53
The Dead Family Diaz (Bracegirdle and Bernatene), 35
"Deconstructing Masculinity in the English Classroom: A Site Reconstituting Gendered Subjectivity" (Martino), 64
Delpit, L., 165
de Magnón, Leonor Villegas, 4
De Paola, Tomie, 48
Día de los Muertos, 33–44, 53–54, 128; in children's literature, 33–44
Disney, Walt, 19, 29
Disney Corporation, 19
DLI. *See* dual language immersion programs
Dolores, Tía, 22, 26–28
Dominguez, Angela, 151, 159
Do-Rodriguez, Marie-Astrid, 137, 139
Downtown Boy (Herrera), 61–75, 91–104; absent fathers, 91–104; conocimiento, 91–104; masculinity, 91–104; as a poetic springboard into critical masculinity studies, 61–75; ridiculous voices, 62–65
dramatic irony, 37
dream-to-activism literature: classroom applications of, 145–46
dual language immersion (DLI) programs, 154

Eagleton, Terry, 148
education: bilingual, 165–66
The Ego and the Id (Freud), 68
EL. *See* English Learners
ELL. *See* English Learners
el mestizaje, 155–56

emergent bilinguals: bilingualism and, 156; current ideologies in schooling of, 156; defined, 156; as English Learners (EL or ELLs), 153; instructional and classroom recommendations for teachers of, 160–61
Empanadas, 51
English for the Children (Proposition 227), 153
English Learners (EL), 121, 153
Entre Tejana y Chicana, 3–14

familia: Chicanx picture books, 50–51
Family Pictures (Garza), 51
fantasy land and myths, 108–11
Fantasy Literature For Children and Young Adults: An Annotated Bibliography (Lynn), 107
Faustro, Tomás Ybarra, 125
Fiesta Femenina (Gerson), 125
Flint, A. S., 50
Flores, B., 153–54, 156
Franciscan missionaries, 25
Fránquiz, María E., 49
Freire, P., 121
Freud, Sigmund, 68
Friends from the Other Side/Amigos del otro lado (Anzaldúa), 139, 144
From the Bellybotton of the Moon: And Other Summer Poems (Gonzalez), 113
Funny Bones: Posada and His Day of the Dead Calaveras (Tonatiuh), 53

Gallego, Carlos, 72
García, O., 153–55
Garza, Carmen Lomas, 51
Gelhaus, Erik, 91–92
gender free and nonconforming identities, 113–15
Gerson, Mary-Joan, 125
Gonzalez, Eric, 35–42
González, Jovita, 4
Gonzalez, Maya Christina, 113; artivism, 128–31; Chicana feminist pedagogy in works of, 123–35; Chicana *testimonios* as text and image, 134–35; Chicanita literary spaces and the making of visual "she" worlds, 131–34; as a pioneer of children's books artivism, 126–28; spiritual call to action from women glowing in the dark, 128–31
Gonzalez, Maya Christine, 106, 113–14, 117, 121
González, Rigoberto, 106, 111–13; same-sex artistic creations, 111–13
Gonzalez, Roberto, 117
Gonzalez-Berry, Erlinda, 25
graduate classroom: theories in, 164–65
Grandma and Me at the Flea (Herrera), 152
"Grandma and Me at the Flea, *Los Meros Meros Remateros*" (Herrera), 158–59
Greene, Maxine, 175
Guevara, Susan, 51–52, 54
Gutierrez, Jorge R., 33

Habell-Pallán, Michelle, 33
Haeger, Erich, 35–43
Happy Birthday, Josefina (Tripp), 21, 27
Herrera, Juan Felipe, 61–75, 91–104, 140–41
The House on Mango Street (Cisneros), 169, 174

identity, 163–75; Chicano, 141–42; proto-Chicana, 3–14; queer, 105–17; sexual, 105–17; U.S.–Mexico borderlands, 4
identity texts: classroom, 167; in culturally sustaining classrooms, 163–75; defined, 166; expanding the concept of, 166–67; in linguistically sustaining classrooms, 163–75; reading and creation of, 167
Iguanas in the Snow and Other Winter Poems/Iguanas en la nieve y otros poemas de invierno (Alarcón), 129

Ikas, Karin, 144
I Know the River Loves Me (Gonzalez), 127
image: Chicana *testimonios* as, 134–35; testimonio as, 123–35
Imagineering: American Girl Place and, 19; architectural, 29; Josefina's historical space, 20–30; Walt Disney and, 19
Imagineering: A Behind the Dreams Look at Making the Magic Real, 29
informal restrictive language policies, 154
In Lak'Ech, Tu Eres Mi Otro Yo (Mayan precept), 52
In my Family (Garza), 51
"In Search of the Ideal Reader for Nonfiction Children's Books about el Día de los Muertos" (Davila), 35

Jiménez, Francisco, 171–72
Jimenez, Joe, 8
Johnson, Leah, 9, 11, 155
Johnston, Leah, 11
Jones, S., 145
Josefina Learns a Lesson: A School Story (Tripp), 21, 27
Josefina Montoya (American Girl character), 17–30; imagineering historical space of, 20–30
Josefina Saves the Day: A Summer Story (Tripp), 21, 27
Josefina's Surprise: A Christmas Story (Tripp), 21
Joyce, James, 73–74
Juan, Ana, 53
Juan and the Jackalope: A Children's Book in Verse (Anaya), 106, 108, 110, 115–17
Just Like Me: Stories and Self-portraits by 14 Artists (Rohmer), 125

Kahlo, Frida, 53, 55
Kate del Castillo, 33
Kincheloe, Joe L., 20
Kinderculture, 20
Knaus, C., 165, 175

Ladson-Billings, Gloria J., 50, 165
La Llorona: The Crying Woman (Anaya), 106, 108–10, 115–17
La Prieta and the Ghost Woman/Prietita y La Llorona (Anzaldúa), 128
"*La Quinceañera:* Making Gender and Ethnic Identities" (Dávalos), 78
Larson, Kirsten, 24
Laughing Tomatoes and Other Spring Poems/Jitomates Risueños y otros poemas de primavera (Gonzalez), 113, 129
La venadita (little deer) (painting), 53
Lewison, M., 50
linguistically sustaining classrooms: identity texts in, 163–75
linguistic terrorism, 127
literary assimilation, 10
literary gentrification, 19
Little Chanclas (Lozano), 51
Little Roja Riding Hood, 54
Lopez, Andy, 91–92, 103
Loving in the War Years (Moraga), 107
Lozano, Jose, 51
Luna, Diego, 33
Lynn, Ruth Nadelman, 107

Maciel, David, 25
"Magical Realism: The Latin American Influence on Modern Chicano Writers" (Bartlett), 106
Mama Drama, 82–87
Mango, Abuela and Me (Medina and Dominguez), 152, 159
Manifest Destiny, 21, 24
Martinez, Martínez, R. A., 156
Martinez, S. C., 159–60
Martínez-Roldán, Carmen, 49
Martino, Wayne, 64
masculinity, 91–104; studies, critical, 61–75
Massey, Doreen, 30
Mattel, 18
McCall, Guadalupe Garcia, 4, 6
Medina, Meg, 151–52, 159
Medina, Veronica E., 21

Meet Josefina: An American Girl (Tripp), 21
Meléndez, Gabriel, 25
Melson, Gail F., 115
Mercado, Carmen I., 49
Mesa-Bains, Amalia, 54, 125, 133
mestiza consciousness: activation of, 145; classroom applications of, 145–46; defined, 143; duality and hybridity and, 4; of mixed-race woman, 139; in *Super Cilantro Girl,* 142–43; in "Tata's Gift," 142–43
mestiza identity and the imperial education system, 7–11
Mexican Americans, 21; cultural heritage, 47; culturally responsive representations of, 47; cultural practices of, 51, 127; legacies of internal colonization and, 21; Treaty of Guadalupe-Hidalgo and, 21
"Mexican-Americans in Children's Literature" (Blatt), 105
"Mexican-Americans in Children's Literature since 1970" (Wagoner), 105
Mexican American War, 24
Mexican artists: Chicanx picture books, 52–54
Mexican Repatriation, 10
Mexican women: hypersexualization of, 10; presumptions by others of their sexuality and educational aspirations, 11
middle-grade cultural studies classroom, 147–48
middle-grade ethnic studies classroom, 147–48
middle-grade language arts classroom, 146
Millán, Isabel, 106, 107, 110, 115–17
Mi Nombre: Fabián's Poem, 171
Mirabal, Felipe R., 19–20
"Mirrors, Windows, and Sliding Glass Doors" (Bishop), 34, 48
Monroe, James, 25

Monroe Doctrine, 25, 27
Mora, Pat, 6, 135
Moraga, Cherríe, 106–7, 111, 113–14, 123, 125, 144
Morales, Yuyi, 52–53, 55
Morgan, W., 6
"Mourning and Melancholia" (Freud), 68
muchachito: portrait of the artist as a, 61–75
multiculturalism: boutique, 42; critical, 35; under representation of, 123
Mungin, Lateef, 92
My Colors, My World/Mis colores, mi mundo (Gonzalez), 113, 127, 131, 132
My Diary from Here to There (Pérez), 124
"My Name" (Cisneros), 169–70; Lilian's reflection on, 169–70
My Very Own Room (Pérez), 124

Nana's Big Surprise! (Pérez), 124, 152, 157–58
Nana Upstairs & Nana Downstairs (De Paola), 48
"Narrative, Ideology, and the Reconstruction of American Literary History" (Saldívar), 106
neighborhood: Chicanx picture books, 51–52; *In Lak'Ech, Tu Eres Mi Otro Yo* (Mayan precept), 52
Neighborhood Odes (Soto), 168
The Newberry Library, 17
New London School House Explosion, 7
"The New Mestiza Nation: A Multicultural Movement," (Anzaldúa), 10
New Mexico: bilingual education in, 165–66; TESOL in, 165–66
New York Public Library, 49–50
New York Times, 148
Niña A Mujer, 79–82
Niño Wrestles the World (Morales), 55

Nodelman, Perry, 74
Norton, B., 163–64

"Ode to the Sprinkler," 168–69
Once Upon a Quinceañera (Alvarez), 77
187 Reasons Mexicanos Can't Cross the Border: Undocuments 1971–2007 (Herrera), 140
Operation Wetback, 100
Out of Darkness (Pérez), 1, 5, 7, 14

Palmer, D., 156
Pancho Rabbit and the Coyote: A Migrant's Tale (Tonatiuh), 52
pedagogies of the home, 51
Pérez, Amada Irma, 124, 152, 156–58
Pérez, Ashley Hope, 1, 5, 9
Perlman, Ron, 33
Pleasant Company, 18, 23, 29–30
"Polka Dots, Self-Portraits, and First Voice Multicultural Children's Books," 134
A Portrait of the Artist as a Young Man (Joyce), 73
Posada, José Guadalupe, 53–54
Pre-Columbian text and images, 125
Prietita and the Ghost Woman/Prietita y la Llorona (Anzaldúa), 129, 139, 144
Prietita y el Otro Lado: Gloria Anzaldúa's Literature for Children (Rebolledo), 129
The Promise of Happiness (Ahmed), 96
proto-Chicana consciousness, 3–14
proto-Chicana identity, 3–14
The Psychic Power of Life (Butler), 68
Pueblo Indian Revolt, 23

queer identities: in Chicana/o-Latina/o children's literature, 105–17. *See also* sexual identities
Quinceañera (film), 78
quinceañera celebration as "tradition," 79–82
quinceañeras, 51, 78

Quince Girl, 77, 81
Quiroa, Ruth, 105

Raleigh, Eve, 4
Read, Benjamín M., 25
"Reading Men Differently: Alternative Portrayals of Masculinity in Contemporary Young Adult Fiction," (Bean and Harper), 61
The Rebel (de Magnón), 4
Rebolledo, Tey Diana, 129
restrictive language spaces: current context of, 153–58; *el mestizaje,* 155–56; *Nana's Big Surprise,* 157–58
Revolutionary War, 23, 24
Rivera, Tomás, 72–73
Rohmer, Harriet, 125, 128, 158
Rosa, J., 154, 156
Rosita y Conchita (Gonzalez and Haeger), 1, 35–44
Rowland, Pleasant, 20–21, 29

Salazar, Lupe, 3–4, 7, 9, 11, 14
Saldana, Zoë, 33
Saldívar, Ramón, 106
same-sex artistic creations, 111–13
San Antonio Public Library's Young Pegasus contest, 3
Sánchez, Marta Ester, 8
Sandoval, Chela, 135, 144
Santa Fe Trail, 20, 23, 25, 27
Schatz, Stephanie L., 137
Second Language Acquisition (SLA), 163, 164, 171
SEL. *See* Standard English Learners
sensibilities: Chicanx picture books, 54–55
Serrato, Phillip, 92
sexual identities: in Chicana/o-Latina/o children's literature, 105–17; and childhood, 115–17
Shame the Stars (McCall), 5
"she" worlds, 131–34
Shulevitz, Uri, 50

The Significance of Theory (Eagleton), 148
Sisters, Strangers, and Starting Over (Acosta), 78
SKU. *See* Stock Keeping Unit
SLA. *See* Second Language Acquisition
Sluys, K. V., 50
Soja, Edward, 24
Soledad Sigh-Sighs (González), 111
Soto, Gary: *Neighborhood Odes,* 168; "Ode to the Sprinkler," 168–69
Spanish colonization, 23
Standard English Learners (SEL), 153
Steinberg, Shirley R., 20
Stock Keeping Unit (SKU), 19
student voice, 163–75
Summer of the Mariposas (McCall), 5–6
Super Cilantro Girl (Herrera), 137–48; mestiza consciousness in, 142–43

tamaladas, 51
"Tata's Gift," 137–48; Chicano identity, 141–42; mestiza consciousness in, 142–43
Tatum, Channing, 33
teachers: bilingual, 154, 156, 160, 168, 172; of Chican@, emergent bilinguals, instructional and classroom recommendations for, 160–61; culturally sustaining pedagogy and, 165–66; DLI, 154; dream journaling and, 146; of students of color, 6; translanguaging pedagogy and, 155
Teachers as Cultural Workers (Freire), 121
The Teacher's Guide, 22
Teaching English to Speakers of Other Languages (TESOL), 163, 165; in New Mexico, 165–66
Tejana young adult fiction and poetry, 3–14
TESOL. *See* Teaching English to Speakers of Other Languages

testimonio as text/image, 123–35
Texas State University, 20
text: Chicana *testimonios* as, 134–35; testimonio as, 123–35
theories in graduate classroom, 164–65
theory of Chicana/o-Latina/o fantasy and queerness, 106–8
This Bridge Called My Back (Anzaldúa and Moraga), 108
Through the Looking-Glass (Carroll), 137
Tibbles, Jean-Paul, 21–22
Tonatiuh, Duncan, 52–54
tourism, 18, 35
"Toy Guns, Deadly Consequences," 91
"Transforming Boys, Transforming Masculinity, Transforming Culture: Masculinity Anew in Latino and Latina Children's Literature" (Serrato), 92
translanguaging, 155; authors, use by, 154; bilingualism and, 153, 155–56; in Chican@ children's literature, 160; in classroom, 155, 160; examples of, 157–58; practices, 155–56
Treaty of Guadalupe-Hidalgo, 21
Tripp, Valerie, 19, 21–22, 26, 29

Under the Mesquite, Summer of the Mariposas (McCall), 4–5
US Census Bureau, 166
U.S.–Mexico borderlands identity, 4

Variety, 34
Varos, Remedios, 53
Virgen de Guadalupe, 33, 51
visual "she" worlds, 131–34
Viva Frida (Morales and O'Meara), 53
Viva La Vida (Watermelons) (painting), 53

Wagoner, Shirley A., 105
Walker, Addy, 24
Wei, L., 153
What Night Brings (Trujillo), 138

"Who the Boys Are: Thinking about Masculinity in Children's Fiction" (Nodelman), 74
Why the Wild Things Are: Animals in the Lives of Children (Melson), 115
Wilding, Michael, 64
women, 11, 128–31; hypersexualization of, 10; role of, conceptualizing, 109
Wong-Fillmore, Lily, 159

World War II, 23–24
Writing with Pictures (Shulevitz), 50

Yarbro-Bejarano, Yvonne, 107–8
y no se lo tragó la tierra (Rivera), 72
Yosso, Tara, 50, 55
"'You Don't Know How Much He Meant': Deviancy, Death, and Devaluation" (Cacho), 91

About the Editors

Laura Alamillo received her PhD from the University of California at Berkeley in Language, Literacy, and Culture. She is currently professor and chair in the Literacy, Early Childhood, Bilingual, and Special Education Department at Fresno State. Her research includes looking at the education of emergent bilingual children specifically at humanizing and culturally sustaining pedagogy in multilingual classrooms.

Larissa M. Mercado-López received her PhD in Latina literature from the University of Texas at San Antonio and is currently an associate professor of women's studies at California State University, Fresno, and children's book writer. Her research focuses on Chicana feminisms, Tejana literature, and intersectional feminist fitness studies.

Cristina Herrera holds a PhD in literature from Claremont Graduate University and is associate professor and chair of Chicano and Latin American Studies at California State University, Fresno. She has published on Chicana literature, motherhood, and young adult literature, among other topics.

About the Contributors

Cecilia J. Aragón is an associate professor of theater and dance and director of Latina/o studies at University of Wyoming.

Enrique Avalos is a MA TESOL student at NewMexico State University.

Elena Avilés joined the faculty at Portland State University in 2014 as an assistant professor of Chicano/Latino studies. She earned a PhD in Hispanic Languages and Literatures (2014) and MA in Spanish (2008) at the University of New Mexico (UNM). Her teaching and research are informed by the fields of feminist, gender, and ethnic studies as well as by the literary and visual arts.

Katherine Elizabeth Bundy is a lecturer of Spanish at University of North Georgia as well as a doctoral student at the University of Georgia in Athens, Georgia. Of Cuban descent, her research interests include hybrid subjectivities, women's studies, technology studies, film and visual studies, as well as Latina/o and Transnational Caribbean Children's and Young Adult's literature. In the future, she aspires to teach, write, and give back to the communities around her.

Lilian Cibils is an assistant professor of curriculum and instruction, in the Bilingual Education/TESOL Program at New Mexico State University.

Virginia Gallegos teaches at La Academia Dolores Huerta Middle School and is in the MA Bilingual Education Program at New Mexico State University.

About the Contributors

Tanya González is an associate professor in the English Department at Kansas State University. She publishes in Latina/o literature and the Gothic and representations of Latinas in popular culture. She is the coauthor, with Eliza Rodriguez y Gibson, of *Humor and Latina/o Camp in Ugly Betty* (Lexington, 2015).

Roxana Loza is a graduate student in children's literature at Kansas State University. She has a BA from Rice University with a triple major in English, French, and psychology. Before graduate school, she was a Spanish Kindergarten teacher in a dual language program outside of Houston, Texas, for four years.

Fabián Martínez is a MA TESOL student at New Mexico State University.

Sonia Alejandra Rodríguez is an independent scholar with a doctorate in English from the University of California, Riverside. Her research project introduces "conocimiento narratives" as a new lens to read and analyze Latinx children's and young adult literature.

Phillip Serrato is an associate professor of English at San Diego State University. His teaching and research interests revolve around matters of identity, sexuality, and gender (especially masculinity) in both children's and adolescent literature and Chicano/a literature, film, and performance. Lately he has also been developing courses in Gothic and horror studies at the undergraduate and graduate levels. Recent publications include "Postmodern Guacamole: Lifting the Lid on *El Tigre: The Adventures of Manny Rivera*," "'What Are Young People to Think?': The Subject of Immigration and the Immigrant Subject in Francisco Jiménez's *The Circuit*"; "Conflicting Inclinations: Luis J. Rodríguez's Picture Books for Children"; and "From 'Booger Breath' to 'The Guy': Juni Cortez Grows Up in Robert Rodríguez's *Spy Kids*Trilogy." Presently he is at work on two books, one an examination of masculinity in Chicano/a literature, film, and performance from the nineteenth century to the present day, and the other a critical survey of the emergence, history, and development of Chicano/a children's literature.

Lettycia Terrones is a doctoral student in the Department of Information Sciences at University of Illinois at Urbana-Champaign, where she researches Chicanx picture books as sites of love and resilient resistance.

Patricia Marina Trujillo was born and raised in the Española Valley and earned her doctorate in US Latina/o Literature at the University of Texas in San Antonio. She has a master's degree in English from the University of Nebraska and bachelor's degrees in English and Law & Society from New Mexico State University. She is an associate professor of English and Chicana/o studies at Northern New Mexico College.